A SPITFIRE'S STORY

A SPITFIRE'S STORY

THE INVISIBLE THREAD
SPITFIRE R6644 AND THE PILOTS WHO FLEW IT

DILIP SARKAR
MBE, FRHistS, FRAeS

AIR WORLD

A SPITFIRE'S STORY
The Invisible Thread: Spitfire R6644 and the Pilots Who Flew It

First published in Great Britain in 2025 by
Air World
An imprint of
Pen & Sword Books Ltd
Yorkshire – Philadelphia

Copyright © Dilip Sarkar, 2025

ISBN 978 1 03613 852 3

The right of Dilip Sarkar to be identified as Author of this work has been asserted by him in accordance with the Copyright, Designs and Patents Act 1988. A CIP catalogue record for this book is available from the British Library All rights reserved.

All rights reserved. No part of this book may be reproduced, transmitted, downloaded, decompiled or reverse engineered in any form or by any means, electronic or mechanical including photocopying, recording or by any information storage and retrieval system, without permission from the Publisher in writing. NO AI TRAINING: Without in any way limiting the Author's and Publisher's exclusive rights under copyright, any use of this publication to "train" generative artificial intelligence (AI) technologies to generate text is expressly prohibited. The Author and Publisher reserve all rights to license uses of this work for generative AI training and development of machine learning language models.

Typeset by SJmagic DESIGN SERVICES, India.
Printed and bound in the UK by CPI Group (UK) Ltd.

The Publisher's authorised representative in the EU for product safety is Authorised Rep Compliance Ltd., Ground Floor, 71 Lower Baggot Street,
Dublin D02 P593, Ireland.
www.arccompliance.com

For a complete list of Pen & Sword titles please contact:

PEN & SWORD BOOKS LTD
George House, Units 12 & 13, Beevor Street, Off Pontefract Road,
Barnsley, South Yorkshire, S71 1HN, England
E-mail: enquiries@pen-and-sword.co.uk
Website: www.pen-and-sword.co.uk

or

PEN AND SWORD BOOKS,
1950 Lawrence Road, Havertown, PA 19083, USA
E-mail: uspen-and-sword@casematepublishers.com
Website: www.penandswordbooks.com

Contents

Author's Note and Glossary..vi
Acknowledgements..xii
Foreword One to the Original Edition, by Group Captain Sir Hugh Dundas xiii
Foreword Two to the Original Edition, by Squadron Leader
    Bolesław H. Drobinski..xv
Foreword to the 2025 Edition xvii
Author's Introduction: Spitfire R6644: The Invisible Thread.......................xix

PART ONE

Chapter One	Birth of a Spitfire...	2
Chapter Two	5 Operational Training Unit: A Roll Call of the Lost..........	23
Chapter Three	616 'South Yorkshire' Squadron	89
Chapter Four	65 'East India' Squadron...	159
Chapter Five	308 'City of Krakow' (Polish) Squadron	203
Chapter Six	The Crash	222

PART TWO

Chapter Seven	Flying Officer Franciszek Surma VM KW	230
Chapter Eight	308 'City of Krakow' Squadron and the Non-Stop Offensive..	240
Chapter Nine	Circus 110: One of Our Spitfires is Missing…	259

Postscript: The Legend Lives On…...273
Bibliography 290
Other Books by Dilip Sarkar..296
Index 299

Author's Note and Glossary

The aviation-minded reader will notice that I have referred to German Messerschmitt fighters by the abbreviation 'Me' (not 'Bf', which is more technically correct), or simply by their numeric designation, such as '109' or '110'. This not only reads better but is authentic: during the Battle of Britain, Keith Lawrence DFC, a New Zealander and an 'ace', flew Spitfires and once said to me 'To us they were just "Me's", "109s" or "110s", simple, never "Bf".'

In another attempt to preserve accuracy, I have also used the original German, wherever possible, regarding terms associated with the *Luftwaffe* and *Regia Aeronautica* (the Italian Air Force), such as:

Abwehrkreis	Essentially a defensive circle formation, each aircraft protecting the tail of the other, but which also had an offensive function, because any enemy fighter entering the circle could be attacked.
Adlerangriff	'Attack of the Eagles'.
Adlertag	'Eagle Day'.
Corpo Aereo Italiano	Italian Air Corps.
Eichenlaub	The Oak Leaves, essentially being a Bar to the *Ritterkreuz*.
Erprobungsgruppe	Experimental group, in the case of *Erprobungsgruppe* 210, a skilled precision bombing unit.
Experte	A fighter 'ace'. Ace status, on both sides, was achieved by destroying five enemy aircraft.

AUTHOR'S NOTE AND GLOSSARY

Fähnrich	Officer cadet.
Fallschirmjäger	Paratroopers.
Freie hunt	A fighter sweep.
Gefechstand	Operations headquarters.
General der Jagdflieger	General of Fighter Pilots.
Geschwader	The whole group, usually of three gruppen.
Geschwaderkommodore	The group leader.
Gruppe	A wing, usually of three squadrons.
Gruppenkeil	A wedge formation of bombers, usually made up of vics of three.
Gruppenkommandeur	The Wing Commander.
Jagdbomber ('*Jabo*')	Fighter-bomber.
Jagdflieger	Fighter pilot.
Jagdgeschwader	Fighter group, abbreviated JG.
Jagdwaffe	The fighter force.
Jäger	Hunter, in this context a fighter pilot or aircraft.
Kampfflieger	Bomber aircrew.
Kampfgeschwader	Bomber group, abbreviated KG.
Kanal	English Channel.
Katchmarek	Wingman.
Kriegsmarine	German war navy.
Lehrgeschwader	Literally a training group, but actually a precision bombing unit, abbreviated LG.
Luftflotte	Air Fleet.
Oberkannone	Literally the 'Top Gun', or leading fighter ace.
Oberkommando der Wehrmacht (OKW)	German armed forces high command.
Oberkommando der Marine (OKM)	German naval high command.
Oberkommando der Heer (OKH)	German army high command.
Oberkommando der Luftwaffe (OKL)	German air force high command.
Ritterkreuz	The Knight's Cross of the Iron Cross.

Rotte	A pair of fighters, comprising leader and wingman, into which the *Schwärm* broke once battle was joined.
Rottenführer	Corporal
Rottenfleiger	Wingman.
Schwärm	A section of four fighters.
Schwarmführer	Section leader.
Seelöwe	Sealion, the codename for Hitler's proposed seaborne invasion of England.
Seenotflugkommando	*Luftwaffe* air sea rescue organisation.
Stab	Staff.
Staffel	A squadron.
Staffelkapitän	The Squadron Leader.
Störflug	Harassing attacks, usually by lone Ju 88s.
Stormi	an Italian Air Force wing.
Stuka	The Ju 87 dive-bomber.
Sturkampfgeschwader	Dive-bomber group, abbreviated StG.
Vermisst	Missing.
Wehrmacht	Armed forces.
Zerstörer	Literally 'destroyer', the term used for the Me 110.
Zerstörergeschwader	Destroyer group, abbreviated ZG.

Each *geschwader* generally comprised three *gruppen*, each of three *staffeln*. Each *gruppe* is designated by Roman numerals, i.e. III/JG 26 refers to the third *gruppe* of Fighter Group (abbreviated 'JG') 26. *Staffeln* are identified by numbers, so 7/JG 26 is the 7th *staffel* and belongs to III/JG 26.

Rank comparisons may also be useful:

Gefreiter	Private 1st Class
Unteroffizier	Corporal, no aircrew equivalent in Fighter Command
Feldwebel	Sergeant

AUTHOR'S NOTE AND GLOSSARY

Oberfeldwebel	Flight Sergeant
Leutnant	Pilot Officer
Oberleutnant	Flight Lieutenant
Hauptmann	Squadron Leader
Major	Wing Commander
Oberst	Group Captain

RAF abbreviations:

AAF	Auxiliary Air Force
AASF	Advance Air Striking Force
A&AEE	Aeroplane and Armament Experimental Establishment
AC1	Aircraftman First Class
AC2	Aircraftman Second Class
ACW1	Aircraftwoman First Class
ACW2	Aircraftwoman Second Class
AFC	Air Force Cross
AFDU	Air Fighting Development Unit
AFS	Auxiliary Fire Service
AHB	Air Historical Branch
AI	Airborne Interception Radar
AOC	Air Officer Commanding
AOC-in-C	Air Officer Commanding-in-Chief
ARP	Air Raid Precautions
ASR	Air Sea Rescue
ATA	Air Transport Auxiliary
ATS	Armament Training School
BEF	British Expeditionary Force
CAS	Chief of the Air Staff
CFS	Central Flying School
CGS	Central Gunnery School
CO	Commanding Officer
CWGC	Commonwealth War Graves Commission
DAF	Desert Air Force

A SPITFIRE'S STORY: THE INVISIBLE THREAD

DES	Direct Entry Scheme
DFC	Distinguished Flying Cross
DFM	Distinguished Flying Medal
DSO	Distinguished Service Order
E/A	Enemy Aircraft
EFTS	Elementary Flying Training School
ENSA	Entertainments National Service Association
FAA	Fleet Air Arm
EFTS	Elementary Flying Training School
FIU	Fighter Interception Unit
FTS	Flying Training School
GPC	Guinea Pig Club
HE	High Explosive
HF	High Frequency
HQ	Headquarters
ITW	Initial Training Wing
LAC	Leading Aircraftman
LFB	London Fire Brigade
LFS	London Fire Service
MC	Military Cross
MG	Machine-gun
MO	Medical Officer
MOD	Ministry of Defence
MRAF	Marshal of the Royal Air Force
MSFU	Merchant Ship Fighter Unit
MT	Motor Transport
MTB	Motor Torpedo Boat
NCO	Non-Commissioned Officer
OR	Other Ranks
ORB	Operations Record Book
OTC	Officer Training Corps
PAF	Polish Air Force
OTU	Operational Training Unit
PDC	Personnel Distribution Centre

AUTHOR'S NOTE AND GLOSSARY

PRU	Photographic Reconnaissance Unit
RAE	Royal Aircraft Establishment
RAFVR	Royal Air Force Volunteer Reserve
RFS	Reserve Flying School
RN	Royal Navy
RNAS	Royal Navy Air Service
R/T	Radio Telephone
SASO	Senior Air Staff Officer
SFTC	Service Flying Training School
SHAEF	Supreme Headquarters Allied Expeditionary Force
SMO	Station Medical Officer
SOO	Senior Operations Officer
SSC	Short Service Commission
SSQ	Station Sick Quarters
TAF	Tactical Air Force
VHF	Very High Frequency
UAS	University Air Squadron
U/S	Unserviceable
UXB	Unexploded Bomb
WDAF	Western Desert Air Force

Also:

'Angels' refers to height measured in thousands of feet, hence 'Angles 15' means 15,000 feet. A 'vector' is a compass course, measured in degrees, a 'Bandit' is a confirmed enemy aircraft whilst a 'Bogey' and an 'X-Raid' are as yet unidentified but potentially hostile radar plots. 'Tally ho!' was shouted when the enemy were sighted and the leader was ordering an attack. To the Germans, hostile aircraft were 'Indians' and the German fighter pilot's victory cry was 'Horrido'.

Acknowledgements

Andy Long will forever have my gratitude for telling me, back in 1986, that R6644 crashed locally – which changed the course of my life, and set us both off on an adventure still yet to end. The members of our original Malvern Spitfire Team, some no longer with us, also deserve a special mention for sharing this incredible journey with us.

All of the wartime survivors, eyewitnesses and relatives of casualties quoted in this and the original book still have my thanks, as do the Madresfield Estate and Mr Nick Nugent of Lower Woodsfield Farm; the former Polish Air Force Association in Great Britain; Polish Institute and Sikorski Museum; Artur Bildziuk, Chairman of the Polish Airmen's Association UK; MOD AHB (RAF); The National Archives; Commonwealth War Graves Commission; the RAF College Cranwell, and Scott Booth of the Laguna Spitfire Legacy Project; my cousin, Pooja Das Choudhury, kindly photographed graves for me in faraway Kolkata.

H.H.J. Brendan Finucane KC, nephew of Wing Commander Brendan Finucane, was most helpful in respect of this new edition, as was Baroness Hodgson CBE, whose late mother's first husband was Wing Commander Howard Frizelle 'Billy' Burton, and John Don, a volunteer at Bentley Priory Museum; Angus Mansfield kindly checked Wing Commander John 'Iggy' Kilmartin's log book for flights in R6644 at 5 OTU, finding none, whilst Professor Jeremy Crang had more success when investigating the log of Flight Lieutenant Colin Hamilton 'Mac' MacFie, courtesy of the pilot's son, Shaun MacFie.

As always, my great friend and commissioning editor Martin Mace was an essential part of the creative process, and all at Pen & Sword a pleasure, as always, to work with.

Last but certainly not least, my wife, Sue, and our family and friends, have my ongoing thanks.

Foreword One

Ostensibly, this book is the story of one wartime Spitfire – and in telling that story Dilip Sarkar weaves a remarkable tapestry, illustrated with portraits of the twenty-five[*] young men identified as having flown Spitfire R6644, and with detailed accounts of the circumstances, some hum-drum, others dramatic, in which those flights were carried out.

I was one of those young men, only a little past my twentieth birthday at the time when I made thirteen flights in that aeroplane – but already a veteran, with both the Dunkirk evacuation and Battle of Britain behind me. Indeed, several of the others who also flew the plane were well-known to me.

Flying Officer Hugh 'Cocky' Dundas in his 616 Squadron Spitfire at Tangmere, 1941.

Spitfire R6644 itself survived for just under a year, from 30 May 1940 when my old and great friend Jeffrey Kindersley Quill, Chief Test Pilot at Supermarine, took it up on its first flight, to 11 May 1941, when the Polish Pilot Officer Franciszek Surma baled out of it near Malvern. It may seem a

---

[*] Author's note: more recent research has identified two more pilots of R6644 – one of whom was killed in action, the other captured.

xiii

short time, but nevertheless the machine outlived some of those who flew her. Of the twenty-five, nine were killed in action and four were shot down to become prisoners of war – a ratio illustrating the rather uncertain future faced by fighter pilots in those now far off days of total war.

It is with nostalgia, as well as with pride and pleasure, that I have responded to Dilip's invitation to write this foreword. Those are three emotions which are easily aroused in all whose lives were touched for any length of time by the Spitfire. It is heart-warming to know that young men, unborn at the time when we were fighting our battles, have themselves been so moved by the Spitfire story as to undertake the monumental amount of loving research which went into compilation of this book.

I salute the author and his team.

Group Captain Sir Hugh S.L. Dundas
CBE DSO DFC DL RAF (Ret'd),
London,
February 1989

Sir Hugh Dundas passed away on 10 July 1995, aged 74.

Foreword Two

When I was asked by Dilip Sarkar 'to write something along the lines of what the project has meant from the Polish side', I replied that I would consider it a privilege and would do so with great pleasure.

I knew 'Franek' Surma when we served together in the Polish air force before the invasion of our country by Nazi Germany on Friday, 1 September 1939. He was a friend of mine; I remember him almost always being cheerful with a very good sense of humour. He was also a very good pilot. Unfortunately, he lost his life fighting to see freedom one day restored to his beloved Poland.

Pilot Officer Bołeslaw H. 'Gandy' Drobinski whilst serving with 65 Squadron during the Battle of Britain.

On Sunday, 11 May 1941, Franek had a narrow escape when his Spitfire, R6644, caught fire, forcing him to bale out over Madresfield. The aeroplane crashed in an open field, not far from where he landed safely by parachute.

On Sunday, 8 November 1941, Flying Officer Franciszek Surma VM KW was reported 'Missing: Presumed Killed'. He was most likely, as the author's research suggests, shot down over the English Channel during an operational flight escorting bombers to Lille; his body was never found.

On Saturday, 12 September 1987, together with fellow former Polish Spitfire pilot Squadron Leader Ludwik Martel, I had the great honour of unveiling the memorial built by the Malvern Spitfire Team commemorating Flying Officer Surma.

On behalf of all Polish airmen, I want to publicly express our gratitude to Dilip Sarkar and his small team. By paying such a unique and moving tribute to Franek Surma, they also unknowingly paid a similar tribute to all Polish airmen who lost their lives during the Second World War. We all greatly appreciate their determined commitment to this project.

I am certain that the original idea of writing this book was stimulated by the author's desire to honour a pilot who successfully managed to steer his burning Spitfire away from the houses of Malvern below. In a masterly way, Dilip has managed to research and write a nostalgic and romantic history of Spitfire R6644, as a result of which the lives of the twenty-five[*] young pilots who flew the machine are now connected by an 'invisible thread'.

I warmly congratulate the author and the team for their excellent work.

Squadron Leader Bolesław H. Drobinski
VM KW DFC RAF (Ret'd),
Chiddingfold,
April 1989

Squadron Leader Bolesław H. Drobinski passed away on 26 July 1995, aged 76.

---

[*] Author's note: now known to be twenty-seven.

Foreword to the 2025 Edition

I have had the pleasure of knowing Dilip Sarkar for many years, having met him at various Polish air force events when I attended with my parents, who both served in the Polish air force during the Second World War. It is an honour and privilege, as Chairman of the Polish Airmen's Association UK, to contribute this foreword to Dilip's book *A Spitfire's Story: Spitfire R6644 and the Pilots Who Flew It*.

I was fortunate to be brought up in the company of Polish airmen, many of whom flew Spitfires during the war, both in Polish air force and Royal Air Force fighter squadrons. Such an elegant, iconic, aeroplane, which came to life in the hands of the pilots that flew it. Every one of the stories of these men, so carefully researched and told in this book, is a glimpse into the lives of these pilots – and for some of the them that life was all too short. The survivors I was privileged to know would often recall with fondness the performance of the Spitfire and the unmistakable sound of its Rolls-Royce Merlin engine. These Polish airmen were the humblest people I have ever known; duty called and they had answered.

Dilip Sarkar is a renowned historian and in this book has addressed the story of a particular Spitfire and pilots from many nations, including Poland, identified as having flown it in the troubled skies of the Second World War. The story of this Spitfire is entwined with the lives of these pilots and is now a document recording their exploits and sacrifices for future generations to read – and discover the history of those who gave so much for us to enjoy the freedom we have today.

I am grateful to Dilip for researching and writing this book, which helps maintain the currency of these brave men and women – and long may their memory remain ever-green, as it deserves to be.

Artur Bildziuk, Chairman, Polish Airmen's Association UK, 2025

Author's Introduction

Spitfire R6644: The Invisible Thread

For Bill Pritchard, a 21-year-old milkman working at Bennet's Dairy in Lower Wick, Worcester, Sunday, 11 May 1941 began, so far as the Second World War was concerned in the Shire, unremarkably.

The war was not yet two years old, and not being of any great military or industrial importance, the 'Faithful City' had only been subjected to one aerial attack, when on 3 October 1940, Ju 88 pilot, *Leutnant* Otto Bischoff of 6/KG 77, mistook Worcester for Coventry, and instead of bombing the latter's Daimler works hit the Mining and Engineering Company factory, known locally as the 'MECO'. To the west of Worcester the Malvern Hills rise up, a magnificent range of heights some 13 miles long, on which Sir Edward Elgar found his inspiration for 'Land of Hope and Glory'. It was to Malvern that Pritchard's milk round would take him that morning, before heading back to the dairy. This tranquil rural scene was, of course, a direct contrast with the events in London that morning, the preceding hours of darkness having seen the crescendo of the terrifying night Blitz, a raid which left 1,400 dead and set 700 acres of the capital ablaze. The war was, however, about to touch Worcestershire – although fortunately not with such malevolence.

Driving his milk truck towards Callow End along Jennet Tree Lane, a country lane connecting that village and Madresfield, all was as it should be – until Pritchard was suddenly shocked by an explosion in the field to his right. Astonished, Bill braked hard, and stopped – as a 3-feet long sheet of metal crashed into the road just in front of his bonnet. Jumping out, Pritchard realised that the debris was from an aircraft, and that the explosion had not been caused by a bomb but a crash. Immediately, the young milkman clambered over a newly laid hedge into the field and ran towards the shattered and burning wreck – although so violent had the crash been, Pritchard realised that if the pilot remained in his machine, he or she would be beyond help. Looking around for signs of life, Pritchard saw no one, so was puzzled when he heard someone shouting, presumably at him. Looking up, he saw an airman descending by parachute, shouting and gesticulating for him to keep away from the crash site because of exploding ammunition. The parachutist drifted overhead towards the cottage at the nearby junction of Jennet Tree and Hawthorn Lanes, disappearing from view. Rightly assuming that soon the scene would be swarming with people, Pritchard returned to the road, picked up the piece of aircraft as a souvenir, and continued on his way back to Manor Farm.

Unsurprisingly, the crash of what was actually Supermarine Spitfire Mk IA, R6644, caused great excitement in sleepy Malvern and surrounding villages – and over forty years later I would find the event indelibly etched into the memories of local people. It is also fair to say that the events of that now far off day also affected the course of my life, even though I was not born until twenty years later.

As Group Captain Sir Hugh 'Cocky' Dundas said in his foreword to my first telling of this story, *The Invisible Thread: A Spitfire's Tale* (Ramrod Publications, 1992), 'Ostensibly, this book is the story of one wartime Spitfire', that story being 'a remarkable tapestry'. In his foreword, the Polish Squadron Leader Bolesław Drobinski observed that R6644 had become 'an invisible thread' connecting the twenty-seven young pilots identified as having flown her, which is very true. That said, apart from its dramatic demise, R6644 itself had a comparatively mundane existence – but the stories of the pilots and others involved are fascinating and inspirational in equal measure. Indeed, this is very much a book about people, people who considered themselves 'ordinary' but who did extraordinary things – and without the Second World War, most would very likely never had the opportunity to fly.

The Spitfire emerged from the Second World War as a symbol of freedom and defiance against all odds, and all these years later has become *the* icon associated with British national pride, courage and excellence. The sight and sound of R.J. Mitchell's little fighter continues to inspire and excite,

AUTHOR'S INTRODUCTION

the wartime darling, the star of every air show – and interest in its story, if anything, increases daily, or so it seems. The Spitfire, however, when all is said and done, is a machine, and until in human hands an inanimate object. A human being, of course, designed the aircraft, others built and maintained it, whilst the stars of the show – the fighter pilots – flew in her to battle. Tragically, the Spitfire's designer, Mitchell, died prematurely, aged just 42, of cancer, in 1937, without ever knowing the contribution he had made, or being aware of just how much the Spitfire excited the public consciousness. Nonetheless, Mitchell designed the Spitfire for one purpose, to defend Britain, and was acutely aware that this was a warplane, built for killing and no other purpose, in which pilots could – and would – be killed. In a foreword to one of my earlier books, R.J. Mitchell's son, the now also sadly late Dr Gordon Mitchell, summed up his father's feelings succinctly:

> My father was heard to say on a number of occasions that 'A Spitfire without a pilot is just a lump of metal', which was meant to show the high regard and respect he had for the pilots whose job it was to fly his 'lump of metal'. I think that this book mirrors those sentiments, in that the first part is devoted to describing the Spitfire in accurate detail, this being followed by in-depth descriptions of eleven individuals who had the task of flying the 'lump of metal' into battle.

The same, in fact, could be said of this particular book, because it develops a similar theme, giving currency to the memories of various young pilots who flew R6644, some of whom failed to return, for one reason or another – killed or captured, others missing. Indeed, here we explore stories of both aces and lesser-known pilots, the latter drawn from the anonymous 'rank and file' – young men who volunteered to serve their country and get in harm's way from the cockpit of a Spitfire, seeking no recognition or reward, and never knowing if each new day was their last.

This book was largely researched forty years ago, when the survivors remained aplenty, as did the widows, siblings and children of casualties with first-hand knowledge of their loved ones. Recording interviews and corresponding with them was an incredible experience, collating in the process a unique archive of memories and photographs – now, with their passing, this material providing a unique and rich primary source enabling me to add essential colour to the 'tapestry'.

The opportunity to completely re-write and update what was the first book I ever wrote, and second to be published, was not to be missed. I have long felt that this Spitfire's tale needed refreshing and re-telling as so much more information is now available – that extra detail making the stories involved even more remarkable…

Dilip Sarkar MBE FRHistS FRAeS BA(Hons),
December 2024

PART ONE

Chapter One

Birth of a Spitfire

When the Second World War broke out, aviation remained a comparatively new phenomenon. Indeed, the 'Wright Flyer', made and flown by the American Wright brothers, Orville and Wilbur, had only become the first powered, heavier-than-air machine to sustain controlled flight with a pilot aboard at Kittyhawk, North Carolina, on 17 December 1903. Just eleven years later, however, the First World War erupted and the aeroplane went to war. Those early warplanes were biplanes, with open cockpits, fixed undercarriages, and two-bladed, fixed-pitch, propellers, which is to say that the angle of 'bite', similar to changing gear in a car, cannot be changed. At first, these primitive machines were used for scouting and reconnaissance work, but inevitably air-to-air combat ensued and so the race began to stay one step ahead of the enemy. Hand-held revolvers and rifles gave way to machine guns, and aircrew were soon dropping bombs, at first by hand. On Christmas Eve 1914, the Germans jettisoned their first of many bombs over England, in fact, which exploded harmlessly in a Dover garden – but was a terrifying indication of things to come. Indeed, from that point on, Britain could no longer rely upon being an island for protection, or exclusively upon the Royal Navy for home security. Warfare had irrevocably changed – owing to the birth of military air power.

Throughout most of the First World War, British military aviation was delivered jointly by the army's Royal Flying Corps and the Royal Naval Air Service, but as the importance of military aviation increased, it was decided to create a new service: the Royal Air Force, which was born on 1 April 1918. Major General Lord 'Boom' Trenchard became the first Chief of the Air Staff and set about building the new junior service. In the wake of the Allies defeating the Central Powers and the guns falling silent on 11 November 1918, the resulting Versailles Peace Conference the following year sought, amongst other things, to so restrict the German military that the jingoistic nation would never threaten peace again. One of Versailles' primary clauses was preventing Germany from having an air force, and so, with the threat apparently neutralised permanently, the Western Allies focused upon disarmament. Moreover, the air power doctrine of the time revolved heavily around the concept that the 'bomber would always get through', as British Prime Minister Stanley Baldwin told the House of Commons in 1932. Trenchard subscribed to this view, stating that 'It is on the destruction of enemy industries and above all in the lowering of morale of enemy nationals caused by bombing that the ultimate victory lies'. Indeed, Trenchard considered fighters 'only necessary to keep up the morale of one's own people'. Consequently, what little spending there was on defence revolved around the bomber force, and in 1932, Britain abandoned what had been a miniscule RAF expansion programme. The following year, however, Adolf Hitler, leader of the Nazis, became Chancellor of Germany – and, again, everything changed.

The *Führer* immediately set about contravening and reversing what Germany saw as injustices arising from the Versailles, namely the severe restrictions on the military and territorial concessions. Already, though, Weimar Germany had begun secretly re-building its prohibited *Luftwaffe*, far away from prying Western eyes, deep in Soviet Russia. The Great Depression caused by the Wall Street stock-market crash of 1929, had not helped, the resulting financial chaos affecting the next decade. The British government, therefore, had serious socio-economic issues to address at home, which it tried its best to do – whilst Germany fervently rearmed. Later, Churchill would write that for defence spending, the years 1931–1935 were those of the 'locust'. Be that as it may, the complete lack of substantial rearmament and deficiencies on doctrinal thinking were caused by three things: fiscal constraints, political indifference or opposition, and Trenchard's unshakeable belief in the bomber. By 1935, however, the threat posed by Hitler's Germany was increasingly plain – and could no longer be ignored. At last Britain tentatively began to rearm. On 25 February 1936, Expansion Scheme 'F' was approved: 124 squadrons (1,736 aircraft of all types) by

April 1937. Unfortunately, whilst Scheme 'F' increased the bomber force to 1,000 aircraft, the number of fighters was only maintained. Ironically, however, there were concurrently exciting developments in fighter design.

The Supermarine Aviation Works Ltd had been formed before the First World War when one Noel Pemberton Billing decided to combine his passions for flying and boating by producing flying boats. The site chosen for the new enterprise was an old coal wharf on the banks of the river Itchen at Woolston, where the proposed 'Super Marine Craft' was to be built. With the advent of war in 1914, this machine never entered production, however, and Supermarine turned its attention to building fighter aircraft. In 1916, Pemberton Billing left the company and was replaced as managing director by Hubert Scott-Paine – after which a great reorganisation followed. Many new faces appeared at the factory and offices, including a gifted young designer: Reginald Joseph Mitchell. At this time, the RN commissioned Supermarine to build its aircraft, as a result of which the company continued an association with flying boats lasting well into the 1940s.

Supermarine's Woolston works, on the River Itchen.

BIRTH OF A SPITFIRE

During the 1920s, both financial constraints and, of course, disarmament, had severely curtailed resources available to the RAF for research and development, restrictions applying equally to the British aircraft industry generally. Paradoxically, in spite of this, it was actually an exciting time for aviation – thanks to the Schneider Trophy competition. The Frenchman Jacques Schneider, son of an armament manufacturer, was perplexed by the demonstrable fact that although seven-tenths of the world's surface was covered by water, marine lagged far behind land-based aviation. Schneider saw the sea providing cheap airports with huge potential for aviation – and so inaugurated an international air race for seaplanes over a water course measured by fixed points. Whichever nation won the coveted silver trophy three consecutive times got to keep it. This was also a period of globally emerging nationalism, meaning that the exciting aerial race became a matter of great national pride. It was this, more than anything else, that drove forward development – leading directly to the fast monoplane fighters of the Second World War.

The genius Reginald Joseph Mitchell, designer of the Spitfire, whose work was continued after his untimely death, aged 42, by Joe Smith.

In 1928, the Supermarine Aviation Works was taken over by Vickers-Armstrong, thereafter operating as Vickers Supermarine. The following year Mitchell won the Schneider Trophy for a second consecutive time, with his sleek S.6 – a monoplane, metal, seaplane. Unfortunately, the economic collapse meant no government funding was forthcoming for Supermarine's next all-important entry. This incensed a wealthy patriot, Lady Houston, who personally funded the £100,000 necessary for Mitchell to compete. Her Ladyship's confidence was well-placed: on 12 September 1931, Flight Lieutenant J.N. Boothman flashed over the delighted crowds at 340.08 mph with the throttle not even wide open – winning the Schneider Trophy for Britain, once and for all. That afternoon, Flight Lieutenant G.H. Stainforth took up another S.6B and set a new world air speed record at 379.05 mph.

A SPITFIRE'S STORY: THE INVISIBLE THREAD

British aviation was supreme, delighting the depressed nation and arousing the interest of the Air Member for Supply & Research: Air Vice-Marshal Hugh Dowding – whose name would become synonymous with the unprecedented aerial battle for Britain's survival which lay ahead.

At the time, owing to the development and investment emphasis, bombers were getting faster – able to outpace existing fighter types. When Mitchell won the Schneider Trophy, the Air Defence of Great Britain relied entirely upon biplanes such as the Bristol Bulldog, which was 10 mph slower than Hawker Hart light bomber introduced in 1929. Although advised by experts that biplanes were superior to monoplanes, Dowding, who had himself flown biplanes during the First World War, disagreed and rightly perceived the monoplane as a major improvement. He also recognised that Mitchell's more advanced designs used more metal parts than the wood framed and fabric covered biplanes – which Dowding saw as a potential advantage in the event of Britain ever being blockaded and timber being in short supply. Dowding believed that the experience of British aircraft designers gained during the Schneider Trophy races could and should be applied to new military, land-based aircraft. Consequently, starting on 1 October 1931, the Air Ministry issued various specifications for a new fighter, inviting British

Mitchell's Schneider Trophy winning seaplane, the S6B.

designers to submit proposals. Eventually, in April 1935, the Air Ministry issued its 'Requirements for Single-Engine Single-Seater Day & Night Fighter (F.10/35)'. This new aircraft, amongst other things, had to feature eight machine guns, an enclosed cockpit, be capable of at least 310 mph at 15,000 feet, and be at least 40 mph faster that contemporary bombers at that height. Interestingly, though, there was no requirement for the new 'real killer fighter' to be a monoplane, indicating not all at Whitehall were as convinced as Dowding that the biplane was obsolete.

On 6 November 1935, Hawker's Chief Test Pilot, P.W.S. 'George' Bulman, successfully flew Sydney Camm's Hurricane on its maiden flight from Brooklands. The flight was successful, and on 3 June 1936, the Air Ministry ordered 600 of the new type – the largest such order to date and indicative of the growing concern regarding German rearmament by this time. That concern was fully justified. The same year, Hitler revealed his new *Luftwaffe* to a disbelieving world in contemptuous disregard of Versailles and the Western Allies. In May 1935, Professor Willy Messerschmitt's new monoplane fighter – the '109' – had flown for the first time. Messerschmitt had followed a simple principal: the smallest and lightest airframe built around the most powerful engine. It would prove a formidable adversary and, ominously, the German prototype was 30 mph faster than Britain's Hurricane. Fortunately, 'a real killer fighter' was on the way: the Supermarine Spitfire.

Mitchell's racing seaplanes were undoubtedly ahead of their time, and the designer soon began work on responding to Air Ministry specification F7/30 and designing a monoplane fighter, using the experience of modern, forward-thinking, technology gained from his Schneider Trophy entrants. The first prototype, a gull-winged brutish machine, was unsuccessful, however, and Mitchell knew full well that it was not up to Germany's challenge. Returning to his drawing board, Mitchell designed the Spitfire, a revolutionary design, whereas Sydney Camm's Hawker Hurricane relied upon tried and tested construction techniques. The Spitfire's fuselage was of three sections: a tubular case accommodating the engine, a monocoque centre section and a detachable tail unit. The wing's mainspar comprised girders of different lengths, a leaf spring, in effect, the thickest part of which was at the wing root, where most strength was required. The wing leading edges were covered in heavy gauge aluminium, the trailing edges in a lighter covering. The Spitfire was, therefore, a superb combination of strength and lightness. With an enclosed cockpit, retractable undercarriage and eight machine guns, powered by the Rolls-Royce Merlin engine, this was a very different aircraft indeed to the Gloster Gauntlet biplanes currently equipping the RAF's frontline fighter squadrons.

On 5 March 1936, a small group of men gathered at Eastleigh airfield, near the Supermarine works, located on the banks of the Itchen Estuary at Woolston, near Southampton. The occasion was an event which could perhaps be considered one of the most important flights since the Wright brothers flew at Kittyhawk: the first test flight of the prototype Spitfire, K5054. Vickers' Chief Test Pilot, 'Mutt' Summers, made a short but successful flight, after which he told excited onlookers that he did not want any of the aircraft's controls altered in any way. Spitfire legend interprets this as meaning that the aircraft was perfect from the off, but such a statement is quite ridiculous even for an aircraft as outstanding as Mitchell's Spitfire. What Summers really meant, of course, was that he did not want any of the controls interfered with before his next flight. Nevertheless, from that very first flight the Spitfire legend was born. It was a profound moment, when this iconic fighter flew for the first time. Soon, the shape and sound of Mitchell's Spitfire would become a potent symbol of British national pride – and to fly one the pinnacle of ambition and achievement for a generation of young men.

On 3 June 1936, the Air Ministry ordered the first Spitfires from Supermarine, the first 49 aircraft costing £8,783 each, the next 26 cost £5,696 each, and the final 31 cost £5,768.10s. According to popular myth, delivery of those machines was delayed by the Spitfire's advanced design, but more accurately this was because Supermarine, a comparatively small company, lacked the facilities and resources for mass production. Camm's Hurricane, the first of the new British fighters to fly, was also first to reach the RAF when 111 Squadron at Northolt took delivery of the first production machine in November 1937. By then, whilst RAF pilots made the quantum leap from biplane to modern monoplane and learned how to fly their very different and more advanced machines, the Me 109 was already available in

BIRTH OF A SPITFIRE

The Spitfire was first flown at Eastleigh on 5 March 1936 by Captain J. 'Mutt' Summers – pictured here on that very day (extreme left) with Major Harold 'Agony' Payn (Assistant Chief Designer), R.J. Mitchell, S. Scott-Hall (Air Ministry Resident Technical Officer) and test pilot Jeffrey Quill.

numbers and being blooded in aerial combat over Spain – as Hitler's *Condor Legion* supported the fascist General Franco in a bitter civil war.

The Spitfire – already supreme in the public's imagination owing to its victorious Schneider Trophy lineage – would not be received by the RAF until 4 August 1938, when 19 Squadron received the first Spitfire at Duxford. As we have seen, powered flight itself was only 34 years old on that date, military aviation younger still – and whereas the Germans had operated their Me 109 monoplane for three years, and even been to war in Spain, RAF fighter pilots now had to convert from their Gloster Gauntlet biplanes, which were little different to First World War types, to the very different, modern Spitfire and Hurricane. The new monoplanes had arrived just in the nick of time; had the RAF gone to war in biplanes, the result would undoubtedly

A SPITFIRE'S STORY: THE INVISIBLE THREAD

Above: The prototype Spitfire, K5054.

Left: Jeffrey Quill over Supermarine in K5054.

have been a catastrophic defeat. Sadly, by the time the Spitfire entered service, though, R.J. Mitchell had succumbed to cancer, aged 42, on 11 June 1937. The Spitfire's creator therefore died without ever knowing of the immeasurable contribution his little fighter made to preserving democracy.

After the devastation of the Basque town of Guernica by the *Luftwaffe* during the Spanish Civil War, the fear of aerial bombardment was almost tangible in Britain. This perception was not assisted by Alexander Korda's film *Things to Come*, screened in 1937, providing a futuristic look at a war beginning in December 1940, in which 'Everytown', deliberately made to resemble London, is flattened by enemy bombers. That same year, *The Gap*, directed by Donald Carter, showed an enemy air attack succeeding because manpower was deficient in Territorial Army anti-aircraft units. On 6 June 1939, *The Warning*, was released, aimed at recruiting volunteers to the Air Raid Precaution network; although Spitfires and Hurricanes were shown scrambling, and described as being 'incredibly fast', the raid succeeded, RAF pilots flying Gladiator biplanes being shot down in droves. These films, at a time when the cinema provided a primary source of entertainment, only emphasised the bomber's apparent invincibility. When the Second World War broke out, an antidote was required to boost public morale and confidence in Britain's aerial defences – hence Korda's *The Lion Has Wings*, the first British film of the war, directed by Brian-Desmond Hurst, Michael Powell and Adrian Brunel, released in November 1939. Featuring the Spitfires of 74 Squadron's 'B' Flight, Powell assured viewers that the RAF was perfectly equipped, able and ready, 'to blow the *Luftwaffe* out of the sky' – and the Spitfire was star of the show.

The early Spitfire Mk Is, however, were far from perfect. The first seventy-four ever produced were powered by the Rolls-Royce Merlin II engine, the remainder of that initial contract receiving the improved Merlin III, and the first seventy-seven were fitted with a fixed pitch, two-bladed, mahogany propeller. This meant that the pilot only had one 'gear', being unable to alter the propeller's angle of bite into the air, which has a similar effect to changing gear in a car. The Me 109, however, already had the three-bladed metal controllable-pitch propeller, produced by Vereinigte Deutsche Metallwerkel (VDM), which was far superior. The German propeller adjusted pitch by way of a reversible electric motor mounted on the engine crankcase, actuation being via a flexible shaft connected to a small primary drive reduction gearbox, which in turn was attached to a large annular gearbox fitted to the rear of the propeller hub – thereby enabling the pilot, via as small control mounted on the aircraft's throttle, to select the optimum pitch for any given situation. It was essential that the new British fighters maintained a close parity to the 109, so from Spitfire K9961 these new aircraft were fitted with the new all mental, three bladed, two-pitch – coarse and fine – de Havilland propeller, although this was only a half-way house between fixed pitch and the VDM airscrew. From L1000 onwards, all production Spitfires became designated Mk IA.

At this time, all Spitfires were still only built at Woolston, where 'Supermariners' toiled long hours at the Woolston and adjacent Itchen Works to fulfil the Air Ministry's orders. On 9 August 1939, came Contract No. B19713/39, an order for 450 more Spitfire Mk Is at a cost of £4,250 each (excluding engine and instruments). The first batch of these aircraft were allocated the serial numbers R6595 to R6644. In the second week of May 1940, a young Sotonian school leaver, Terry White, joined the Supermarine workforce as a 'handy lad'. In 1988, Terry recalled that he was 'utterly bewildered by the noise and, what appeared to me, confusion of what was a very, very busy factory'. At that time, R6644 would have been being built in its jig, and undoubtedly Terry saw the Spitfire under construction, adding that 'When the Germans attacked the West on 10 May 1940, everything went up many gears, there being a great sense of urgency and responsibility'. On that day, Winston Churchill replaced Neville Chamberlain as Britain's Prime Minister, and four days later the last appointments in the new leader's administration were announced – the most significant of which was arguably Lord Beaverbrook, who became Minister of Aircraft Production; immediately the dynamic 'Beaver' would supercharge aircraft production, not least at Supermarine. Another young Sotonian Supermariner was Cyril Russell, who recalled that Beaverbrook's appointment 'soon made its effect felt and our company was instructed to concentrate exclusively on Spitfire production'. It was against this backdrop of events that R6644 was built – and an indication of the increased urgency is reflected by the fact that seventy-seven Spitfires were built by Supermarine in May 1940, compared to the thirty-three of September 1939.

BIRTH OF A SPITFIRE

Above and overleaf: Spitfires being produced at the busy Supermarine factory in 1940.

Completed Spitfires were taken to nearby Eastleigh airfield for final assembly in the newly camouflaged flight sheds there, after which each aircraft would be given a thirty-minute production test flight by one of Supermarine's test pilots. This standard test was formulated at Eastleigh by Jeffrey Quill and George Pickering upon assembly of the first Spitfire Mk Is, and other than

A Spitfire from the same production batch as R6644 – of which we have no photographs – having its markings applied.

catering for changes in Spitfire design, remained largely constant throughout the decade of Spitfire production. On Thursday, 30 May 1940 – just days before conclusion of the Dunkirk evacuation and the final Fall of France – R6644 received its maiden flight at the hands of Jeffrey Quill, who, in 1986, remembered that:

> It usually took a few short flights of not more than five minutes duration each at the start of a production test to clear the engine and propeller settings. This would be followed by a flight of at least twenty minutes to check performance and full throttle settings. For simplicity we usually entered in our log books a total of thirty minutes per aircraft under the general heading of 'Production Test'. No doubt we did ourselves out of a lot of logged airborne time as a result of this form of clerical laziness; one's mind was not focussed [*sic*] on posterity in 1940!
>
> In addition to the essential functional tests of the whole aeroplane (which were listed), the basic performance and

handling should also be checked at selected points throughout the flight envelope. This meant that each aeroplane was to be climbed at maximum continuous climbing power and best climbing speed to its full throttle height of at least 18,000 feet and all instrument readings checked. This was to be followed by a two-minute level run at maximum combat power settings to check the indicated top speed and performance of the engine and supercharger. The aeroplane was then to be put into a full-power dive to its limiting indicated air speed of 470 mph and its trim and control behaviour checked in this extreme condition. In general, and allowing for two or three short initial flights for trimming the ailerons and adjusting boost and propeller settings, this schedule took about forty minutes' flying time and gave the aeroplane a thorough shake down. A minimum of three take-offs and landings was also required before the aeroplane could be passed for delivery. There would be no concessions on any aspect of the schedule.

The question arose as to what was to happen when the weather was too bad to permit the schedule to be carried out. My answer to this was that the aeroplane would stay on the ground until the weather was fit, since no aircraft would ever be delivered until the schedule was completed. I argued that in the immediate short term and with determined piloting, hold-ups due to weather would be minimal and insignificant.

As soon as each new Spitfire emerged from the factory we proposed to fly it whatever the state of air raid alerts, whatever the time of day, balloons up or down, ack-ack guns or no ack-ack guns, rain or shine, Germans or no Germans, and Sundays included. By studying the exact location of the balloon winches we were able to work out a route through the balloon barrage which, by keeping right down to ground-level, enabled us to take off and come into land picking our way through the barrage without hitting a cable while the balloons were flying. It was also arranged that when we were operating through heavy cloud cover, we would have a specific area out to sea south of the Isle of Wight where we could climb to height to complete our test schedules. This would cause minimum inconvenience to the Fighter Command radar stations and the understanding was that if we got picked off by a marauding Me 109, that was our hard luck.

Clearly, test flying Spitfires was a demanding and dangerous business. Jeffrey Quill, of course, was a highly skilled and experienced pilot – and a very brave man.

Jeffrey Kindersley Quill was born in Littlehampton, Sussex, on 1 February 1913, taking a Short Service Commission in the RAF in October 1931, upon

Jeffrey Quill: having delivered the RAF's first Spitfire to 19 Squadron in 1938, he is seen here post-war having flown Spitfire AB910 to Coltishall, where the aircraft joined the RAF Historic Aircraft Flight (now the Battle of Britain Memorial Flight).

A SPITFIRE'S STORY: THE INVISIBLE THREAD

Left: Jeffrey Quill's aluminium knee pad, on which he made notes during production test flights.

Below: Jeffrey Quill's log book, indicating R6644's production test flight on 30 May 1940.

leaving Lancing College. After successfully completing flying training, his first posting was to fly Bristol Bulldog biplane fighters with 17 Squadron at Upavon in September 1932. By November 1934, 'J.K.Q.' was commanding Duxford's Station Flight when offered the role of assistant to the Chief Test Pilot at Vickers, so left the service, joining the reserve of RAF officers, and became a civilian test pilot. In 1936, J.K.Q. became heavily involved with testing the new Spitfire, becoming Chief Test Pilot and being awarded the Air Force Cross that same year. Having delivered the RAF's first Spitfire to 19 Squadron at Duxford on 4 August 1938, in November he was transferred to Supermarine, working full time on the Spitfire programme.

'The Fall of France in June 1940', J.K.Q. recalled, 'had created a most desperate situation, and I felt I simply must get back into a fighter squadron' – which indeed he did, joining 65 Squadron at Hornchurch on 6 August 1940. Soon in action, J.K.Q. soon shared in the destruction of a Me 109, probably destroying another in addition to claiming two He 111 probables. On 24 August 1940, now with the benefit of first-hand combat experience, J.K.Q. returned to Vickers-Armstrong, filing a comprehensive report with certain recommendations regarding how to improve the Spitfire. One suggestion was cannon, the 109 having two 20mm Oerlikon guns in addition to a pair of rifle-calibre machine guns, whereas the Spitfire was less hard-hitting with eight .303 machine guns. 19 Squadron, in fact, was already equipped with the experimental and problematic Spitfire Mk IB, armed only with a pair of 20mm Hispanos, but frequent jamming would soon lead to a loss of confidence in the type, which were replaced by Mk IAs, so it would be a while yet before the Spitfire caught up.

By 1942, the radial engined Fw 190 held sway, completely outclassing the Spitfire Mk V equipping frontline squadrons at that time. Consequently Operation *Airthief* was conceived, a commando raid on a German airfield in France, during which a 190 would be seized and flown back to England by J.K.Q. Fortunately, this hazardous undertaking became unnecessary when a German pilot, disorientated after combat, mistook the Bristol Channel for the English Channel and landed by mistake at RAF Pembrey in South Wales – thereby delivering a perfectly intact 190 to RAF Intelligence. Nonetheless, that J.K.Q., who passed the commando fitness course during his preparation for the operation, was prepared to undertake such a dangerous and audacious operation speaks volumes about the man's personal courage. The following year, J.K.Q.'s contribution to test flying was recognised when he was made an OBE.

Holding the rank of lieutenant commander in the RN Volunteer Reserve, in 1943, J.K.Q. spent five months serving with the Fleet Air Arm whilst working on the Seafire, the carrier version of the Spitfire. Having worked so intensively testing aircraft for so long, by 1947, unsurprisingly, J.K.Q. was exhausted and took enforced leave – having recorded over 5,000 flying hours on 90 different types of aircraft. Returning to work for Vickers, even after the Spitfire was retired from service, J.K.Q.'s association with Mitchell's fighter was still not over: until 1965, he displayed Spitfire AB910 at numerous airshows. His work did not solely concern piston-engined machines, because as head of Vickers' Military Aircraft Office at Weybridge he was directly involved with the TSR2, Sepecat Jaguar and Panavia Tornado jet projects. In 1978, J.K.Q. retired to Andreas on the Isle of Man, where he died on 20 February 1996, aged 83.

Returning to R6644, after J.K.Q.'s successful production test flight, the Spitfire remained at Eastleigh until the following day, when collected by a ferry pilot and flown to RAF Llandow, near St Athan in South Wales, and taken on charge by 38 Maintenance Unit. In 1987, former Air Transport Auxiliary pilot Miss Lettice Curtis, explained to me the impossibility of identifying who made this flight:

> It is quite likely that the pilot who ferried R6644 from Eastleigh to Llandow was not an ATA pilot, and there are a number of reasons for this. Although the ATA ferry pool at White Waltham came into being in February 1940, it was only in mid-May, with the arrival of Winston Churchill as Prime Minister, and his appointment of Lord Beaverbrook as Minister of Aircraft Production, that the ATA became a properly organised body. During May 1940, the RAF ferry pools were still in existence and the one based at Bristol Whitchurch may well have sent a pilot to collect R6644. There are, I fear, none of the thirty or so

Above and below: Spitfire R6644's Form 78, or Aircraft Movement Card, providing the baseline of data for this book.

original ATA pilots still alive, and women did not fly Spitfires until late 1941. If a civilian pilot collected R6644, he could well have been from British Overseas Airways Corporation (BOAC). At the start of the 'hot' war, RAF pilots began being withdrawn from non-operational duties, so a number of BOAC captains, unoccupied as a result of the war, were seconded to the ATA. The nearest serial I have in my log book was R6602, which I flew in 1942 when it had been converted to a Mk V.

Like nearby St Athan, Llandow was originally built as a massive Aircraft Storage Unit (ASU), where new aircraft would be prepared for operational service and stored. On 1 April 1940, 38 Maintenance Unit formed at Llandow to undertake this process, and on 31 May 1940 took R6644 on charge.

Spitfire R6644 now awaited allocation to an operational unit.

Chapter Two

5 Operational Training Unit: A Roll Call of the Lost

After just six days at Llandow, on 6 June 1940, R6644 was allocated to 5 Operational Training Unit at Aston Down, near Stroud in Gloucestershire, and flown there by an unknown ferry pilot.

Due to the fighting in France and the casualties suffered, the matter of pilot training was now a vexing one for Fighter Command, given the need to carefully shepherd limited resources. At the outbreak of the Second World War, Fighter Command was the only RAF Command to oppose Air Ministry plans for establishing special units to convert pilots to the type of aircraft they would fly operationally. Air Chief Marshal Sir Hugh Dowding, Fighter Command's commander, considered that allocating operational aircraft for conversion training away from squadrons was a waste of aircraft when such instruction could be given by the squadrons themselves – as indeed it previously had been. Ironically, though, at the time, Fighter Command was the only Command to possess such a unit: 11 Group Pool had been formed at Andover on 16 January 1939, and equipped with four Demon biplane fighters with which to train eight pilots at a time on two-month courses. The Air Ministry considered that three pools would actually be required to back the thirty-six squadrons, but shortages of aircraft, personnel and aerodromes delayed the expansion process. By March 1939, 11 Group Pool had moved to St Athan in South Wales, and re-established itself with more modern aircraft, namely eleven Battles and twenty-two Hurricanes.

In September 1939, however, the unit was seriously below establishment whilst focusing upon the advanced service flying training of volunteer reservists. Shortly after the outbreak of war, the unit's Battles were replaced with Harvard trainers, and soon 11 Group Pool was only five Hurricanes short of its authorised establishment. The course length was halved to four weeks, and syllabus hours reduced from forty-five to thirty hours per pupil. Producing twenty-four pilots every four weeks, it was hoped that the Pool would provide three hundred pilots trained to operational standard per year.

Still Fighter Command HQ remained sceptical regarding the value of Pools for training at the expense of front-line strength. Dowding continued to vigorously contest the need, making it clear at conferences on 15 and 21 September 1939 that, in his opinion, new pilots from FTS should be trained in squadrons, 11 Group Pool at St Athan being used only for reinforcements to France. The commander-in-chief went further by saying that the need for a 12 Group Pool based at Aston Down in Gloucestershire was unnecessary. The Air Ministry parried with the argument that the lack of Group Pools would mean a lack of casualty replacements when the fighting became intense, and if necessary Group Pool aircraft could be taken for operational use. Fighter Command therefore agreed, albeit reluctantly, to this compromise and opened 12 Group Pool on a limited basis, on the understanding that it did not absorb any Spitfires or Hurricanes. Training was still to be ongoing in squadrons, and the constant need for it was impressed upon group commanders.

No. 12 Group Pool became operational at Aston Down on 25 September 1939, equipped with six Harvards, three Blenheims and eleven Gladiators. The schedule was to train some 230 pilots per year. Both pools were initially handicapped, though, by a shortage of cine-camera guns, reflector gunsights, lack of proper armouries, and no ground-to-air radio-telephony facilities. Nonetheless, when the general adequacy of Group Pools was compared with FTS output in October, it was found to be satisfactory. The planned Group Pool capacity at full establishment almost equalled that of the FTSs with a projected figure of 1,100 fighter pilots per year. In reality the Group Pools were far below establishment and therefore capable of dealing with less than half of those proposed numbers. Due to lack of aircraft, the Pools were able to do little Blenheim training and no Spitfire training at all. To remedy the former deficiency, a few pupils were given conversion courses at Hendon during December 1939.

5 OPERATIONAL TRAINING UNIT: A ROLL CALL OF THE LOST

In January 1940, Fighter Command eventually agreed in principle that an adequate operational training system for fighter squadrons should be established. Both 11 and 12 Group Pools were renamed Operational Training Units (OTU) the following March, and became 6 and 5 respectively. The OTUs remained under the command of their respective Fighter Command Group areas (but in June 1940 were placed under the direct control of 10 Group). By 1 April 1940, the fighter training organisation had expanded and three OTUs were planned with a total strength of forty-eight Hurricanes, thirty-four Spitfires, twenty Blenheims, four Defiants, two Gladiators and twenty-four Harvards or Battles.

These decisions were not altogether welcomed by Dowding, who disagreed that the recent spate of flying accidents prompting the Air Ministry's action was due to inadequate training, and still saw OTUs as an unaffordable luxury. Dowding particularly objected to a third OTU being formed before all front-line squadron requirements were met. His arguments were once again to no avail as the Air Ministry decided to go ahead, regardless. At that time the total strength of operational aircraft held by OTUs was 20, as opposed to the authorised 132. Their combined pilot output was barely enough to back the Hurricane squadrons in France serving there with the Advanced Air Striking Force (AASF), and also fulfil the requirement to supply ninety Blenheim pilots to Fighter Command. In France the fighter squadrons criticised the standard of training provided by OTUs, the replacement pilots being received direct from St Athan and Aston Down having just ten hours flying experience on Hurricanes or Spitfires, and no high altitude, oxygen or fighter attack experience.

In May 1940, the urgent need for replacement, operational, fighter pilots suddenly became acutely apparent when the Hurricane squadrons in France began suffering heavy losses. Nos. 5 and 6 OTUs were at that time achieving a maximum output of eighty pilots per month, against a monthly requirement of 200 for casualty replacement alone. Hitler's attack on the West that month brought the realities of modern warfare into sharp focus, emphasising the urgent need to step up operational training. With the Dunkirk evacuation having concluded on 3 June 1940, fighter pilots who had fought in France and survived returned home with valuable combat experience. Some of these men were rested from operations and posted as flying instructors to OTUs, there to pass on their knowledge of air fighting to new pilots. On 30 May 1940, for example, Wing Commander Patrick 'Bull' Halahan, who commanded 1 Squadron during the Fall of France, arrived at Aston Down to take command of 5 OTU. A week later, Halahan's DFC was gazetted, the citation describing how he had destroyed a Do 17 in November 1939, and led an attack on sixteen enemy aircraft near Maastricht, six of which were destroyed, two by Halahan himself. The 'Bull', the citation reads, 'has at all times set an excellent example to his pilots and is mainly responsible for the fine spirit of his squadron, which, under his command, has destroyed approximately seventy enemy aircraft'. Given this experience and obvious leadership skills, there could have been no better officer appointed to command 5 OTU. With Halahan came his two former 1 Squadron flight commanders, namely Flight Lieutenants Peter 'Johnnie' Walker and Prosser Hanks – both were aces, which is to say they were credited with five or

Squadron Leader 'Bull' Halahan (sixth from left) with 1 Squadron's pilots at Nueville-sur-Ornaine during the 'Phoney War'. After the Fall of France, Halahan commanded 5 OTU at Aston Down, taking with him Prosser Hanks (fourth left) and John 'Iggy' Kilmartin (third right) as flight commanders.

5 OPERATIONAL TRAINING UNIT: A ROLL CALL OF THE LOST

more enemy aircraft destroyed, and both would be decorated with the DFC for their efforts on the continent. On 11 June 1940, another 1 Squadron ace, Flying Officer John 'Iggy' Kilmartin, also arrived to instruct, so there was no shortage of combat experience amongst Halahan's staff.

The Basic Fighter Course provided by the OTUs at this time lasted a fortnight. Having already completed advanced flying training, student pilots would first be checked out by an instructor in a North American Harvard, a two-seater monoplane trainer, before soloing on the Spitfire. Thereafter flights consisted of aerobatic practice, to master the aircraft and increase confidence in handling, dogfight practice, formation practice, battle climbs, mock interceptions, and cross-country navigation exercises. Such was the shortage of ammunition, however, that there was no opportunity for air-to-air firing, only popping off a few rounds into the Severn Estuary. After the Fall of France came a lull, until 19 June 1940, when German bombers attacked targets in East Anglia by night, and son afterwards, on 2 July 1940 (although officially eight days later) the Battle of Britain began. Fought to deny the *Luftwaffe* the aerial supremacy necessary for a seaborne invasion of southern England to succeed, this unprecedented contest would last sixteen weeks; thanks to Lord Beaverbrook the supply of replacement aircraft was never

The North American Harvard, which student pilots flew at 5 OTU before soloing in a Spitfire or Hurricane.

an issue for Fighter Command – but replacement pilots were. Consequently this meant reducing the Basic Fighter Course in order to rush pilots through the conversion process – so these young men arrived at their squadrons with rarely more than just ten hours flying time on Spitfires recorded in their log books. Nonetheless, the course reduction was dictated by the urgency of the hour – and Aston Down was a hive of activity when R6644 arrived.

It is a fact that between the wars air power doctrine revolved around the bomber delivering a 'knockout blow' against an enemy's military and industrial means, or causing dissent, and even uprising, against people's own governments by targeting civilian populations. So much faith was there is these theories, propagated by the Italian General Douhet, that what little spending there was in Britain on re-armament was heavily loaded in favour of the 'Bomber Barons'. This, of course, was at the expense of the fighter force, which, indeed, Lord Trenchard considered only necessary 'to keep up the morale of one's own people'. Fortunately Air Chief Marshal Dowding disagreed, and was single-mindedly dedicated to the concept of 'security of base', arguing that unless there was a robust defence, the 'Bomber Barons' would never be able to deliver a 'knockout blow'. After Dowding became Fighter Command's first chief in 1936, ably assisted by Air Commodore Keith Park, his Senior Air Staff Officer, he set about honing to perfection the System of Air Defence, which far-sightedly included the new science of radar, thanks to Dowding's technical mind and understanding. So little was that of fighters, in fact, that army cooperation flying was seen as more important. Flying generals around in light communications aircraft like the Westland Lysander was hardly the exciting life most young men had volunteered for, and so after the Fall of France many such bored pilots answered Fighter Command's call for volunteers – amongst them, on 23 June 1940, Pilot Officer Richard Hillary who was previously serving at No. 1 School of Army Co-operation at Old Sarum. In his classic memoir, *The Last Enemy*, Hillary described his first flight in a Spitfire, which occurred at Aston Down:

> The Spitfires stood in two lines outside 'A' Flight's pilots' room. The dull-grey-brown of their camouflage could not conceal their clear-cut beauty, the wicked simplicity of their lines. I hooked

5 OPERATIONAL TRAINING UNIT: A ROLL CALL OF THE LOST

up my parachute and climbed awkwardly into the low cockpit. I noticed how small was my field of vision. Kilmartin swung himself onto a wing and started to run through the instruments. I was conscious of his voice but heard nothing of what he said. I was to fly a Spitfire. It was what I had most wanted through all the long, dreary, months of training. If I could fly a Spitfire, it would all be worth it. Well I was about to achieve my ambition and felt nothing. I was numb, neither exhilarated nor scared…

I taxied slowly across the field, remembering suddenly what I had been told: that the Spitfire's prop was long and that it was therefore inadvisable to push the stick too far forward when taking off; that the Spitfire was not a Lysander and that any hard application of the brake when landing would result in a somersault and immediate transfer to a Battle squadron. Because of the Battle's lack of power and small armament, this was regarded by everyone as the ultimate disgrace.

I ran quickly through my cockpit drill, swung the nose into wind, and took off. I had been flying automatically for several minutes before it dawned on me that I was actually in the air, undercarriage retracted and half way round the circuit without incident. I turned into wind and hauled up on my seat, at the same time pushing back the hood. I came in low, cut the engine, and floated down on all three points. I took off again. Three more times I came round for a perfect landing. It was too easy. I waited across wind for a minute and watched with satisfaction several machines bounce badly as they came in. Then I taxied rapidly back into the hangars and climbed out nonchalantly. Noel, who had not yet soloed, met me. 'How was it?' he said. I made a circle of approval with my thumb and forefinger. 'Money for old rope', I said. I didn't make a good landing for a week.

The 5 OTU Operations Record Book records the names of over 100 pilots who converted to Spitfires at Aston Down in June and July 1940. Truly, this list of names makes for sad reading, a veritable roll call of the lost, as

A SPITFIRE'S STORY: THE INVISIBLE THREAD

Pilot Officer Richard Hillary, author of *The Last Enemy* chronicling his personal journey having been shot down and grievously burned during the Battle of Britain, who may well have flown R6644 at 5 OTU – possibly beneath the Severn railway bridge!

so many were to die in the Battle of Britain or the wider war. For example 19-year-old Pilot Officer Robert Dewy was shot down and killed flying Spitfires with 603 Squadron on 27 October 1940; Pilot Officer Ray Aeberhardt, also 19, lost his life on 31 August 1940 flying Spitfires with 19 Squadron at Fowlmere when he crashed back at base whilst landing his combat damaged fighter without flaps; on the same day, 24-year-old Pilot Officer Gerald Maffett, a Hurricane pilot on 257 Squadron, was shot down and killed by Me 109s, crashing at Walton-on-the-Naze; the previous day, 30 August 1930, saw Pilot Officer Colin Francis – another 19-year-old and a Hurricane pilot with 253 Squadron – reported missing after combat and would remain so until discovered in the wreckage of his aircraft in 1981. A sad list indeed.

The Operations Record Books are a primary source of information for researchers, and these essential documents are preserved at The National Archives. Unfortunately, they are inconsistent in terms of content, some being excellent, others scant in detail. Most comprise two forms, the Form 540, being a daily summary of events, and Form 541, which is essentially a unit flying log book, recording the pilot, aircraft, time up, down, sortie and any other remarks. Unfortunately, there is no Form 541 for 5 OTU, and so it is impossible to compile a list of pilots who flew R6644 during the Spitfire's time at Aston Down, which was 31 May 1940–4 July 1940. Unfortunately the flying log books of most aircrew killed, or even captured, were destroyed by the Air Ministry during the early post-war period, only preserving a handful of specimens, so the log books of those we know not to have survived, including Pilot Officer Richard Hillary and his friends, Pilot Officers Peter Pease and Noël le Chevalier Agazarian, there is no means of confirming their flights with 5 OTU. After the war, the Air Ministry recognised those Fighter Command aircrew who flew operationally during the Battle of Britain, between 10 July 1940–31 October 1940, with the award of the Battle of Britain Clasp to the 1939–1945 Star. Many of these men – the fabled Few – joined the Battle of Britain Fighter Association, membership of which was exclusive to clasp holders. During the 1980s, the Honorary Secretary was Wing Commander Pat Hancock, who kindly passed letters on my behalf to members known to have converted to Spitfires at Aston Down when R6644 was there. The question, of course, was did their log books record a flight in this Spitfire? From that investigation eight pilots were identified as having flown R6644 at 5 OTU – and also confirmed that Flight Lieutenant Kilmartin did not.

These are their stories.

Flight Lieutenant Peter Prosser Hanks

Hanks made R6644's first flight at Aston Down, on 7 June 1940, an air test of just five minutes' duration. He next flew the Spitfire on 28 June 1940, a formation exercise lasting forty minutes, and finally for an hour on 2 July 1940, practising Fighter Command attacks.

From York, Hanks was commissioned into the RAF during 1935, and at this juncture it is appropriate for us to explore the structure of the service's flying personnel and commissioning system.

When Trenchard originally created the RAF, his vision was that all officers would be pilots, permanently commissioned and trained at the RAF College Cranwell. Cranwell, which was fee paying and really an extension of the public-school system, was too small, however, to produce the quantity of pilots required by the RAF, especially in time of war, and, of course, in reality not all officers were capable of being pilots, a skill above and

Flight Lieutenant Peter Prosser Hanks DFC pictured at Vassincourt whilst serving in France with No. 1 Squadron.

beyond normal duties. In 1921, Trenchard, to achieve the number of pilots he needed and create a trained reserve, permitted a small number of non-commissioned officers to re-train as pilots. The concept was that these men would fly for five years before resuming their original trades, whilst eligible for recall to flying duties in the event of an emergency. The initiative was both popular and economic, but numbers remained small: in 1925, 13.9% of pilots were NCOs, rising to 17.1% in 1935. Trenchard's next initiative was revolutionary: Short Service Commission.

In the two senior services, officers usually served for the duration of their working lives (hence the term 'Permanent Commission'). This, however, lead to a 'dead man's shoes' scenario, which Trenchard wished to avoid, recognising that flying is a strenuous physical activity for young men. The SSC scheme, therefore, provided for officers to serve a fixed contract of four years active

5 OPERATIONAL TRAINING UNIT: A ROLL CALL OF THE LOST

service, followed by six on the reserve list. Such officers were only eligible for promotion so far as flight lieutenant but could transfer to a Permanent Commission upon successfully passing the required examination. The pre-war SSC initiative also reached out to young men of the Empire and Commonwealth, who travelled to England and became both RAF officers and pilots. Together with Direct Entrants from the University Air Squadron, SSC officers were not trained at Cranwell, which remained exclusively for professional career officers, but at Service Flying Training School. Furthermore, the Direct Entry Scheme provided a small number of permanent commissions offered to university graduates via competition for limited places.

Pilot Officer Hanks learned to fly at 6 Flying Training School, Netheravon, making his first flight on 28 October 1935, as a passenger in Avro Tutor K3390 flown by an instructor, Flight Lieutenant Dickson. Having gone solo on 5 November 1935, Hanks completed both elementary and advanced flying training at Netheravon before being posted to 1 Squadron at Tangmere. Flying Hawker Furies, Demons and Harts, and Gloster Gauntlets and Gladiators, Hanks excelled at aerobatics and became a member of the Squadron's prestigious aerobatics team. Indeed, on 26 June 1937, he displayed with the team at the enormously popular Hendon Air Pageant.

Having previously only flown open cockpit biplanes with an open cockpit and fixed undercarriage, on 31 January 1938, he flew a Hurricane, L5941, for the first time – a very different aeroplane only having in common with the biplanes a fixed pitch propeller at that time. Some pilots, including the legless Douglas Bader in due course, found the transition difficult, not least having to remember to lower and retract the monoplane's undercarriage. Hanks flew L5941 three times that day, noting in his log book having practised operating the undercarriage and sliding the cockpit canopy back and forth. The following year, on 3 September 1939, Hanks recorded in his log 'Great Britain and France declare war on Germany' – by which time he had accumulated 767.45 flying hours.

According to the 1 Squadron Operations Record Book (ORB), 'The declaration of war found No. 1 Squadron fully prepared'. Indeed, for days previously the Squadron had received orders for 16 Hurricanes to be ready at one hour's notice to move to France with 100 personnel and stores for two weeks. With the CO, Squadron Leader Halahan, having flown to France on 7 September 1939, the following day saw Flight Lieutenant Walker lead the Squadron from Tangmere to Octeville. There 1 Squadron joined the RAF Advanced Air Striking Force (AASF), formed on 24 August 1939, the French component comprising ten squadrons of Fairey Battle light bombers, two of Blenheims and now, in addition to 1 Squadron, the Hurricanes of 73 Squadron. The idea was that flying from airfields around Rheims, the bombers would attack strategic targets in Germany, although in the event Anglo-French command was reluctant to provoke a German attack on the West, and so instead the German military and communications were targeted. No. 1 Squadron's first commitment in France, however, was less violent: a morale-boosting exercise on 9 September 1939, as the ORB recorded: 'At 1135 hrs the Squadron took off and flew over Le Havre. A demonstration of squadron, flight, and section formation air drill was given. This greatly impressed the people and thereby did much good for the Squadron.'

This was, of course, the so-called 'Phoney War', when nothing much happened as both sides awaited the following year's campaigning season. 1 Squadron's pilots patrolled uneventfully and undertook dogfight practice with French Morane and Curtis fighters – monoplanes but inferior to the Hurricane, Hanks noting in his log book having 'won' two such 'combats' in October 1939. By April 1940, however, the *Luftwaffe* was more active, and on the 1st of that month Hanks, now a flight lieutenant, would see action for the first time – indeed, this was the first time that any future pilot of R6644 pilot would experience combat. On that day, from 0630 hrs onwards, operating from Vassincourt, 1 Squadron maintained patrols on the Metz front between Thionville and Boulay, and at 1140 hrs, Hanks was patrolling with Flying Officer Clisby and Pilot Officer Mould at 22,000 feet when the pilots sighted anti-aircraft fire over Thionville. Three minutes later, nine twin-engined Me 110s were sighted flying west over Thionville, 4,000 feet above the three Hurricanes. Immediately, Hanks climbed his Section to 'get on their tails'; he later reported that:

> As we were climbing below and a little to one side of the enemy, they saw us and turned to attack. Three of their aircraft remained

in position, while the rest followed the leader. The leader turned straight for me, and he and I fired at each other head-on. His burst was canon and incendiary bullets, and one cannot shot penetrated my port leading edge, went through the main spar, the oil tank and petrol tank, and shrapnel pierced the Perspex hood. Oil poured out of the mainplane but I decided to finish my ammunition off before leaving the combat. I fired at about four different aircraft and saw one go spinning down, completely out of control, but as I watched it go down, another got on my tail and I lost sight of it.

All three Hurricane pilots claimed an Me 110 destroyed, which the ORB noted 'proved to be exceptionally manoeuvrable for a twin-engined aircraft and very fast' – at odds with the popular narrative telling us that the 110 was not. Moreover, in a head-on attack, as Hanks discovered, with a pair of 20mm Oerlikon cannons and twin 7.92mm machine guns, the 110 packed a heavyweight punch. None of the I/ZG 26 Me 110s involved, however, were actually destroyed in the combat, although one returned to Niedermendig damaged and with a wounded crewman aboard, and another crashed on landing there with damaged undercarriage. Fortunately, Hanks managed to safely land his Hurricane, N2380, at Etain-Rouvres and was unhurt.

More action followed for Hanks on 20 April 1940, again over the Metz front:

> A He 111 escorted by two Me 109s and a He 112 was attacked by Flight Lieutenant Hanks, Pilot Officer Mould, Sergeants Berry and Albonico near Charnay at 23,000 feet. In the action that followed, the He 111 was shot down by Flight Lieutenant Hanks and landed within our lines. One Me 109 was shot down by Berry, Albonico also claimed a 109. The He 112 was attacked by Pilot Officer Mould and last seen diving steeply for Germany with black smoke pouring from it. Sergeant Berry, who saw the He 112 fire from a front view states that it bore wing armament placed much the same as our Spitfire and may have been six or eight guns. This was the first He 112 ever engaged in this war on the Western Front. [ORB]

Surprisingly, considering the report that the He 111 crashed behind Allied lines, there is no record of any German bomber coming down in this area on this day. The reference to the 'He 112' is erroneous: this was a German single-engined, single-seater prototype fighter which never saw operational service – although the Nazi propaganda machine managed to convince the Allies that many of this type were on charge with *Luftwaffe Jagdgeschwadern*. Given the speed of combat, aircraft identification is frequently either questionable or incorrect, and throughout the battles over France and Britain ahead, innumerable combats would be reported by RAF pilots with 'He 112s' – which in reality were either Me 109s or even friendly fighters mistaken for enemy machines. This, though, is clear: Sergeant Berry did not see a He 112 that day, and nor could it have been a Spitfire, given the foresight of Air Chief Marshal Dowding in only sending Hurricanes to France in order to preserve his less numerous but superior Spitfires for home defence.

On 22 April 1940, Hanks was leading a section of Hurricanes on patrol when fifteen Me 109s were sighted at 30,000 feet; in his log book, Hanks wrote 'They refused to fight. Moral victory for us!'

On Friday, 10 May 1940, the 'Sitzkrieg' ended abruptly with Hitler's shocking attack on the West. Beginning at 0435 hrs, the 'Blitzkrieg' achieved total surprise, German troops pouring across the Dutch, Belgian, French and Luxembourg borders. Anticipating that the Germans would replicate their strategy of 1918, and advance from the Netherlands into Belgium from the north, the BEF was forced to pivot forward 60 miles into previously neutral, across unreconnoitred ground with no supply dumps or prepared positions. In doing so, the Allies had fallen for the bait: the actual *Schwerpunkt*, the point of main effort, was actually cleverly disguised. As Gort's men marched into Belgium, *Panzergruppe* von Kleist was successfully negotiating the supposedly impassable Ardennes forest, thereby outflanking and neutralising the much-vaunted French Maginot Line – and soon the *panzers* would be racing for the Channel coast in a totally unanticipated uppercut movement. Overhead streamed German aircraft, as the AASF valiantly but ultimately hopelessly fought back. On that fateful day, Hanks flew six patrols, claiming a Do 17 destroyed and after the final sortie landing at Berry-Au-Bac,

5 OPERATIONAL TRAINING UNIT: A ROLL CALL OF THE LOST

where 1 Squadron was bombed on the ground within half an hour. As the Blitzkrieg progressed, the tempo of fighting rapidly increased: on 11 May 1940, Hanks claimed two Me 110s destroyed, one of these, shared with Flying Officer Clisby and Pilot Officer Mould, being a 3/ZG 2 machine escorting II/KG 53 He 111s and which crash-landed near Vendresse where the two crewmen were captured. Another 110 was claimed destroyed the following day, and on 13 May 1940 Hanks shared the destruction of an 8/KG 55 He 111 bent on bombing Allied troops near Charleville-Mézières and which also crash-landed near Vendresse. Two days later, Hanks was shot down by an Me 110, over St Rémy-le-Petit, baling out unhurt. Back in action, on 19 May 1940, what was left of 1 Squadron attacked thirty He 111s, during which six of Hanks's eight machine guns jammed, forcing him to break off the combat. Four days later, the Squadron's losses were such that it was withdrawn back to England; three days afterwards Lord Gort, his BEF in danger of envelopment, decided to evacuate his BEF from the flat beaches around Dunkirk: the unthinkable had happened.

Arriving at Aston Down to instruct at 5 OTU on 30 May 1940, by the time his DFC was gazetted on 15 July 1940, Operation *Dynamo*, the Dunkirk evacuation, had concluded on 3 June 1940; on 22 June 1940, France had surrendered, and, as the British Prime Minister, Winston Churchill rightly but ominously predicted 'What General Weygand called the Battle of France is over. I expect the Battle of Britain is about to begin', which, at least according to the Air Ministry, it did on 10 July 1940. Hanks would not actually receive his medal until attending an investiture at Buckingham Palace on 3 September 1940 – the first anniversary of Britain and France's declaration of war on Nazi Germany.

Even though flying in a non-operational role, there was always the chance of action, as lone or small formations of German bombers, engaged on reconnaissance or nuisance raids – as Flight Lieutenant Hanks discovered on 25 July 1940.

On that day, a Ju 88 crew of 5/KG 51, based at Paris-Orly, was briefed to carry out a solo Störflug, a nuisance attack, on the Gloster Aircraft Factory at Hucclecote, near Gloucester. Having passed over the Isle of Wight at 18,500 feet, the enemy navigator and aircraft captain, *Unteroffizier* Wilhem

Hugelschäfer, noted that the weather was fine and clear – completely unsuitable conditions for such a raid, which relied upon heavy cloud to approach and escape undetected. Nonetheless, the pilot, *Unteroffizier* Friedel Dörner, pressed on, flying east of the intended target before turning to pass directly over the factory. Given the weather, however, the bomber's progress had not gone unnoticed, and as it passed over Kemble airfield near Cirencester, some 6 miles west of Aston Down, two ferry pilots, Pilot Officers Alec Bird and Richard Manlove, spotted the Ju 88 and scrambled in their Hurricanes. Giving chase, Bird's Hurricane, fitted with the new and superior Rotol Constant Speed Propeller, drew ahead.

As Pilot Officer Bird closed in and *Unteroffizier* Walter Theiner, the flight engineer, shouted his warning, Hugelschäfer jettisoned the bombs, Dörner turning south-south-west, racing for the coast and home. Anti-aircraft fire then burst between the two Hurricanes, Manlove, being slightly behind, watching his comrade close or a stern attack on the Ju 88, level with the bomber at 18,000 feet. As the bombs fell, Dörner changed course abruptly and dived for the nearest patch of thin cloud. No sooner had he done so that Hugelschäfer felt 'A severe jolt in the back'. Whilst converging from the port side, Manlove saw Bird 'close right in and deliver his attack from very close quarters before turning away upwards and to port'. At the top of the break, Manlove watched Bird's Hurricane suddenly go into a spin.

Alone, Manlove then opened fire from long-range, some 500–600 yards, at which point the Ju 88's starboard engine broke up and a parachute left the aircraft. Inside the bomber was chaos. At 12,500 feet, Dörner lost control, ordering the crew to bale out. Manlove followed the bomber's downward spiral, observing Pilot Officer Bird's Hurricane still spinning but down to only 500 feet. Then, he saw '… a flock of Spitfires arriving', which orbited the burning Hurricane. Reluctantly accepting that Bird's fate was sealed, Manlove returned to Kemble.

The 'Spitfires' were from nearby 5 OTU at Aston Down, and was actually Flight Lieutenant Hanks DFC in Spitfire P9501, and a pupil in a Hurricane. The pair were engaged on dogfight practice when informed by the Duty Controller of the Ju 88's presence and hurried to investigate. In 1985, Hanks remembered that:

5 OPERATIONAL TRAINING UNIT: A ROLL CALL OF THE LOST

> When I first saw the Ju 88, he was well above me, being chased by a Hurricane, presumably Bird's. I went after them, leaving my pupil a long way behind. When the 88 entered cloud, Bird's Hurricane was about 800 yards astern of it and followed the bomber into the cloud. I was still about a thousand feet below. I carried on below cloud in the general direction of the Ju 88, which after only a short while broke cloud about a thousand yards ahead of me. It looked to be flying quite normally and I saw no damage or pieces falling off. I closed with it and started firing. I must admit to having been surprised to have received no return fire, and almost immediately the crew began baling out.

At 1415 hrs, the Ju 88 crashed into Bidcombe Bottom, between Oakridge and France Lynch, near Stroud. Pilot Officer Bird's Hurricane crashed at Bournes Green, Oakridge, on the Bisley Road. Soon a posse of special constables arrived on the scene, finding the fighter burnt out and the pilot's remains being removed by a Mr P. Handy of Painswick. What, though, had caused the crash? Hugelschäfer, an experienced combat flyer, always remained convinced that his aircraft had been deliberately rammed by Bird. Certainly, in the opinion of Pilot Officer Manlove, 'there is no doubt that the aircraft (Ju 88) was destroyed by Pilot Officer Bird'. Upon hearing of Bird's involvement and fate, Hanks retracted his claim for the raider's destruction, which was accredited to Pilot Officer Bird.

Interestingly, although they had seen action flying fighters between 10 July 1940–31 October 1940, the dates between which the Air Ministry later considered that the Battle of Britain had taken place, the names of Hanks, Manlove and Bird – who gave his life – will not be found amongst the ranks of 'The Few' because they were not flying operationally with one of the seventy-two Fighter Command or appended units considered to have fought the battle.

Hanks would remain at Aston Down until his next operational posting, on 17 December 1940, which was as a flight commander on 257 Squadron at North Weald, again flying Hurricanes. Near the east coast, the majority of sorties during the winter months would involve routine but essential convoy protection patrols. By that time, cutting a very long story short, Air Chief Marshal Dowding had been retired and replaced by Air Marshal Sholto Douglas, and Air Vice-Marshal Park, the tactical victor of the Battle of Britain, sent to Training Command and replaced by Air Vice-Marshal Leigh-Mallory. The new brooms were obsessed with the idea of using mass formations in both attack and defence, and were determined that Fighter Command should go on the offensive, 'reaching out', 'leaning into France', and taking the war to the Germans instead of fighting another defensive campaign. So it was that the so-called 'Non-Stop Offensive' began in earnest during the spring of 1941, which also saw a significant reorganisation of Fighter Command. The machine-gun armed Spitfire Mk IIA and the cannon-armed B were in the process of replacing the Hurricane as the RAF's frontline fighter, and all sector stations now accommodated wings of three Spitfire squadrons. To command these new formations came the first 'Wing Commander (Flying)' appointments in March 1941, and that same month 257 Squadron began training for and flying sweeps over France (of which much more later). For Flight Lieutenant Hanks, though, action was found much closer to home: on 28 March 1941, he claimed a He 111 destroyed 20 miles out over the North Sea, and on the night of 7 May 1941, as the night Blitz drew towards its destructive crescendo, he shot down a Ju 88, also over the sea.

Following an interview with Air Vice-Marshal Leigh-Mallory on 16 June 1941, four days later Hanks was promoted to acting squadron leader and posted to command 56 Squadron, also at North Weald and flying Hurricanes. In September 1941, 56 re-equipped with the new Hawker Typhoon, a brute of a single-engined fighter bomber which, not without initial difficulties, Squadron Leader Hanks helped introduce to operational service. Following this pioneering contribution, a further promotion followed and a posting to command the Duxford Wing on 20 December 1941. Something that had caused problems with the Typhoon was carbon monoxide poisoning of pilots, and on 21 December 1941, Wing Commander Hanks flew Typhoon R7589 on a carbon monoxide test flight. Having survived the experience, many similar flights followed, in various 'Tiffies'. On 22 February 1942, Hanks moved on, to command the Spitfire-equipped Coltishall Wing. On 15 March 1942 the 'Wingco' damaged a North Sea E-boat, and on 29 April

5 OPERATIONAL TRAINING UNIT: A ROLL CALL OF THE LOST

1942, flying in the defence of Norwich, claimed one and a shared Do 215 probable, and another damaged, following these successes up with a shared Ju 88 destroyed on 16 May 1942.

In June 1940, another battle had begun far from East Anglia when fascist Italy declared war on the Western Allies, and began to attack the island of Malta, Britain's essential strategic base in the Mediterranean. Between then and December 1942, the tiny, heavily built-up, island, no bigger than the Isle of Wight, famously became 'one of the most bombed places on earth'. At first, the island's aerial defence was provided by three Gloster Gladiators, *Faith*, *Hope* and *Charity*, Flight Lieutenant George Burgess destroying the first Italian bomber over Malta in the former aircraft on 22 June 1940. 2 August 1940 saw reinforcements arrive in the shape of twelve Hurricanes flying off HMS *Argus*, with a second delivery of twelve more following in November 1940. 27 April 1941 saw Operation *Dunlop*, the delivery of twenty-four Hurricanes via HMS *Ark Royal*, all but one of which arrived safely, and forty-five more, again flying off that carrier and HMS *Victorious*. Slowly but surely, although dreadfully outnumbered, Malta's aerial defences were strengthened, until eventually, in March 1942, following an abortive attempt the previous month, thirty-one Spitfires were flown off HMS *Eagle*, all of which were most welcome on the besieged island. Further deliveries followed as the fighting became intensely visceral, both in the air and at sea. In August 1942, Wing Commander Hanks DFC and other passengers travelled to Malta via Gibraltar in a Lockheed Hudson communications aircraft, where he took over as Wing Leader at RAF Luqa – and was soon back in action, damaging an Italian Savio Marchetti 79 bomber on 13 August 1942.

On 10 October 1942, Hanks damaged a Me 109F over Malta, flying his personal Spitfire Mk VC, BR498, its fuselage sporting his initials, P.P.-H., as was the Wing Leader's privilege. The following day, Hanks claimed another 'Franz' destroyed and one damaged off Sicily, and on 12 October 1942 he destroyed another, in flames. The next day Hanks damaged a Ju 88 but was himself shot down, forced-landing Spitfire AB464 with a bullet in the sump. So hectic was the fighting now that the next day he damaged an Italian Macchi 202, and destroyed another 109F on 15 October 1942.

Two days later, Hanks led seven Spitfires to intercept seven Ju 88s escorted by thirty Me 109s. Three of the bombers and a 109 were destroyed against the loss of just one Spitfire. This action led to Hanks being invested in the Distinguished Service Order on 3 November 1942, the citation describing him as 'a fearless fighter whose example and leadership have instilled great confidence in his fellow pilots'.

Hanks' final combat claim over Malta came on 18 December 1942, a probably destroyed Savio Marchetti, and on 21 December 1942 he became Station Commander of RAF Hal Far. By that time the tide had turned in the defenders' favour, and although Hanks flew further patrols, and supported Operation *Husky*, the Allied invasion of Sicily on 9 July 1943, no further claims followed. On 20 February 1944, Hanks was promoted to group captain and posted to Italy, the Allies having landed at Salerno on 3 September 1943 (Operation *Avalanche*), to command 286 Wing.

More uneventful flying followed until Group Captain Hanks was posted home in October 1944, becoming Duty Group Captain at Fighter Command HQ, Bentley Priory, and on 4 May 1945 returned to Aston Down, this time as Station Commander. Four days later, the war in Europe was over, and finally, on 15 August 1945, the Japanese also surrendered. Remaining in the post war service, Group Captain Hanks went on to fly de Havilland Vampire and Venom jet fighters before eventually retiring in 1964, with an AFC also to his credit, thus concluding a flying career which began in a biplane, ending in a fast jet. An accomplished pilot, officer and fighter ace, Group Captain Hanks died some years ago.

Squadron Leader Graham 'Minnie' Manton

The next pilot to fly was R6644 also a SSC officer: Squadron Leader Graham Ashley Leonard Manton – known universally as 'Minnie'. Born in Margate on 18 June 1910, Manton was commissioned on 26 June 1931, and after successfully completing flying training at Digby, joined 111 Squadron at Hornchurch on 20 June 1932, flying the Bristol Bulldog biplane fighter. On 29 March 1934, Flying Officer Manton became the assistant adjutant and a

5 OPERATIONAL TRAINING UNIT: A ROLL CALL OF THE LOST

Squadron Leader G.A.L. 'Minnie' Manton pictured when serving in the Far East.

flying instructor on 605 'County of Warwick' Squadron of the Auxiliary Air Force (AAF) – which requires some explanation.

Another sound initiative by Trenchard to create a substantial reserve was creation of the AAF in 1924, based upon the territorial concept: locally-raised squadrons of part-time airmen, who flew at weekends and attended an annual summer camp at an RAF station, representing an essential trained reserve, there to be mobilised in time of emergency. By 1930, the AAF represented 5% of the service's strength, and was demonstrably a *corps d'elite*, the circumstances and attitude of which was perfectly explained by a distinguished auxiliary, namely Group Captain Sir Hugh 'Cocky' Dundas:

> In all the history of arms there can seldom have been a body of men more confident and pleased with themselves than the pilots of the AAF. We wore a big brass 'A' on the lapels of our tunics and no amount of official pressure during the war would

persuade us to remove them. The regulars insisted that the 'A' stood for 'Amateur Airmen', or even 'Argue and Answer Back'. To us they were the symbols of our membership of a very special club. The pilots of the AAF were lawyers and farmers, stockbrokers and journalists; they were landowners and artisans, serious-minded accountants and unrepentant playboys. They had two things in common: a passion for flying and a determination to prove that anything the regulars could do the auxiliaries could do better.

By 1939, there were twenty auxiliary squadrons. In this elite, all pilots were officers, social background and class everything. Many of these young men were of independent means, who even owned their own aeroplanes and flew for pleasure. James Edgar 'Johnnie' Johnson, on the other hand, was a policeman's son from Melton Mowbray:

> I was a member of the local territorial yeomanry but rather fancied flying a Spitfire in preference to riding a bloody great horse. So, I went along for an interview for the AAF and the senior officer present, noting that I was from Leicestershire, said 'With whom do you hunt, Johnson?'
> I said 'Hunt, Sir?'
> He said 'Yes, Johnson, hunt; foxes. With whom do you hunt?'
> I said, 'Well, Sir, I don't hunt, I shoot, pheasants and such on the wing with a 12-bore'.
> He said 'Thank-you, Johnson, that will be all'.
> I simply didn't have the right social background so that was that.

No. 605 Squadron had been formed at Castle Bromwich as a daylight bomber unit, recruiting its personnel from the Birmingham area, at first flying DH9s before converting to the Westland Wapiti. In October 1934, 605 became a fighter squadron, operating the Hawker Hart until August 1936, when these were replaced by Hawker Hinds. By that time, Flight Lieutenant

5 OPERATIONAL TRAINING UNIT: A ROLL CALL OF THE LOST

Manton had become a permanently commissioned officer, having decided, in June 1936, to make a life-long career of the RAF. His next posting was on 1 January 1937, to the Directorate of Flying Training at the Air Ministry – which is where it gets interesting.

When war broke out on 3 September 1939, Manton was still flying a desk at the Air Ministry, by which time he was an experienced officer, one of many now desperate to return to an operational fighter squadron. The only problem was that these men had no experience of flying the new monoplane fighters. Nonetheless, after the Fall of France, when the need for replacements became a priority, a number were provided this opportunity – amongst them Manton, who was promoted to squadron leader and posted to 5 OTU. There, at Aston Down, Manton would convert to the Spitfire and Hurricane, making three flights in R6644: a formation attack practice of fifty-five minutes duration on Sunday, 9 June 1940, a similar exercise of fifty minutes later the same day, and dogfight practice, of an hour and five minutes, on 19 June 1940. His course completed, on 1 July 1940, Squadron Leader Manton was posted to command 56 Squadron at North Weald – a regular Hurricane squadron with a proud fighting tradition dating back to the First World War.

After the German invasion of France and the Low Countries on 10 May 1940, 56 Squadron fought in the Battle of France, for four hectic days 'B' Flight operating from Vitry-en-Artois. During this ill-fated campaign, 56 claimed thirty-five enemy aircraft destroyed, then re-grouped at Digby on 31 May 1940, returning to North Weald a day later. Then, 56 Squadron began receiving new replacement pilots, including Squadron Leader Manton, who succeeded Squadron Leader E.V. Knowles in command. July 1940 began with a variety of training flights: cloud flying, air firing at Sutton Bridge, practice attacks, re-arming and re fuelling practice, and practice 'attacks' on the aerodrome, these training flights punctuated by convoy protection and other patrols, 56 Squadron frequently operating from Martlesham Heath, Manston and Rochford. This gave Manton an opportunity to gain operational experience, which he lacked, and was sensible enough to allow a more experienced man to lead the Squadron in the air, whilst he adjusted to his new role. Nonetheless, 'Minnie' was soon in action, three days after the Battle of Britain began, at least according to the Air Ministry, on 13 July 1940:

> I left Rochford at 1745 hrs to patrol Canterbury, then vectored to Dover, subsequently to carry out sweep to within 10 miles of French coast. Flew westwards, then turned east near French coast, intercepting E/A (enemy aircraft), of which Ju 87s were in sections of three (vic formation) and climbing at the time. I was leading two aircraft (Yellow Section) and followed Red Section into attack. Red had dived onto the formation, which then broke up and turned towards the French coast. Dogfight ensued. I attacked three 87s, one after the other, the first two without visible effect. I sat behind the third, firing continuously, expending all my ammunition, and I last saw it diving steeply towards the sea with petrol pouring from port tanks, then at a height of 2,000 feet. I was then attacked by a He 113 from above and from the rear. I then broke off the engagement and returned to North Weald at 2005 hrs via Manston. The rear-gunner of the third 87 fired only one short burst, so I presume that he was knocked out. On the way back I observed a large circle of foam on the water, in the direction of which a destroyer was proceeding.
>
> I claim one Ju 87 as an unconfirmed casualty.

At this time, the enemy was probing the Channel, attacking convoys between the Thames Estuary and Portland, as Hitler increasingly played 'Air Fleet Diplomacy', which increasingly larger formations, in the deluded hope of frightening Britain into accepting Germany's peace terms. The Ju 87 *Stuka* dive-bomber was heavily involved in these operations – but Manton's reference to a 'He 113' is erroneous, this being the same as the mythical 'He 112'; undoubtedly, he was actually attacked by either a Me 109 or, as often happened given the speed of combat, a friendly fighter.

Commanding 'A' Flight of 56 Squadron was Flight Lieutenant Steve 'Squeak' Weaver; years later, 'Minnie' Manton recalled:

5 OPERATIONAL TRAINING UNIT: A ROLL CALL OF THE LOST

> From those hectic times I remember well one particular incident… probably because it occurred shortly after I had taken over the Squadron following two-and-a-half years at the Air Ministry. Every moment with 56 Squadron, therefore, was new and exciting for me. After only my first or second combat, I was returning to North Weald, trying to gather my wits, when another 56 Squadron Hurricane came alongside and formated on me. The pilot opened his hood, gave me a great grin, a thumbs up and then one finger to indicate that he had made a kill: it was 'Squeak'.

Although a damp squib owing to bad weather and a communications failure, the *Luftwaffe* launched its main offensive on mainland Britain, targeting airfields, on 13 August 1940. By Sunday, 18 August 1940, '*Adlerangriff*' (Attack of the Eagles) had intensified, this day seeing the heaviest fighting yet. That lunchtime, Biggin Hill and West Malling airfields were bombed, and Kenley was subjected to an audacious low-level attack by Do 17s of 9/KG 76. Late afternoon, fifty-eight KG 2 Do 17s were despatched to bomb Hornchurch, whilst fifty-one He 111s of KG 53 droned towards North Weald, the two bomber formations escorted by 140 Me 109s and 110s, drawn from JGs 3, 26, 51 and 54, and ZG 26. Of this impressive fighter force, twenty-five Me 109s of JG 51 were closely bound to the Hornchurch raiders, whilst twenty Me 110s shepherded KG 53 to North Weald. The remaining enemy fighters were tasked with a *freie hunt* to soften and divert RAF defences ahead of the bombers. In response, the 11 Group Controller brought thirteen squadrons either to a state of immediate readiness or scrambled them to patrol specific lines. No. 56 Squadron, scrambled at 1700 hrs with orders to patrol Manston, and was the first of Park's squadrons to engage, rapidly reinforced by 54 Squadron's Spitfires. At 1730 hrs, Squadron Leader Manton, now leading 56 in the air, engaged an Me 110 over Bradwell, which he subsequently claimed as a probable. Ten days later, 'Minnie' led 56 Squadron to intercept thirty Dorniers escorted by a similar number of Me 109s, combat taking place at 1250 hrs, 15,000–16,000 feet 10 miles north of Whitstable, the 'Boss' claiming a 109 probable.

A SPITFIRE'S STORY: THE INVISIBLE THREAD

During yet another bitter day of fighting on 31 August 1940, 56 Squadron suffered a sad loss, as 'Minnie' later recalled:

> 'Squeak' was posted missing the very day I left the Squadron on posting to command RAF Manston, or at least what was left of it! They rang me from North Weald the next day to tell me the news, that he was missing, such was Flight Lieutenant Weaver's standing in the Squadron.

For the newly promoted Wing Commander Manton, the Battle of Britain, so far as it was concerned from the cockpit of a Hurricane, was over. It was not, though, the end of his operational flying: in March 1941, Manton was posted to Northolt as Wing Leader, surviving being shot down on 16 April 1941. On that day, he flew a Hurricane, Z2492, with 601 Squadron on a 'Circus' operation, escorting Blenheims attacking a target in the Pas-de-Calais. Off the French coast, however, 601 Squadron's CO, Squadron Leader John O'Neill, sighted some Me 109s, one of which he destroyed. On the return flight, however, O'Neill was bounced by a 109 and shot down himself, ditching in the sea off Dungeness with a leg wound, and fortunately picked up by a rescue craft. It was not a great operation so far as Northolt's senior officers were concerned: in addition to 601's CO, the Station Commander, Group Captain Theodore McEvoy, who was also flying with 601 Squadron, was shot-up by a 109 and forced-landed at Lydd with a damaged aircraft and a slight head wound; Wing Commander Manton was also jumped, crash-landing at Dungeness, also with a head wound. Moreover, Northolt's Spitfire-equipped 303 Squadron, flying high cover, was also hit by Me 109s on the return journey: Pilot Officer Wiktor Strzembosz was wounded and survived, but both Pilot Officers Bogusław Mierzwa and Mieczyslaw Waskiewicz were both killed. The three Hurricanes or 601 Squadron, and three Spitfires of 303, were Fighter Command's only operational losses that day, pilots of JG 51 and 53 claiming seven Spitfires destroyed and four Hurricanes; noteworthy is that one of the Hurricanes was claimed SW of Dungeness by that great fighter pilot *Major* Werner Mölders, *Kommodore* of JG 51, although which of 601 Squadron's pilots this was, is impossible to say. In response, the Northolt Wing's only combat claim was O'Neill's Me 109, although this cannot be substantiated.

For Wing Commander Manton, a period of restricted duties followed, at RAF Colerne, after which he joined the staff of Fighter HQ, Belfast, flying another desk. By 1942, he was a group captain and SASO at 82 Group HQ, then HQ Northern Ireland. In 1943, Group Captain Manton commanded both RAF Coltishall and Church Fenton, and served as Group Captain Operations at 12 Group HQ. In 1944, he volunteered for service in the Far East, and in September 1944 consequently went out to Burma, taking command of 907 Fighter-Bomber Wing, flying Spitfires. After the war ended with Japan, Group Captain Manton came home, remaining in the post-war service, finally retiring in 1960 when Chief Instructor, Air Defence Wing. Having later made a new life in Australia, he died there, aged 95, in 2005.

Sergeant Jack Stokoe

On 12 June 1940, Sergeant Jack Stokoe practised aerobatics in R6644, a flight of fifty-five minutes.

Jack Stokoe was born on 1 February 1920, the son of a miner in West Cornforth, Durham. After leaving school, he travelled south in search of work and a better life than depressed north-east England was likely to offer, finding an administrative position with Buckinghamshire County Council at Aylesbury. In June 1939, he joined the RAF Volunteer Reserve – another Trenchard initiative aimed at creating a substantial and trained reserve. Indeed, it was undoubtedly the most far-sighted feature of 1936's Expansion Scheme 'F', intended to have wide appeal based upon the Citizen Volunteer, as opposed to the territorial basis of the AAF, and unlike the AAF, the VR was not socially elite. So far as aircrew training was concerned, the system was based upon local population centres for spare time ground training, and on aerodrome centres associated with those places for flying training at the weekend and a fortnight's annual camp'. All such volunteer aircrew were automatically made sergeants – much to the chagrin of professional NCOs who had taken years to attain that exulted rank.

A SPITFIRE'S STORY: THE INVISIBLE THREAD

Sergeant Jack Stokoe.

Jack Stokoe recalled that:

> Only a year before the Battle of Britain began, my contemporaries and I were pursuing our civilian careers whilst learning to fly with the RAFVR in our spare time. The majority of us were 18 or 19 years old and given the rank of sergeant on call-up, which at first caused much dismay amongst the ranks of professional sergeants, many of whom had taken twenty years to reach that exulted rank!
>
> Most of us had only fifty or sixty hours flying on elementary types like Tiger Moths and Magisters when we were called up. After a brief spell at ITW to instil some discipline into us, we had about 100 hours on Harvards at FTS, which included a few

trips actually firing guns. We were then posted to an OTU, in my case Aston Down, before being posted to an operational fighter squadron with just ten to fifteen operational hours on combat aircraft.

So it was that Sergeant Stokoe reported for duty at Aston Down on 10 June 1940, along with fellow sergeants Eddy Egan and Don Kingaby, and Pilot Officer Colin Francis. There, Stokoe accumulated 13.20 hours on Spitfires before a posting, on 26 June 1940, to 263 Squadron at Drem, which was in the process of converting from Hurricanes to the twin-engined, cannon-armed, Westland Whirlwind.

Jack Stokoe:

> I eventually joined 603 'City of Edinburgh' Squadron, an AAF squadron, and there were only three sergeant pilots, the remainder already being pilot officers. By 27 August 1940, the Squadron moved south to Hornchurch, by which time I had about seventy hours on Spits and had sighted, but not engaged, two Heinkel reconnaissance aircraft in the north of Scotland.
>
> On 29 August 1940, we flew four patrols, intercepting Me 109s on two of them. I claimed one damaged but the trimming wires of my own aircraft were shot away. On 30 August 1940 we made four more interceptions, during the course of which I was credited with one Me 109 confirmed and one damaged. My own aircraft was damaged, by a cannon-shell in the windscreen, and my hand slightly cut by splinters.
>
> On 1 September 1940 came three more interceptions of 20 plus bandits, one of which I shot down in flames in the Canterbury area.
>
> On 2 September 1940, I was involved in two interceptions, during the course of which I damaged two enemy aircraft but was myself shot down in flames and baled out. On that occasion, as I was attacking an enemy aircraft I remember machine-gun bullets, or maybe cannon shells, hitting my Spitfire, followed by flames

in the cockpit as the petrol tanks exploded. I thought 'Christ! I've got to get out of here and *quick*!' I undid the straps and opened the hood, but this turned the flames into a blowtorch. I was not wearing gloves, as during our hasty scramble I had forgotten them, but had to put my hands back into the fire to invert the Spitfire so that I could drop out (no ejector seats in those days!). I remember seeing sheets of skin peeling off the backs of my hands before I fell out of the plane. I was then concerned regarding whether the parachute would function or whether it had been damaged by fire, but I pulled the ripcord and the chute opened.

I landed in a field, but the Home Guard queried whether I was an enemy agent! A few choice words in English soon convinced them I was genuine, and thereafter I was rushed into the emergency hospital at Leeds Castle, suffering from shock and severe burns to my hands, neck and face.

I was in hospital for six weeks before returning to operational duties on 22 October 1940, with further combat successes. A second tour of duty with 54 Squadron followed, which included a second baling out, into the North Sea, before secondment to a training unit and night-fighter duties later in the war.

The point about the incident when I was shot down over Kent on 2 September 1940 is that at the time 603 Squadron was suffering such heavy casualties that that things got pretty chaotic, so for four days after baling out, I was reported 'Missing in Action'!

Commissioned in January 1941, Stokoe joined 54 Squadron at Catterick on 3 February 1941, to fly Spitfires, later that month flying south and back to Hornchurch for another tour of frontline duty in 11 Group. On 5 March 1941, Pilot Officer Stokoe claimed a 109 destroyed off Boulogne, and a 110 off Clacton on 20 April 1941 – although therein lies a tale, as he recalled:

I have had some difficulty remembering the sequence of events just before and after being shot down on 20 April 1941 – not entirely surprising as when I was admitted to hospital I was suffering from shock, concussion, exhaustion and hypothermia, aided and abetted by a generous helping of Navy Rum, for which at the time I was extremely grateful!

As far as I remember we were patrolling about ten to 20 miles out in the North Sea, off Clacton, probably vectored there by Control reporting 'bandits' in the area, then suddenly we were in a combat situation and I was firing at an enemy aircraft. Then – a blank! I was still in the air, but minus an aircraft, which had disappeared entirely (probably as a result of one or more direct hits from cannon shells behind the armour-plated seat).

I had not opened the hood, or disconnected my oxygen supply or intercom, or unstrapped the seat harness, and I seemed not to be surprised or unduly worried that I was apparently flying without any visible means of support. Nor did I seem to have any sensation of falling! My helmet was missing, as were my gloves and one of my flying boots, and when I got around to looking, my parachute looked somewhat worse for wear. However, I pulled the ripcord, the chute opened, and I landed in a very cold and somewhat wild sea.

My hands did not seem to be functioning properly, and I was unable to free myself from the parachute (which remained attached to me and shows quite clearly in the photograph). I slowly recollected that I ought to have an inflatable dinghy, and after another struggle managed to inflate it, only to have it burst. Whether it was damaged, or whether I inflated it too quickly we will never know, but I certainly reached a new low in the survival stakes. However, I managed to hang on grimly to a certain amount of air in an undamaged corner of the deflated dinghy and struggles feebly to stay afloat.

When I had just about given up hope, I heard voices, a ship was near me and ropes were thrown. I grabbed one and was hauled aboard. I remember little else, but was told the rest of the story by a couple of the crew members (possibly the Captain and his Mate) when they visited me in Harwich Hospital and presented me with the photograph you now have.

Apparently, they wrapped me in blankets, gave me an unspecified hot drink, and laid me to rest in a bunk. An RAF Air Sea Rescue launch then arrived and wanted to take me back but fortunately the Skipper said I was comfortably resting aboard and he was returning to port anyway. So, I remained where I was. I say '<u>fortunately</u>' because I was told that the launch overturned in rough sea outside the harbour, and I was in no state to face another struggle.

They also reported seeing an enemy aircraft crash into the sea before fishing me out.

I was in hospital for seven days and had seven days' leave, but strangely enough I have no recollection of whether I went home or not, although it is likely that I did. I returned to duty with 54 Squadron and was back in action again on 6 May 1941.

On that day, 54 Squadron had taken off from Hornchurch at 1625 hrs to patrol Barrow Deep. Upon arrival, a *staffel* of Me 109s were sighted above, one of which attacked the Spitfires head-on, passing above them before turning to assault 'A' Flight from astern. The Squadron broke in all directions, after which Pilot Officer Colebrook was last seen heading seawards, streaming glycol. *Oberleutnant* Winfried Balfanz of *Stab*/JG 51 claimed a Spitfire destroyed, that most likely being Colebrook. The Royal Navy, however, claimed the destruction of two Me 109s, but there were, in fact, no such actual casualties. Given how Jack Stokoe's aircraft dramatically disintegrated around him, it is likely therefore, that he was hit by anti-aircraft fire, not by a 109 – a victim of so-called 'Friendly Fire'. When I put this to Squadron Leader Stokoe, his response was perfectly understandable: '"Friendly Fire"? Wasn't very bloody "friendly", you take it from me!'

During his time flying Spitfires in 1940 and 41, Stokoe destroyed seven enemy aircraft and was commissioned on 26 June 1941. After spells instructing, his DFC was gazetted on D-Day, 6 June 1944. In 1946, Jack was de-mobbed, going to work for Rochester County Council as a weights and measures inspector. Keen to fly again, in 1947 Jack re-joined the RAFVR, instructing in his spare time on Tiger Moths and Chipmunks until 1952.

5 OPERATIONAL TRAINING UNIT: A ROLL CALL OF THE LOST

Considering that he was such a successful ace and aviation enthusiast, it always surprised me that when I found Jack back in the late 1980s, this retired trading standards officer was living in obscurity in East Kent. Sadly, Squadron Leader Jack Stokoe DFC died on 1 October 1999, aged 79.

Sergeant Don Kingaby

On 12 June 1943, another pilot is also known to have flown R6644 on aerobatic practice, namely Sergeant Kingaby – destined to become a legend – who made two such flights of 1.10 and 45 minutes respectively.

A Londoner, Donald Ernest Kingaby was born on 7 January 1920, the son of a vicar, and attended the King's cathedral school in Ely. Whilst working as an insurance clerk when aged 19, he joined the RAFVR

Don Kingaby, the '109 Specialist', pictured at Hornchurch when commanding 122 Squadron in 1943.

in April 1939. Mobilised when war broke out, conversion to Spitfires at 5 OTU was the last segment of flying training before a posting to an operational squadron, and on 24 June 1940, Sergeant Kingaby was posted to fly Spitfires with 266 'Rhodesia' Squadron at Wittering. On 9 August 1940, the Squadron was placed under Coastal Command's orders and flew to Eastchurch, via Tangmere, the move completed three days later. A flight of 19 Squadron's Spitfires was also at Eastchurch, the idea being for the fighters to escort Coastal Command light bombers to attack the invasion ports. On that day, 12 August 1940, Sergeant Kingaby opened his account as a fighter pilot damaging two Ju 88s over the Solent and just south of Portsmouth. The following day, however, Eastchurch was heavily bombed, with twelve fatalities, and 266 Squadron's hangar was set ablaze, destroying a Spitfire and the unit's ammunition. Consequently the offensive scheme was dropped, 19 Squadron returned to Fowlmere in the Duxford Sector and 266 moved to Hornchurch. On 18 August 1940, the Squadron engaged the enemy over Dover whilst en route to Manston, where the Spitfires were later strafed on the ground whilst re-fuelling – Sergeant Kingaby being hit by enemy gunfire but fortunately not seriously wounding him. On 22 August 1940, 266 Squadron, having lost its CO killed in action, returned to Wittering and the comparative inactivity of 12 Group. This, however, would not last long for Sergeant Kingaby – who was posted to 92 'East India' Squadron at Biggin Hill on 25 September 1940.

No. 92 Squadron was another fighter squadron with a proud history. First formed in September 1917, flying SE5A scouts over the Western Front, the Squadron accounted for thirty-seven aerial victories before the Armistice. With no war to fight thereafter, 92 was disbanded in 1919, but, with Britain once more at war with Germany, reformed at Tangmere on 10 October 1939. Although a regular RAF squadron, unusually the nucleus of its original personnel was drawn from 601 'County of London' Squadron of the AAF, which, certainly before the casualties suffered during the Dunkirk fighting, gave 92 Squadron a somewhat unique identity. During the evacuation, 92 Squadron operated from Hornchurch, losing its auxiliary CO, Squadron Leader Roger Bushell, a barrister, who was captured but later executed by

5 OPERATIONAL TRAINING UNIT: A ROLL CALL OF THE LOST

the Gestapo having masterminded the 'Great Escape' from Stalag Luft III. Thereafter replacement pilots arrived from the regular service, AAF and VR, forever changing the Squadron's identity. Indeed, this was especially so with AAF squadrons, which soon lost their elite status as their strength became diverse. Bushell was replaced by a Cranwellian, Squadron Leader P.J. 'Judy' Sanders, who, on 19 June 1940 had led his pilots to Pembrey in South Wales, from where the Squadron afforded some protection to South Wales and the West Country's aircraft factories. From there, 92 Squadron intercepted various lone raiders and reconnaissance aircraft, and on 18 August 1940 sent 'A' Flight on deployment to Bibury in Gloucestershire. By that time, the Battle of Britain was in full swing over southern England, and 92 Squadron was eager for a return to 11 Group – which came on 8 September 19430, when the Spitfires left South Wales for Biggin Hill. Almost immediately, 92 Squadron was in action, defending London, and by the time Sergeant Kingaby arrived had lost five pilots killed and eight wounded during the current deployment.

27 September 1940, two days after Kingaby's arrival at Biggin Hill, was a bad day for Fighter Command – which requires explanation. The first phase of the Battle of Britain had seen fighting over Channel-bound convoys; the second coastal ports and radar installations; the third heavy attacks on 11 Group airfields; the fourth round-the-clock bombing of London, and on 17 September 1940, convinced that the *Luftwaffe* could not defeat Fighter Command in short order, Hitler postponed the proposed invasion. Then began the sixth phase, concentrating, too late, on the British aircraft industry, which concluded on 30 September 1940 with the daylight defeat of the German bombing effort. The final phase began the following day, featuring nuisance fighter-bomber attacks and high-altitude fighter sweeps, the contest arguably ending on 12 October 1940, when Hitler cancelled the invasion indefinitely, although 31 October 1940 was the concluding date chosen by the Air Ministry. During the sixteen-week long battle, Fighter Command lost 544 aircrew, the worst days having been 8 August 1940 (15 pilots killed), 11 August 1940 (25), 15 August 1940 (13), 18 August 1940 (10), 7 September 1940 (13), 15 September 1940 (11) – and yet, with the battle all but won, 19 pilots were lost on 27 September 1940. Why? Because on

that day German fighters were constantly active during daylight hours over south-east England, operating in strength with the advantage of height and surprise. It would be on this significant day that Kingaby met the lethal Me 109 in combat for the first time.

At 1445 hrs that day, 92 Squadron scrambled from Biggin Hill, at 15,000 feet encountering a dozen Ju 88s escorted by Me 109s. Kingaby attacked the leading Ju 88 from abeam, delivering a short burst of two seconds – but was unable to see the result due to being attacked himself by Me 109s:

> I dived, doing an aileron turn to evade the attack but five Me 109s followed me down. I straightened out and a 109 overshot me. I got him in my sights and gave him a short burst and pieces came out of his starboard wing. Cannon fire from behind came too close to be comfortable and I went into an aileron turn dive again. When I came out the 109s had disappeared. There was no damage to my machine.

The 109 was claimed as damaged.

Having also damaged a 109 on 30 September 1940, on 12 October 1940, Sergeant Kingaby, claimed one 109 destroyed and another probably so; Blue 3, was in combat again on 15 October 1940, having scrambled with 92 Squadron at 0830 hrs:

> At 20,000 feet over Eastchurch we began to chase fifty Me 109s. We came into range in mid-Channel. I opened my hood and my goggles blew off, nearly pulling me out of the cockpit. In the confusion of regaining them I lost the rest of the Squadron. I cruised about in mid-Channel for two or three minutes and then, at 17,000 feet, I sighted nine Me 109s below at about 2,000 feet, heading for the French coast. I opened fire at 250 yards and closed fire at about 10 yards, aiming slightly ahead of the Hun. He rolled onto his back, burst into flames and went straight into the sea. I turned back before the other eight

5 OPERATIONAL TRAINING UNIT: A ROLL CALL OF THE LOST

> 109s had time to turn and attack me. The 109 went in about 16 miles east of South Foreland.

On this day, the Germans lost eight Me 109s with others returning to France badly damaged; German records, however, indicate no candidate for this claim – which is not uncommon.

On 20 October 1940, a section of 92 Squadron Spitfires, including Kingaby, and a section of 222 Squadron's, intercepted a Me 110 of 7(F)/LG 2 on a sortie to photograph the damage to London's docklands. The Spitfires made short work of the snooper, which crash-landed at Bockingfield, where the pilot was captured and his *Bordfunker* killed. The RAF pilots involved were each awarded 1/6th of a confirmed victory.

Although Air Ministry decided that the Battle of Britain concluded on 31 October 1940, there was no abrupt end to the fighting, as suggested by the 1969 film *Battle of Britain*. In reality, the fighter forces of both sides clashed by day until bad weather finally brought proceedings to a close in February 1941, and by the night Blitz on British cities continued until May 1941. As ever, 92 Squadron – and Sergeant Kingaby – remained in the thick of it all.

On 1 November 1940, Kingaby claimed another Me 109 destroyed over the sea, and was in action again, twice, on 15 November 1940, as the fighter-bomber attacks continued. At 1220 hrs, 92 Squadron scrambled to patrol the Thames Estuary, fifty minutes later intercepting a large formation of Me 109s at 24,000 feet. Sergeant Kingaby, Blue 3, chased a *Schwärm* of four 109s eastwards in a slight dive, attacking the leader from astern: 'Glycol and black smoke came from him and he went into a vertical dive. I last saw him east of Gravesend going straight down and out of control at 9 or 10,000 feet. An AA battery confirms that it crashed east of Gravesend'.

It is possible that Kingaby shot down *Oberfeldwebel* Robert Schiffbauer of 3/JG 26, who was captured having forced-landed at Eastchurch, east of Gravesend, at 1345 hrs, although, as was frequently the case, it appears that other pilots also attacked and claimed the 109.

At 1515 hrs that afternoon, Blue Section of 92 Squadron, including Sergeant Kingaby again flying Blue 3, scrambled from Biggin Hill and was vectored to Selsey Bill at 20,000 feet. At 1615 hrs the Spitfires encountered forty Me 109s at 21,000 feet over Selsey Bill, which immediately made to attack the outnumbered RAF fighters. Kingaby reported that:

> … I saw three of them break away in a slight dive close to me as if to run for France. I immediately closed on them; they were in a straggly vic, No 3 being behind the other two. I gave him a 5 second burst and he went down in flames and crashed in the sea [confirmed by Pilot Officer B. Maitland-Thompson].
>
> No 1 of the formation kept straight on, No 2 broke off to the right, to get on my tail. Meanwhile, I delivered a quarter attack on No 1, giving a long burst at about 150 yards range – the 109 blew up into about a thousand pieces. No 3 had by this time got on my tail and was shooting cannon very erratically on my port side. I went into a steep right-hand turn and after three turns got in a quarter attack at 80 yards range. My ammunition gave out after a 4 second burst, after the 109 had started to pour forth glycol. The last I saw of him he was diving through cloud very steeply at 2,000 feet with black smoke and glycol coming out.

Blue 3 claimed two Me 109s destroyed, the third as a probable. Certainly, *Unteroffizier* Rudolf Miese of 4/JG 2 baled out to become a prisoner, his 109 crashing off Felpham, Sussex, east of Selsey Bill, and 4/JG 54 lost a pilot killed, *Oberfeldwebel* Paul Hier, who was presumed to have crashed into the sea, and apart from Flight Lieutenant Bob Holland and Pilot Officer Tony Bartley sharing a damaged 109 over Selsey, Kingaby's were 92 Squadron's only other claims. It had been quite a day for Blue 3, who in total had claimed three Me 109s destroyed and a probable.

Kingaby went on to claim another Me 109 destroyed on 1 December 1940, off Dungeness, and on 6 December 1940 his DFM was gazetted: 'This airman has displayed great courage and tenacity in his attacks against the enemy. He has destroyed at least nine hostile aircraft, four of which he shot down in one day.' To the press, Kingaby became 'The 109 Specialist', although in a radio broadcast in January 1941, he downplayed this, saying

5 OPERATIONAL TRAINING UNIT: A ROLL CALL OF THE LOST

that: 'The reason I've got so many Messerschmitts may be that it's just my luck to run into more of these enemy machines than any other type'.

Kingaby's success continued into the New Year, claiming eight more Me 109s destroyed, and others probably destroyed or damaged; a Bar to his DFM followed on 29 July 1941, and a second Bar on 11 November 1941 – making Kingaby the only man to have ever won three DFMs. November 1941 also saw Kingaby commissioned, and the new, highly decorated Pilot Officer left 92 Squadron for a rest period, serving as an instructor at 58 OTU. Returning to operations in March 1942, joining 111 Squadron at Debden, Flight Lieutenant Kingaby became a flight commander on 64 Squadron at Hornchurch the following month. On 2 June 1942, Kingaby met a new adversary for the first time, the superlative Fw 190, the brutal 'Butcher Bird', although by this time the balance had been redressed with introduction of the Spitfire Mk IX. Further combat successes ensued until in August 1942 Kingaby was posted to command a flight of 122 Squadron, also at Hornchurch. On 19 August 1942, Flight Lieutenant Kingaby flew on Operation *Jubilee*, destroying a Do 217 off Dieppe in what was the greatest air fighting since the Battle of Britain. Having taken command of 122 in November 1942, and more combat success, Squadron Leader Kingaby's DSO was gazetted on 9 March 1943, and the following month he was promoted to Acting Wing Commander and appointed to lead the Hornchurch Wing. By September 1943, it was time for another rest from operations, this time as a staff officer at HQ Fighter Command. Nonetheless, during that time he still managed to make the odd operational sortie, making his final victory claim, a shared Me 109 destroyed over Czelle on 30 June 1944, whilst flying with 501 Squadron. Kingaby's final tally was 21 enemy aircraft destroyed, two shared destroyed, six probables and eleven damaged; in addition to his British decorations, he was also honoured with the Belgian Croix de Guerre and American DFC.

The war's end found Wing Commander Kingaby commanding the Advanced Gunnery School, and having elected to remain in the post-war service his AFC was gazetted on 5 June 1952. Having retired from the service in 1958, he emigrated with his wife to Westfield, Massachusetts, the one-time '109 Specialist' and twice R6644 pilot dying there, aged 70, on 31 December 1990.

A SPITFIRE'S STORY: THE INVISIBLE THREAD

Pilot Officer David Scott-Malden

Francis David Stephen Scott-Malden was born on Boxing Day 1919, at Portslade, Sussex. The son of a school teacher, Scott-Malden was an academic, achieving a Goddard Scholarship to Winchester before going up to King's College, Cambridge, to read classics – winning the Sir William Browne Medal for Greek Verse in 1939. The previous year, however, he joined the Cambridge University Air Squadron and learned to fly in what was another important reserve initiative. Created in 1925, the Cambridge UAS was the first such squadron, encouraging an interest in aviation and flying amongst undergraduates, and was soon followed by the universities of Oxford and London. Concentrated at elitist universities, however, numbers remained small, on 3 September 1939, for example, the Oxford UAS provided just 500 trained pilots for the RAF.

A month later, Scott-Malden was commissioned into the RAFVR and mobilised. After 'square bashing' at an Initial Training Wing, Pilot Officer Scott-Malden was posted to the FTS at Cranwell, and upon completion of advanced flying training was posted, in May 1940, to No. 1 School of Army Co-operation at Old Sarum – which, as previously explained, was seen by many as more important work than flying fighters; it is unlikely, however, that many of the young pilots posted to Old Sarum agreed. Salvation was at hand, however, due to Fighter Command's demand for replacements, and Scott-Malden

David Scott-Malden pictured when a highly decorated group captain in 1945.

5 OPERATIONAL TRAINING UNIT: A ROLL CALL OF THE LOST

was delighted to find himself transferred to fly fighters soon after his army cooperation course began. Consequently, on 10 June 1940, Pilot Officer Scott-Malden arrived at 5 OTU, Aston Down. His diary entries perfectly capture the atmosphere of the time:

> <u>Wednesday, 12 June 1940</u>: Had a test on a Harvard and passed successfully into Spitfire flight. First solo an indescribable thrill. Felt a pretty king man.
>
> <u>Friday, 14 June 1940:</u> Paris falls Astonishing to think of it in the hands of the Germans. Reynaud declares 'Will fight on, even if driven out of France'. Marvellous days doing aerobatics in Spitfires.
>
> <u>Monday, 17 June 1940</u>: The French give up hostilities. Cannot yet conceive the enormity of it all. I suppose it will not be long before we start defending England in earnest.
>
> <u>Thursday 20 June 1940</u>: Reports of another raid in South Wales. Fired eight Brownings into the river Severn for the first time. This getting up at 0430 hrs is beginning to tell.

The previous day, 'Scottie' flew R6644 for an hour's dogfighting practice.

On 23 June 1940, Pilot Officer Scott-Malden, together with Pilot Officer J.W. 'Tommy' Lund, was posted to 611 'County of Lancashire' Squadron at Digby. On that same day, a certain Pilot Officer Richard Hillary and friends, including Pilot Officers Peter Pease, Peter Howes and Noël le Chevalier Agazarian, arrived for instruction at Aston Down. All three had also come from Old Sarum, Hillary recalling in his classic memoir *The Last Enemy* that Agazarian 'was the most elated. His face wore a permanent fixed grin, which nothing could wipe off. "Spitfires at last", he kept repeating.' Hillary and friends regarded their decorated instructors 'with considerable awe', and from them learned something of the skills and tactics of a fighter pilot – but Hillary's 'clearest memory of the course was the bridge' – wherein lies a tale.

A SPITFIRE'S STORY: THE INVISIBLE THREAD

Near Sharpness, at the time a railway bridge of multiple arches spanned the Severn estuary and 'became the occasion of a long-brewing quarrel' between Hillary and Agazarian. The friends had been together for some time, 'and beginning to get on one another's nerves'. For the quick-tempered Hillary and Agazarian, 'there had to be a show-down: the bridge provided it'. The latter, 'low-flying down the Severn, came to the bridge and flew under it', returning to tell Hillary about it – after which the bridge 'fascinated and frightened' Hillary, who 'had to fly under it':

> There was a strongish wind blowing, and as I came down to a few feet above the river I saw that I had on quite an amount of drift. The span of the arch looked depressingly narrow; I considered pulling up but forced myself to hold the stick steady. For a moment I thought I was going to hit with the port wing, and then I was through.

Any of those flights could have been in R6644; sadly neither Hillary or Agazarian survived the war.

David Scott-Malden:

> I remember very clearly that we treated flying under the Severn bridge rather as a parting gesture when we were already safely posted to a fighter squadron, and reasonably safe from any complaints to the authorities. There were several large arches in the railway bridge, and two smaller ones on the Welsh side. I had long arguments with my great friend George Barclay about whether a Spitfire could get through one of the smaller arches. He decided that it could get through on the diagonal, i.e. with the wings at 45° to the horizontal, and we watched while he did so, with some relief at seeing him emerge safely the other side! Personally, I played safe and used one of the larger arches. I am afraid you will never discover if R6644 was used for that purpose, as it would certainly not be recorded in anyone's log book, not if they were wise.

5 OPERATIONAL TRAINING UNIT: A ROLL CALL OF THE LOST

The former Severn railway bridge near Sharpness – the temptation to fly under it was too great for certain daring 5 OTU pilots.

Another fighter ace, George Barclay also joined the 'Roll Call of the Lost' when shot down and killed near El Alamein in 1942.

For Scott-Malden, though, a distinguished service career awaited.

Flying with 611 Squadron at Digby in 12 Group, Pilot Officer Scott-Malden experienced the usual round of patrols, chasing 'X-Raids', which is to say unidentified radar plots, convoy protection patrols off the east coast, and also flying to Duxford to reinforce that Sector when necessary. In September 1940, operating from the Duxford satellite at nearby Fowlmere, 611 Squadron also participated in the Duxford-based 'Big Wing' operations, led by the legless Squadron Leader Douglas Bader. Scott-Malden, however, did not engage the enemy on any of these sorties, and together with Sergeant Alfred Burt was posted to 603 'City of Edinburgh' Squadron at Hornchurch on 4 October 1940, which needed replacement pilots owing to casualties sustained in protracted heavy fighting.

On 12 October 1940, Scott-Malden opened his account as a fighter pilot when he claimed a Me 109 probable off Gravesend. The following month came more success – against the Italians. Although Mussolini's offer of sending an air detachment to support the *Luftwaffe* during the Battle of Britain was initially rejected by Hitler, by October elements of the Corpo Aero Italiano were based in Belgium. On the night of 24 October 1940, the Italians targeted Harwich, then bombed Deal five days later, and sent an unopposed fighter sweep across Kent on

A SPITFIRE'S STORY: THE INVISIBLE THREAD

1 November 1940. On 11 November 1940, the Italians were roughly handled by 257 Squadron, and on 23 November 1940, 603 Squadron intercepted a formation of Italian CR 42 biplane fighters off Dover, twenty-nine of which were sweeping from Margate to Dungeness. In the ensuing combat, two Italian pilots were killed, another severely wounded, and three pilots crash-landed in France. Scott-Malden damaged two of the CR 42s, 603 Squadron claiming seven destroyed and several probables, all for no loss. The Italian contribution to the air war over Britain was ineffective, causing little damage, destroying no RAF aircraft but losing some two dozen machines in the process. The fighter sweeps continued until the end of November 1940, after which the majority of units involved returned to Italy.

On 29 November 1940, Scott-Malden shared in the destruction of a Do 17 off Ramsgate, and would shine in the New Year ahead. Still at Hornchurch, in the spring of 1941, 603 Squadron was amongst Fighter Command's units taking the war across the Channel, as the 'Non-Stop Offensive' began in earnest. Between 28 May 1941 and 18 September 1941, Scott-Malden destroyed three Me 109s, probably destroyed two and damaged six more. In August 1941, his DFC was gazetted, and the following month he was promoted to command 54 Squadron, also at Hornchurch. On 4 November 1941, he damaged another 109 before being rested as 14 Group staff officer at the end of that month. In March 1942, he returned to operations, as a Wing Commander leading the North Weald Norwegian Wing. More combat successes followed, leading to a Bar to his DFC gazetted in June 1942, the DSO in September 1942, and the Norwegian War Cross, presented personally by King Haakon of Norway. Another rest period followed, a public relations tour of American universities, and between July–October 1943, Wing Commander Scott-Malden was RAF Liaison Officer to the United States Eighth Air Force. Aged only 23, between October 1943 and February 1944, he commanded RAF Hornchurch and then joined a mobile Ground Control Unit of Second Tactical Air Force, preparing for D-Day. After the invasion, the GCU went to Normandy, and then, in August 1944, 'Scottie' was promoted to group captain and took over 126 Wing. That posting would see the end of his operational flying, and the end of the war

5 OPERATIONAL TRAINING UNIT: A ROLL CALL OF THE LOST

in Europe found Group Captain Scott-Malden at the Air Ministry, planning for the movement of RAF units from Europe to the Far East – the war with Japan, of course, being ongoing. Remaining in the post-war service, after various senior appointments David Scott-Malden retired in 1966 as an Air Vice-Marshal; he died on 1 March 2000.

Pilot Officer Arthur Vokes

Pilot Officer Vokes was in the same Aston Down intake as Pilot Officer Scott-Malden, and flew R6644 on the same day, 19 June 1940, an interception exercise of an hour and five minutes.

Arthur Frank Vokes was born in Birmingham on 2 June 1918, the son of a civil engineer, Frank Charles Vokes, and his wife, Elsie. After leaving school, Vokes worked as a clerk at one of the city's banks, and in 1938 joined the RAFVR, learning to fly at 6 EFTS, Sywell. Taught by civilian and service instructors, Vokes soloed in a Tiger Moth on 13 June 1938, and by 31 August 1939, his flying training was complete, had also flown the Hawker Hart and Hind, accumulating 61 hours dual and 117 solo flying hours. Vokes then passed an instructor course at Sywell, and having been mobilised, reported to Cambridge ITW in mid-October 1939. On 18 November 1939, Sergeant Vokes arrived at 15 FTS, Lossiemouth, for advanced service flying training, flying a monoplane,

Pilot Officer Arthur Vokes.

the Harvard, for the first time. The course completed, on 9 April 1940, Vokes was assessed as 'above the average' and moved on to 8 FTS at Montrose. From there, he wrote to his father:

> We heard yesterday that due to present events we shall finish here on Saturday and not go to practice camp but straight to a squadron. It only concerns a few of us. After tonight's news even this order may be speeded up, so I thought I would write to you at the office and let you know how things stand.
>
> I recently confirmed with the bank that my life policy covers me for any war risks. It is for £200 and the policy is kept at the bank's head office in London. My only commitment, apart from your honourable self, is the old car. The unscrupulous financiers are United Motor Finance Corporation, Slough. I have paid eight monthly instalments of £4.1s,8d, apart from the original deposit of £32. This leaves the car well covered, even for a forced sale.
>
> This is in no way a despondent letter, but merely a rough draft of my affairs. What with your help in life, mother's love and Peggie's hopes and love, I should be a very difficult target, and have any amount of faith in the attack.

In what were uncertain times indeed, on 1 June 1940, Sergeant Vokes arrived at the School of Army Cooperation at Old Sarum, on No. 8 War Course, and the following day was commissioned as a pilot officer in the general duties branch of the service, 'for the duration of hostilities'. At Old Sarum the students flew Lysanders and Hectors, and relieved when, on 9 June 1940, the course was cancelled and they were posted to 5 OTU – to become fighter pilots.

On 10 June 1940, Pilot Officer Vokes arrived at Aston Down, making a local familiarisation flight in Miles Magister R1838, and after four flights in Harvard P5869, soloed in Spitfire K9976. Upon conclusion of the course on 22 June 1940, Vokes was posted to 19 Squadron at Duxford – a most famous squadron indeed, having been the RAF's first Spitfire squadron. Up in 12 Group, near Cambridge, things were much quieter than they would soon be for 11 Group, covering London and the south-east, providing an opportunity for new pilots to gain further experience in operational conditions. By 19 July 1940, Pilot Officer Vokes was declared combat ready, and practised firing at Sutton Bridge in Spitfires R6882, R6889 and R6924 – all of which had been converted to Mk IB status. These experimental, Spitfires had their eight machine guns replaced by two 20mm cannons, but frequent stoppages exasperated the pilots and would lead, in early September 1940, to their replacement by standard machine-gun-armed Mk IAs.

With the Battle of Britain in progress, notes recorded by Vokes indicate the action:

> 13 August 1940: Aerodrome [author's note: 19 Squadron was temporarily detached to Eastchurch] heavily bombed at 0700 hrs. 250 bombs dropped. Big air battle above the clouds over the Thames Estuary.
>
> 18 August 1940: Interception patrol, South London. Kenley and Biggin Hill bombed.
>
> 31 August 1940: Intercepted 30 Do 215s with Me 110 escort. Beam attack on bombers, Pilot Officer Aeberhardt killed, Flying Officer Coward wounded.
>
> 5 September 1940: Intercepted a large formation of enemy aircraft over London. Chased at Me 110 out to sea but unable to catch up. Blue 3 with Squadron Leader Pinkham, Flying Officer Haines one Me 110. [That day, Pinkham, flying his first combat sortie, was shot down and killed when his parachute failed, and was succeeded in command of 19 Squadron by the commander of 'A' Flight, Squadron Leader Brian Lane DFC.]
>
> 9 September 1940: I was No. 2 in Yellow Section, climbing to attack some Me 109s. I saw six Do 215s below and dived down onto the nearest one. He was flying south and by the time I attacked, was separated from the others and had his wheels down. I fired all my ammunition into him and saw bits coming

off. Just before breaking away I experienced a heavy bump from beneath, which I think was AA fire. I then saw another Spitfire attack the Do 215, so I returned home, my ammunition exhausted.

15 September 1940: Green 2 with Flying Officer Haines, 19, 310, 611 and 242 Squadrons flying as a wing. B Flight attacked six Do 17s, one breaking away, chased by Sergeant Steere and self. One Jerry baled out. One Me 110 surprised me and bored a hole in my starboard wing. After two or three turns I got on his tail and gave him everything. He dived vertically into cloud, starboard engine smoking – one probable 110. Hundreds of Jerries, 19 Squadron scored 16, Duxford 50 certs!

On 5 October 1940, Vokes collected a cannon-armed Spitfire from the Air Fighting Development Unit at Wittering, a booster coil having been fitted to push a round into the breech as the magazine spring ran down.

9 October 1940: Firing cannons at Sutton Bridge. No stoppages, target bounced up in the air.

5 November 1940: Green 2 with Sergeant Charnock who got a Me 109 cert. 'Farmer' [author's note: Flight Lieutenant Walter Lawson DFC, commander of 'A' Flight] blew another to bits with the cannon, its first success since July. No stoppages.

After a convoy patrol on 15 November 1940, Vokes wrote to his parents:

Feeling very excited. This morning three of us shot down an Me 110 into the Thames Estuary after a thrilling chase from Felixstowe – North Sea – London – Buckinghamshire – Southend. We eventually set him on fire and he crashed near a convoy with an enormous splash. The pilot baled out and had a long dip.

Yesterday we did four hours flying and nothing happened, so it was good to have some fun today. A Flight is catching up with

5 OPERATIONAL TRAINING UNIT: A ROLL CALL OF THE LOST

B Flight. I fly with the CO and Jock [author's note: Squadron Leader Brian Lane and Pilot Officer Wallace Cunningham]. It's a glorious day, so we may have some more fun yet.

<u>16 January 1941</u>: Red 2 with Flight Lieutenant Lawson and Jock in security patrol for King and Queen visiting Duxford. Farmer and Jock received their gongs [author's note: DFCs].

Throughout the winter and spring of 1941, Pilot Officer Vokes flew numerous patrols and training flights, and even the odd 'fighter night', nocturnal patrols of London with the night Blitz in progress. The Spitfire, with its narrow-track undercarriage and forward vision impaired by a row of glowing exhaust ports either side of the nose, was not a good night-flying aircraft, but with Britain's nocturnal defences in their infancy, desperate was the hour. On these 'fighter nights', Spitfires would overfly the capital, or perhaps Birmingham, entering the area via a 'gate' in the searchlight beams. Without any night vision aids or airborne radar, the pilot simply hoped to catch sight of a German bomber. Few did.

From the spring of 1941 onwards, 19 Squadron was also engaged on the sweeps and bomber escort sorties of the Non-Stop Offensive. On 27 June 1941, for example, Pilot Officer Vokes flew Spitfire P7260 on an operation in which the 12 Group Wing of 19, 266 and 65 Squadrons escorted six Blenheims attacking Lille power station. Four Me 109s crossed over in front of 19 Squadron, Vokes managing several bursts at one enemy fighter before losing it in thick haze.

On 20 June 1941, Squadron Leader Lane was rested and replaced by Squadron Leader Roy Dutton DFC, who left for the Air Ministry a month later, being succeeded in command by Vokes's friend and 'A' Flight commander, Squadron Leader Lawson DFC. An experienced pilot by now, Vokes was promoted to Acting Flight Lieutenant and became commander of 'A' Flight.

On 16 August 1941, 19 Squadron moved from Fowlmere to Matlask, inland of Cromer in Norfolk. Five days later, 19 was re-equipped with long-range Mk IIA Spitfires formerly operated by 234 Squadron and featuring a large, bulbous, fuel tank beneath the port wing. With range thus extended, 19 Squadron was to fly bomber escort sorties to the Netherlands, across the North Sea, the first such operation taking place on 25 August 1941, when the Squadron escorted Blenheims to attack a convoy off IJmuiden. The next came three days later – beginning a run of bad luck with implications for Flight Lieutenant Vokes.

The 19 Squadron diary for 28 August 1941 records:

> 1800 hrs: Squadron took off from Matlask together with 12 long range Spits of 152 Squadron before rendezvousing with 17 Blenheims from 21, 89 and 11 Squadrons. Course was set to cross the Dutch coast south of Oostveine, the bombers being in three boxes of five, six and six at 2,000 feet with 19 Squadron in sections of four on their port side and 152 on the starboard side at 2,000 feet. The Dutch coast was crossed at 1900 hrs and the formation then turned to port so that the bombers could cross the target area, the Rotterdam docks, in line abreast. Whilst the bombers went in to bomb their target, 19 Squadron kept to the west to pick up the bombers as they came out. Very heavy flak was encountered over Holland between Rotterdam and the coast both from the ground and ships in the river south of Rotterdam, particularly from a ship which appeared to be an armed merchantman. Some of the flak had a low trajectory of about 100 feet and range of about a mile. Pilot Officer Marsh reported seeing flak coming from a church tower. The result of the bombing was not observed as the squadron was not over the target area, but one bomber was seen to go down in flames.

The Blenheims certainly had it rough:

> Low-level attack made from 20 feet, and each aircraft dropped two 500 lb and four dropped 24 incendiaries. Aircraft 'H', flown by Sergeant Jenkinson, scored a direct hit on a red painted ship

5 OPERATIONAL TRAINING UNIT: A ROLL CALL OF THE LOST

of 8,000 tons just off dock 14 – flame and bright red smoke was observed. During these operations, Wing Commander Cree reported seeing a Blenheim crash into a warehouse on the north-west corner of Maashaven, which started a large fire. The same pilot also reported seeing a Spitfire going down in flames. Aircraft 'H' reported a further Blenheim seen to crash into the river from low-level shortly afterwards. Considerable AA fire encountered and aircraft 'K' hit several times although damage not serious.

The Spitfire down was Sergeant Savidge of 152 Squadron. Whilst all of 110 Squadron's Blenheims returned safely, 21 Squadron was not so lucky: 'Four of our aircraft did not return'.

No. 19 Squadron reported that:

Whilst over Holland, Pilot Officers Marsh, Stuart and Strihavka shot up a ship in the river south of Rotterdam. Sergeant Charnock and Pilot Officer Edmunds shot up a machine-gun post each and Sergeant Sokol a factory. When the bombers came out from the target area they were escorted home. Pilot Officer Marsh landed 25 minutes after the rest of the squadron to report Squadron Leader Lawson DFC missing. Both pilots had apparently become separated from the rest of the squadron and were coming home on the starboard side of the bombers. When fifteen miles off the Dutch coast, Pilot Officer Marsh saw his leader on the tail of an aircraft which he thought was a Spitfire. Squadron Leader Lawson did not appear to go into action and had no aircraft on his tail. Likewise, there, was no flak, but Squadron Leader Lawson broke away and Pilot Officer Marsh did not see his leader again, so joined up with 152 Squadron and returned to base.

Squadron Leader Lawson was missing over the North Sea in Spitfire P7995. The 6/JG 53's Me 109s had been scrambled, *Feldwebels* Krantz and Gothe each subsequently claiming Spitfires destroyed.

A SPITFIRE'S STORY: THE INVISIBLE THREAD

Pilot Officer Wallace 'Jock' Cunningham, a close friend of Vokes and who may also have flown R6644 when at 5 OTU.

Squadron Leader Walter 'Farmer' Lawson DFC, another close friend of Vokes, shot down and killed off Rotterdam on the same day Cunningham was captured.

5 OPERATIONAL TRAINING UNIT: A ROLL CALL OF THE LOST

Flight Lieutenant Wallace 'Jock' Cunningham:

> Crossing the 100 miles of North Sea, we flew so low that the Blenheim airscrews made a furrow on the sea's surface. Our height was held down so that we did not show up on the German radar. 19 Squadron with Squadron Leader Lawson leading crossed the coast south of Rotterdam and continued flying east for a few miles. The Blenheims turned more sharply after crossing the coast and went for their targets in the harbour. By this time, we had turned 180° and flew down the estuary just above the Blenheims' height. Farmer Lawson was hit and we lost sight of his aircraft. I took over the lead and continued drawing fire from the motor vessels in the harbour. There was no sign of any German aircraft, and in any case we were too low to be useful in that respect. I was hit by a multiple pom-pom and started streaming glycol. My No 2 called 'Jock, you're on fire, better climb.' I started to do so but the engine began labouring. I could not gain enough height to bale out, so I made for the beaches south of Amsterdam. I crash-landed on the sand – in front of a gun post. A machine-gun there from fired a few warning shots and two soldiers came over and took possession. My efforts to start a fire were unsuccessful. As I had descended, my No 2, Peter Stuart, a fine Canadian, said 'Cheerio, Jock – good luck.' Sadly, he was killed the next day – shot down off the Dutch coast.

Flight Lieutenant Cunningham's war had come to an end, shot down not in aerial combat but by flak. The German machine-gunners of *Küstenposten 3 der 9 Kompanie III Battalion, Infantrie Regiment 723*, were credited with having shot Jock down. That claim, however, Jock also disputed:

> That is horsecock! I was absolutely positive, beyond question, that the hits which knocked me down came from multiple pom-poms on a ship in the estuary. The hits ruined my engine,

> I became a streamer and after comment by Peter Stuart, my number two, instead of heading out to sea, I tried to gain height. As I got back to the coast (going west), my engine seized and so I turned south to make a wheels-up landing on the sand. At this stage '*Küstenposten 3 der 9 Kompanie III Battalion, Infantrie Regiment 723*', fired a few machine-gun bullets at me from a post in the dunes. Then a platoon of 'goons' took over.
>
> I suppose that the episode of our trip to Rotterdam at least provided a paragraph in the *Daily Mirror*: 'Yesterday our aircraft bombed ___'.

The loss of both its CO and a flight commander – both popular and long-serving members of 19, – hit the Squadron hard. As the only remaining flight commander, Arthur Vokes found himself in temporary command of 19 Squadron. The following morning, he led eleven of 19 Squadron's Spitfires on a search for Squadron Leader Lawson:

> East coast was crossed at 12,000 feet and the squadron proceeded on a vector of 130° from base in order to arrive in the area where our missing pilot was last seen, about 10-15 miles off the Dutch coast from the Hague. Our aircraft swept the area but without success and were just about to return home when they encountered a formation of about ten Me 110s at about 500 feet. The enemy aircraft were in line astern and apparently engaged in bombing practice as there were smoke floats in the sea.

The Me 110s belonged to 6/ZG 76, which was employed on coastal defence. The ensuing combat was ferocious – and must represent one of the rare occasions when the twin-engined Me 110 came off better than the Spitfire: 19 Squadron lost four aircraft. Pilot Officers Stuart, Edmunds and Parkin, were all killed, whilst Sergeant Clifford Davies crash-landed at Bulskamp in Belgium. In response, the Squadron claimed the destruction of two Me 110s and two more damaged, but in reality only one Me 110 suffered '15%' damage. For 19 Squadron the sortie was an absolute disaster.

5 OPERATIONAL TRAINING UNIT: A ROLL CALL OF THE LOST

On 5 September 1941, just days after these disastrous operations, Flight Lieutenant Vokes took off at 1550 hrs in Spitfire P8166 on a ferry flight from Coltishall to Matlask. Visibility, however, was poor, and during this short hop the cloud base descended dangerously low. As the Spitfire pilot lost height, he emerged from cloud at too steep an angle and too low to flatten out – and was killed in the resulting crash at Langham, near Bircham Newton. The 22-year-old was buried in the service plot at St Mary's Great Bircham.

On 2 February 1942, Flight Lieutenant Cunningham wrote to Mrs Vokes from *Oflag* XC:

> Pilot Officers Andrews, Cowley and myself, all of the same Squadron send our very deepest sympathies to you and Mr Vokes. Arthur and I were together for a very long time. We were on duty together and spent our leisure time together. I don't know how I should have felt if I had been left with both he and Farmer gone. Arthur was always happy in what he was doing and most certainly fulfilled the greatest duty asked of him by his country.

Pilot Officer Bill Read

The next pilot known to have flown R6644 at Aston Down was Pilot Officer William Albert Alexander Read, who did so for fifty minutes on 20 June 1940, firing his guns into the Severn.

Read was born on 11 August 1918, in Palmer's Green, London, and joined the RAFVR in July 1938, accumulating 46 flying hours by the time war was declared. After mobilisation and ITW Cambridge,

Pilot Officer Bill Read.

A SPITFIRE'S STORY: THE INVISIBLE THREAD

Sergeant Read completed flying training at 15 FTS, Lossiemouth, and then, in May 1940, undertook a bombing course at Middle Wallop. Commissioned on 10 June 1940, Read was posted to Aston Down for conversion to Spitfires. Having done so, on 26 June 1940 Pilot Officer Read was posted to 263 Squadron at Grangemouth, flying Hurricanes; a further posting followed on 7 July 1940, to 603 Squadron and Spitfires at Turnhouse. Off Aberdeen on 24 July 1940, Read shared in damaging a He 111, which would be his only combat claim.

On 4 March 1941, Read became an instructor on 53 OTU, first at Heston, then at Llandow, and in September 1941 sailed for Archangel in Russia on the River Aston. Another pilot on this mission, Operation *Benedict*, was Flying Officer John 'Tim' Elkington, who remembered that:

> I went to Russia on the first convoy there – the only one to get through unscathed. Aboard HMS *Argus*, on 18 August 1941, the First Sea Lord briefed us, telling us that we, 151 Wing, had been promised by Churchill in response to Stalin's demand for support. Our role was to be the defence of the naval base of Murmansk, and cooperation with Soviet forces in that area. We were to instruct the Soviets in the operation and maintenance of our aircraft and ground equipment, which was then to be handed over to them. And so it was that we joined the first ever convoy to Russia, together with merchantmen carrying the rest of the Wing and our crated Hurricanes. We were escorted by HMS *Victorious*, a cruiser and several destroyers. Whilst in Scapa Flow, outbound, from 20 August, we received typical naval hospitality on several of the ships anchored there. Mindful of events a few months later, it is painful to reflect on those present: HMS *Prince of Wales*, *Repulse*, *King George V*, *Victorious*, *Furious*, *Malaya*, *Sheffield* and *London*. We finally sailed for Iceland on 30 August, together with a convoy bound for North America, and were escorted by Sunderland and Catalina flying boats. For a few days, we were down to seven knots, in thick fog. On 3 September, the weather cleared, and the Martlets from

5 OPERATIONAL TRAINING UNIT: A ROLL CALL OF THE LOST

Victorious got a Do 17; one Fulmar was lost in the engagement. Then, more days of thick fog.

Flying off *Argus* at 0600 hours on 7 September, some 200 miles north of Murmansk, our compasses were unreliable. We were told to pass over *Argus*, then a pre-positioned destroyer, and keep going! After over-flying miles of desolate tundra, we landed at Vaenga, a vast expanse of pot-holed sand which, later, became a soggy mess. Breakfast, however, was more welcoming – caviar, smoked salmon, Finnish ham, wine and champagne.

In the first month, we were unfortunate, as a squadron, to miss out on engagement with the enemy. Apart from reconnaissance, our first real work did not come until 17 September, with three patrols that day over the front line. Even then we saw nothing but flak, directed both at us and the bombers we were escorting. A few days later, close to Petsamo, one Pe2 was hit and crashed in flames after the crew had jettisoned their bombs and baled out. Their bombs came close to hitting the ships that were firing.

October opened with attacks on our airfield. Advanced warning was unsophisticated. On the first occasion, some twenty Ju 88s dropped their loads, and we took off to intercept through a hail of bullets, dodging the bomb craters. One 81 Squadron pilot, whose engine was stopped by a blast on take-off, was then blown off the wing by another explosion. Of 134 Squadron, I was first away and managed to catch up with them at 7,000 feet. My Number 2 joined me and we damaged one Ju 88, which later failed to reach home. The excellent DVD on the Russian episode, by Atoll Productions, has an over-generous simulation of the event showing a 'flamer', which we did not achieve. No surprise – I was rated below average in air gunnery.

The weather was now closing in and our efforts were devoted more to the conversion of Russian pilots, who seemed oblivious of fog, snow and ice, and the instruction of their technicians. On one occasion we watched with disbelief as a protégé attempted his third approach in dense fog.

Came the time for return home, and the most testing time of the expedition, for me at least, began. On 16 November, I was put in charge of an advance party of seven officers and sixty airmen, which I had to lead in deep snow, in virtual night, down the 10 miles or so of treacherous track to Rosta oiling jetty. We knew when we reached our destination, at 5 pm, when all our kit became black with oil. Our only casualty was one airman with a broken arm.

We waited there six hours for the fleet minesweepers we had to board for the voyage to Archangel – HMS *Hussar*, in our case, and *Gossamer* and *Speedy*, but they had docked at a different jetty. (If anything suggests that we had a tough assignment, read up their sea logs!) Eventually bed, without having had any food for fourteen hours, at 0200 hours. Next day, up to Polyarny, and a drink aboard the submarine *Seawolf*, before she left on patrol.

Transferring to an icebreaker, captained by a very large lady, and following the *Lenin* – the world's largest – we struggled through six-inch deep ice for the last 20 miles into Archangel. On one occasion we passed a merchantman loaded with crated Hurricanes and tanks. On the icebreaker, I made the acquaintance of General Gromov – the pre-war long-distance flyer.

On 24 November, we were transferred to MV *Empire Baffin*, a 10,000-ton cargo ship. Despite the icebreakers, moving yards at a time, it was not until 28 November that we were steaming past the Gorodetski light and into the open sea. We were held to 7.5 knots for the Russian boats with us – their first convoy to the UK. It was only then that we found the two Esthonian stowaways who had crossed the ice at night to board us. On 29 November, HMS *Kenya*, with most of the Wing personnel on board, joined us. The following day we hove to in gale and heavy seas – our lifeboat was washed away, and slag ballast on deck shifted. We had to rope ourselves into our bunks at night. No chance of sleep. Everything heavy with frozen spray which had to be constantly chipped off with shovels. We were sleeping in our clothes in case we had to get Vic Berg – who was in full

5 OPERATIONAL TRAINING UNIT: A ROLL CALL OF THE LOST

plaster after his terrible crash – to the lifeboats. On 1 December we were attacked by a U-boat, which destroyers depth charged – no casualties, but an outgoing convoy later lost several ships. Ballast shifting again. Our airmen helped to re-locate it. On 4 December, our engines cut out, with propellers racing, in the heavy seas. Steering gear damaged. Still semi-dusk all day. Several mines seen – one uncomfortably close. By 8 December we had reached Iceland, and eight days later, Scotland & home!

Above and below: Hurricanes in Russia.

Pilot Officer Read's experiences in Russia would doubtless have been very similar to Elkington's, whose recollection provide an idea of the operations and conditions involved. At Kineshma, between 3 November 1941 and 13 January 1942, Read test flew assembled Hurricanes and formed five Russian squadrons, the pilots of which he converted to the Hurricane. Back in the UK and whilst instructing at 51 OTU, Cranfield, in April 1942, Read was awarded the AFC for his work in Russia, which King George VI discussed with him at the subsequent investiture.

A return to operations came in March 1943, a posting to 29 Squadron at West Malling, first flying Bristol Beaufighters from Bradwell Bay, then the new de Havilland Mosquito. In September 1943 he returned to test flying, serving with the Intensive Flying Development Unit at Boscombe Down, and in February 1944 he served with the AFDU, testing the suitability of various types of aircraft to be armed with rockets. In July 1944, Read was seconded to BOAC, in Egypt, joining the airline as a junior captain when demobbed in March 1946. Many years of flying airliners followed, from Constellations to Comets, until he finally retired in 1963 to farm in England. Known to all as 'Bill', Read died in May 2000.

R6644 crash-landed

Unsurprisingly, considering the intense flying programme and pilots' inexperience, accidents during training were not uncommon; some were also down to headstrong pilots pushing the limits. Such, sadly, was the case of Pilot Officer Lancelot Steele Dixon, stepson of the famous novelist Rafael Sabatini, and son of the sculptor Christine Sabatini: on 9 April 1940, three days after arriving at 5 OTU, Dixon undertook a straight-forward cross-country navigation exercise in a Harvard but was soon performing unauthorised low-level aerobatics over his family's home at Clock Mill, on the banks of the river Wye at Winforton in Herefordshire; tragically, a wingtip clipped a tree and the young pilot crashed in flames. Buried in Hay-on-Wye cemetery, his unique grave can be found there today, a bronze effigy, sculpted by the pilot's mother and in his likeness, depicting Icarus having fallen to earth, the wax holding his feathers together having melted owing to flying too close to the sun – a poignant image and sentiment indeed.

Other 5 OTU accidents, fortunately, were not fatal and caused by minor technical faults or pilot error. On 1 July 1940, for example, Spitfire R6640 inexplicably caught fire forcing the pilot, Sub-Lieutenant Viv Bellamy of the Fleet Air Arm to crash-land on Kemble airfield, and Sub-Lieutenant John Sykes, also of the FAA, similarly escaped unhurt having forced-landed R6684 at Aston Down (both pilots, in fact, are worthy of note, being volunteers for Fighter Command and who were amongst the fifty-six FAA pilots who fought in the Battle of Britain, serving in RAF squadrons – Bellamy and Sykes survived the war).

On 4 July 1940, Spitfire R6644 was crashed on landing at Aston Down by Sergeant 514976 John Stenton, who therefore made the aircraft's last flight with 5 OTU.

Sergeant John Stenton

Born in Oldham in Lancashire on 19 March 1913, the son of a cotton mill worker, John Stenton's mother died whilst giving birth. Cared for by his grandmother for the first ten years of his life, Stenton attended Oldham School and then went to live with his father, new step-mother, and two sisters. On 28 July 1931, he left home, enlisting in the RAF as 514976 Aircraftman Second Class/ Aircrafthand. Initially the new airman served at the CFS, then re-mustered in December 1933 as a wireless operator under training at the Electric and Wireless School. Earlier that year, whilst

Flight Lieutenant John Stenton.

serving at RAF Bircham Newton, John met Marian, who would become his wife in 1937.

In 1921, however, in what was a far-sighted move during a time when society was strictly hierarchical, Trenchard permitted a small number of airmen and NCOs to become pilots, who, after five years' flying, would revert to their original trades and be available for recall in the event of a crisis. Consequently, in July 1937, Corporal Stenton re-mustered again – as a pilot under training at 11 FTS, Wittering. The following year he spent periods at No. 7 Armament Training School and No. 2 Air Observers' School, both at Acklington, but was hospitalised between November 1938 and May 1939, due to a motorcycle accident in Newcastle. During 1938, the Stenton's first child, Keith, was born; at first, Marian Stenton had been a 'camp follower', but having become homesick returned to her native Heacham in Norfolk, where the couple established a permanent home.

Upon discharge from hospital, Sergeant Stenton again re-mustered as a pilot under training, but was hospitalised once more, owing to ongoing treatment, the following month. Eventually, Sergeant Stenton completed his service flying training at Cranwell, and on 4 May 1940 reported to 15 OTU at RAF Harwell for conversion to the Vickers Wellington twin-engined bomber. On 1 June 1940, he was posted to RAF Upwood and 17 OTU, on Bristol Blenheims, then, having volunteered for Fighter Command, arrived at 5 OTU, Aston Down, on 24 June 1940. Fortunately, Sergeant Stenton was uninjured during the R6644 crash-landing – and a week later his daughter, Jean, was born. Apparently uniquely, however, Stenton appears to have remained at 5 OTU for an extraordinary length of time, not leaving until 18 December 1940 and thereby missing the Battle of Britain. Even then, it was not to a Spitfire squadron that he was posted, instead joining the recently formed and Defiant equipped 256 Squadron at Catterick. There were, of course, similarities between the Spitfire and Defiant turret fighter: both were single-engined interceptors powered by the Rolls-Royce Merlin, although the Defiant was bigger and heavier, with a crew of two. By this time, the daylight battle won, the night Blitz was at its height, and the Defiant, which had been withdrawn as a day-fighter due to horrendous losses during July and August 1940, was now performing better as a night fighter.

5 OPERATIONAL TRAINING UNIT: A ROLL CALL OF THE LOST

On 31 January 1941, 256 Squadron moved to Pembrey in South Wales, where the unit found itself carrying out nocturnal patrols and training flights. On 22 February 1941, Stenton survived another landing accident when returning from a night-flying practice sortie in Defiant N1697. Soon afterwards 256 Squadron moved north, to Squire's Gate, near Liverpool, unsuccessfully searching the night sky for German bombers on many occasions. By 7 April 1941, Stenton had accumulated 369 flying hours, 69 of which were on Defiants – but that night became lost above cloud on a moonlit night, baling out with his air gunner, Sergeant William Ross. The Defiant (T3480 according to 256 ORB, N1694 according to the MOD AHB (RAF)) crashed at Houghton, near Southport, at 2345 hrs, the cause of the accident attributed to an electrical fault resulting in radio failure. Ross was injured upon landing and admitted to Ormskirk General Hospital; Stenton jumped at 2,500 feet, landing safely 8 miles NE of Southport. On 9 April 1941, 256 Squadron's CO informed Irvin Airchutes Co. Ltd of Stenton's decent, using parachute A77150, as a result of which the pilot was admitted to membership of the 'Caterpillar Club' – reserved for those whose life had been saved by an Irvin parachute.

On 7 July 1941, 256 Squadron moved south again, to Colerne in Wiltshire – where, four days later, the hapless Stenton again crashed on landing (Defiant T3981); fortunately both pilot and air gunner, Sergeant Low, were unhurt. Promoted to warrant officer, three days after what was his fourth flying accident, Stenton was posted as an instructor, serving consecutively with 60 OTU at Leconfield, 51 at Debden, and 58 at Grangemouth, converting pilots to Defiant and Blenheim night-fighters. On 12 January 1943, by which time Stenton had been commissioned, the chance came at last to fly Spitfires when Flying Officer Stenton was posted to fly the Spitfire Mk VB with 222 Squadron at Ayr. Owing to the winter weather, there was very little flying, however, and Flying Officer Stenton would not make his first flight until 21 February 1943, in AD452, patrolling a convoy.

In April 1943, 222 Squadron returned to 11 Group, based at Martlesham Heath, the North Weald satellite, from where further patrols were flown protecting North Sea shipping. On 10 April 1943, Flying Officer Stenton and Sergeant Cooper escorted some RN motor torpedo boats, providing more cover for same four days later. A month later, 222 Squadron moved to Hornchurch, from where the usual round of offensive sorties and bomber escort flights were made. On 4 May 1943, Flying Officer Stenton flew Spitfire BL516 escorting Ventura bombers attacking the aerodrome at Abbeville, and after several similar sorties on 19 May 1943 left on posting to the Merchant Ship Fighter Unit (MSFU) at Speke.

Owing to the limitations of range, there was an area of the Atlantic in which Allied convoys had no air cover and were at the mercy of U-boats and the long-range, four-engined, FW *Kondor*. As a drastic means of addressing this, it was decided to convert certain merchantmen into Catapult Assisted Merchantmen, better known as 'CAM ships', these vessels having a ramp from which Hurricanes – known as 'Hurricats' – were launched assisted by rockets. The problem, of course, was that the pilot was unable to land his machine back on deck, so after a launch and interception his only option was to bale out near his ship and hope to be picked up. Fortunately, there were few of these dramatic launches, but one always springs readily to mind: on 25 May 1942, Pilot Officer John Kendall, one of The Few, having flown Spitfires with 66 Squadron during the Battle of Britain, was launched to protect Convoy QP12, returning from Murmansk; having destroyed a Ju 88, the gallant pilot's last radio message was to pinpoint the enemy crew, having taken to their dinghy, but upon baling out his parachute malfunctioned and Kendall was picked up dead. On dry land at Speke, however, the MSFU was training replacement pilots, Flying Officer Stenton making many practice flights before the unit was disbanded on 8 June 1943.

Afterwards, on 10 July 1943, Flying Officer Stenton joined the Communications Flight at RAF Northolt, where he was promoted to flight lieutenant and remained until November 1943, when posted to 131 'County of Kent' Squadron. Previously engaged on home defence, in October 1944, 131 had been posted to the Far East, flying the Spitfire Mk VIII, and after a spell in Bombay, reassembled at Amarda Road airfield, near the village of Rasgovindpur village in the Mayurbhanji district of West Bengal. Flight Lieutenant Stenton followed 131 Squadron to India, eventually arriving in May 1945, where there was very little flying ongoing. On 1 June 1945, by which time the war in Europe was over but the fighting continued in the Far

East against the Japanese, Stenton was posted to the Communications Flight of RAF Burma HQ.

At 0300 hrs on 11 July 1945, Flight Lieutenant Stenton left RAF Comilla in Beechcraft Expeditor HB158, a twin-engined communications aircraft, bound for Rangoon. Also aboard were the navigator, Flying Officer Arthur Rhodes, co-pilot Flight Lieutenant James Stephen, and two passengers, Wing Commander Arthur Saunders, a Mosquito pilot with 110 Squadron, and Warrant Officer Dennis Whiskin, a P-47 Thunderbolt pilot of 135 Squadron. Sadly, HB158 never arrived at its intended destination: 'Lost on communications flight between Comilla and Akyab, possibly due to bad weather, technical or pilot error, but no evidence' (Accident Record Card). Simply put, there was 'no evidence' because HB158 and its occupants disappeared, never to be found despite intensive search and recovery operations continuing until October 1956.

The names of Flight Lieutenant John Stenton and those lost with him are inscribed on the Singapore Memorial, situated in Kranji Cemetery, which commemorates 24,000 casualties of the Commonwealth land and air forces who have no known grave.

R6644 moves on…

As the damage necessitated the machine being sent away, by road, to No. 4 MU, a repair depot at RAF West Ruislip. From there, the job of making good was sub-contracted to Scottish Aviation Ltd, one of many firms contributing to the Civilian Repair Organisation, although at which of the nine locations the company operated at is unknown (most likely Hendon or Melton Mowbray).

As previously explained, during the first months of the war, the Spitfire was disadvantaged owing to having a two-pitch de Havilland propeller, providing only coarse or fine pitch, for take-off and cruising – unlike the German VDM constant speed airscrew. The Dowty Rotol company, based at Staverton in Gloucestershire, soon produced a Constant Speed Propeller, which was trialled by certain 54 Squadron Spitfires during the

Dunkirk fighting – convincing all concerned that the CS airscrew was superior. Unfortunately, Rotol was unable to supply the new propeller in numbers until August 1940, and with the Battle of Britain impending the requirement was urgent. Consequently, a speed-regulating device, known as a governor, was produced by de Havilland, converting their existing two-pitch propeller to CS. On 13 June 1940, de Havilland engineers worked non-stop for thirty-six hours to manufacture and fit such a unit to a Spitfire, which was allocated to 65 Squadron at Hornchurch on 15 June 1940. It was found that the converted CS propeller reduced take-off run by 95 yards, decreased climbing time to 20,000 feet by nearly four minutes, and increased maximum ceiling to 39,000 feet, as opposed to the 32,000 feet provided by the two-pitch propeller. Having analysed the results, on 22 June 1940, the Air Ministry contracted de Havilland to convert all of Fighter Command's Spitfires, Hurricanes and Defiants to CS, this work to take precedence over all other commitments with the priority being Spitfire conversion. This work began on 25 June 1940 at twelve Fighter Command Sector Stations – which did not, therefore, include the Spitfires at operational training units. It is likely, therefore, that this modification was undertaken on R6644 by Scottish Aviation.

After the necessary repairs and modification, on 15 August 1940, the hardest-fought day of the entire Battle of Britain, R6644 was taken on charge by 24 MU at RAF Tern Hill, in Shropshire – where it would remain in storage until allocated to an operational unit.

Chapter Three

616 'South Yorkshire' Squadron

On Monday, 7 October 1940, the *Luftwaffe* made its last heavy daytime assault on Britain, a raid by KG 51's heavily escorted Ju 88s on Westland Aircraft at Yeovil. On the same day, Spitfire R6644 was taken on charge by 616 'South Yorkshire' Squadron of the AAF, based at Kirton-in-Lindsey, Lincolnshire – and so begins another chapter, literally, in this Spitfire's story.

On 1 November 1938, 616 Squadron had been formed at Doncaster, and at the start of 1939 was equipped by obsolete Gloster Gauntlet biplanes. In August 1939, the auxiliaries were called to full-time service and in October 1939, thankfully re-equipped with Spitfires (being the original machines of 66 Squadron, the RAF's second Spitfire squadron). That month the Squadron moved to Leconfield, where conversion to the modern fighter was completed. On 27 May 1940, 616 Squadron flew south, to Rochford, from where it participated in the Dunkirk evacuation, seeing combat, returning to Leconfield on 6 June 1940. From there, the pilots flew the usual interception patrols, chasing lone German bombers and reconnaissance machines, until 15 August 1940, when *Luftflotte* 5, based in Norway, sent Ju 88s of KG 30 to attack north-east England. Owing to the range involved, the bombers were only escorted by twin-engined Me 110s – and suffered accordingly. Ten miles off Flamborough Head, combat ensued as squadrons of 12 and 13 Groups intercepted the Germans, 616 Squadron claiming eight Ju 88s destroyed, four probables and two damaged for no loss – somewhat exaggerated claims but a great morale booster on a day recalled by the RAF as the 'Junkers Party' and 'Black Thursday' by the *Luftwaffe*; indeed, *Luftflotte* 5 would play no further part in the Battle of Britain, and Air Chief Marshal Dowding's strategy of not concentrating his strength in the south-east alone, in case of just such an attack on northern England, was described by Churchill as 'genius of generalship'.

On 19 August 1940, 616 Squadron returned to 11 Group, operating from Kenley – which had been heavily bombed the previous day. Over the next fifteen days, 616 would lose a total of eleven Spitfires destroyed and three damaged; five pilots killed, six wounded and one captured. In response, the Squadron claimed the destruction of ten enemy aircraft destroyed, three probably destroyed, and six damaged. On 3 September 1940, just eight of the Squadron's pilots who had arrived at Kenley were left to withdraw to Coltishall. On the same day, Squadron Leader Marcus Robinson was succeeded in command by Squadron Leader Howard 'Billy' Burton (of whom much more later), whose job it was to re-build the depleted Squadron. On 9 September 1940, 616 Squadron moved to Kirton, where this work would be completed.

During the Battle of Britain, the supply of replacement aircraft for Fighter Command was never an issue – but the loss of pilots was. On 7 September

Above and opposite: 616 Squadron Spitfire Mk IAs at Leconfield early in 1940. At that time, the underside of the port wing was black, the remainder of the under-surface white, green and brown upper surfaces and black spinner. Serial numbers were black, fuselage codes medium sea grey. In the head-on photograph, the red doped canvas patches over the gun ports, preventing debris entering during take-off, can clearly be seen.

1940, therefore, Air Chief Marshal Dowding decided upon the 'Stabilising Scheme' which saw his squadrons categorised thus: 'A' at frontline operational strength, 'B' being those re-building but able to provide a flight for operations if necessary, and 'C', those, like 616 Squadron, which were no longer efficient fighting units and needed to withdraw and re-form. Naturally, 'A' units remained at the sharp end, whilst 'B' and 'C' squadrons were based further north. As 'A' squadrons were worn down and were re-categorised, their place was taken by a 'B' squadron now back at full strength and operational efficiency. In this way, limited resources were preserved whilst maintaining the strength of front-line units. Under Burton's leadership it was not long before 616 rose from 'C' to 'B', and on various days in September 1940 was able to provide a flight to join other Spitfire squadrons at Fowlmere, the Duxford satellite, to participate in 'Big Wing' operations, until released from this commitment on 28 September 1940. Thereafter, 616 Squadron remained at Kirton as an extension of the OTU process, receiving new pilots direct from OTU and providing extra training. Some of these men were posted out of 616 to reinforce frontline squadrons in 11 or 12 Groups, whilst others remained with the Squadron in readiness for its next deployment to the sharp end.

The training was intense, and 7 October 1940, the day R6644 was taken on charge by 616 Squadron and given the fuselage code letters QJ-R, was a typical day, pilots flying such sorties as AA cooperation, dogfighting and a dummy interception with the Defiants of 264 Squadron. As a precaution, three sections were maintained at 'readiness', but no scramble order came. As ever, training was not without mishap: on 14 October 1940, Sergeant Hogg belly landed when his undercarriage refused to come down, and on 23 October 1940 Sergeant Wilson misjudged his approach, breaking an undercarriage leg. Previously, on 20 October 1940, Red and Yellow Sections were scrambled twice during the afternoon, making no interception, whilst six Spitfires completed air firing practice at Manby. When bad weather prevented or curtailed flying, training continued by way of lectures in the Armoury. There was action, however, on 27 October 1940, when a lone He 111 attacked the airfield from 2,000 feet, dropping six 50kg bombs, damaging offices and a hangar roof, although an AA gun opened up, the raider made good its escape.

On 5 November 1940, 616 Squadron was scrambled to patrol base, Withernsea, Caistor and Spurnhead at Angels 13, but only Red Leader, Flight Lieutenant Jerry Jones, contacted the enemy: sighting a He 111 at 6,500 feet, he expended almost all of his ammunition but upon breaking away was wounded in an elbow by return fire. Fortunately the Spitfire pilot returned safely to Kirton – the Heinkel crashed into the Humber.

No. 616 Squadron's pilots at Kirton-in-Lindsey, October 1940. Squadron Leader Billy Burton (seventh from left, standing), flanked by his flight commanders, Flight Lieutenants Ken Holden (on Burton's right, 'A' Flight) and Colin MacFie (on Burton's left, 'B' Flight). Others identified are Sergeant Bob Morton (second left, standing); Pilot Officer 'Buck' Casson (with dog); Pilot Officer John Brewster (fourth left, standing); Pilot Officer Phillip 'Nip' Hepple (between Holden and Burton); Sergeant Sydney 'Thug' Mabbett (standing, next to MacFie); Sergeant Jerrold 'Chem' le Cheminant (third right, standing), and Sergeant Jenks (kneeling, extreme right).

Three days later, whilst on a battle climb practice to 19,000 feet, Pilot Officer Roberts lost control and was killed when his Spitfire crashed 8 miles south-east of the airfield. The cause of the accident was believed to have been the use of elevator trim tab whilst the aircraft was in a steep dive – and such high speed did to the Spitfire reach that both wings were actually torn off.

Early on 13 November 1940, even before 616 Squadron had risen for readiness, a lone intruder overflew the aerodrome, dropping incendiaries from just 50 feet, although fortunately no damage was caused. On the same day, 'B' Flight, comprising Flight Lieutenant Colin MacFie, Pilot Officers Hugh Dundas and Lionel 'Buck' Casson, with Sergeants Tompson, Gilders and Gilmour, flew to Ringway, providing protection for troops embarking at Liverpool. 17 November 1940 saw the weather close in, and at 0750 hrs an 85 Squadron Hurricane landed at Kirton after a nocturnal patrol, but crashed into a parked Spitfire, wrecking both machines. Christmas Day 1940 dawned foggy, but 12 Group HQ ordered two sections of 616 Squadron to remain at twenty minutes availability throughout the day, although no flying took place and neither side carried out any bombing raids on either Christmas Eve or Christmas Day nights.

Bad weather saw in the New Year. On 2 January 1941, Flight Lieutenant MacFie was scrambled at 1635 hrs to patrol Donna Nook. Forty miles out to sea he sighted a He 111, flying east. After two bursts of four seconds, the bomber vanished into thick cloud. Having observed no result of his fire, Blue 2 returned to Kirton.

On 8 January 1941 another flying accident occurred when a 255 Squadron Defiant overshot the flare path on landing, chopping the tail off a stationary Spitfire; fortunately the Spitfire's engine and wings were undamaged, and later used on another machine. The following day saw three 616 Squadron Spitfires participating in a 'practise blitz of Sheffield' [ORB], patrolling the city at various heights. On 15 January 1940, Red Section, Pilot Officers Hugh Dundas and James Edgar 'Johnnie' Johnson, scrambled to protect a convoy which an enemy aircraft was rapidly approaching. Sighting a Do 17 at 16,000 feet, Red Section attacked from out of the sun, both pilots firing two bursts, silencing the rear gunner; although the bomber's starboard undercarriage dropped, the damaged raider made off into cloud. Although only claimed as damaged by Dundas and Johnson, it was nonetheless an historic combat, being the first time Johnson fired his guns in anger – who would go on to become the RAF's officially top-scoring fighter pilot of the Second World War.

Continuing bad weather, however, preventing flying, was making 'the pilots restless' [ORB]. The following month this got worse, snow bringing all flying to a standstill for several days. On 10 February 1941, Flight Lieutenant MacFie and Sergeant Arnold intercepted a lone Ju 88 which was also lost in cloud. 22 February 1941 saw 616 Squadron fly to RAF Wittering, from where it undertook a wing practice flight with 266 Squadron – during which a lone Me 110 inadvertently crossed the Spitfires' path: Pilot Officer Johnnie Johnson managed a short but ineffective burst at the fleeting enemy before blacking out in the turn.

616 'SOUTH YORKSHIRE' SQUADRON

Pilots of 616 Squadron whiling away their time at readiness in Kirton's dispersal hut. Those identified are Sergeant Jenks (extreme left); Sergeant Jerrold 'Chem' le Cheminant, a Channel Islander (second left); Pilot Officer Phillip 'Nip' Hepple (third left); Sergeant Syd 'Thug' Mabbett (fourth left); Pilot Officer John Brewster (standing, third right); Sergeant McCairns (standing, second right); Sergeant MacDevett (seated at right).

On 25 February 1941, came the news 616 Squadron had been impatiently awaiting: the Squadron was to move south, to Tangmere, and there relieve 65 Squadron.

At 0943 hrs on 26 February 1941, Squadron Leader Burton led fourteen Spitfires, amongst them R6644, from Kirton, arriving at Tangmere at 1054 hrs. The two squadrons then exchanged Spitfires, 616 Squadron receiving 65's new Mk IIAs, whilst 65 returned 616's former and now obsolete Mk IAs to Kirton, where that squadron too would re-fit and receive new pilots. For 616 Squadron, exciting times were ahead: in March 1941, the first of the new wing leaders were appointed, with the swashbuckling Wing Commander Douglas Bader going to Tangmere; in what became a blood-stained summer, Bader would base himself at Westhampnett, the Tangmere satellite, and exclusively lead the Tangmere Wing at the head of 616 Squadron – heady days indeed.

During the time R6644 was with 616 Squadron, from 7 October 1940–26 February 1941, as with 5 OTU, identifying pilots who flew the Spitfire proved problematic. This was because, again, the ORB is completely unhelpful, failing to identify individual aircraft serial numbers, or even fuselage code letter, instead recording simply 'Spitfire' or 'Red Section', 'Blue Section' etc. Consequently, as with 5 OTU, it was necessary to identify and trace pilots who were still alive who had flown with 616 Squadron at the material time, requesting that they check their log books accordingly. Again, those who had flown in the Battle of Britain were easily accessible via the Battle of Britain Fighter Association, but not so those who flew after the Battle of Britain. Nonetheless, a number of pilots from both camps were located, although the majority returned a nil verdict. However, four 616 Squadron R6644 pilots who survived the war were ultimately identified, and one who was reported missing in 1943.

No photographs of R6644 with 616 Squadron could be found, and it is worth mentioning that for some time both 92 and 616 Squadrons, due to an administrative oversight, both used the squadron code 'QJ', meaning that over the years historians have often confused photographs of 'QJ' coded Spitfires. In 1941, when with the Tangmere Wing, 616 Squadron was switched to 'YQ', although this is unhelpful so far as the R6644 period is concerned.

As for the pilots identified as having flown R6644 with 616 Squadron, these are their stories…

Squadron Leader Howard 'Billy' Burton

The first pilot known to have flown R6644 at Kirton was the CO, Squadron Leader Burton, whose maiden flight was on 8 October 1940, a forty-minute hop to and from Duxford; he would fly this Spitfire eight times, on such exercises as battle climb, cloud flying, air firing and VHF radio testing, the last of which was on 27 December 1940.

616 'SOUTH YORKSHIRE' SQUADRON

Above: Squadron Leader Billy Burton pictured at Tangmere, April 1941.

Right: Squadron Leader Billy Burton at Westhampnett, 1941.

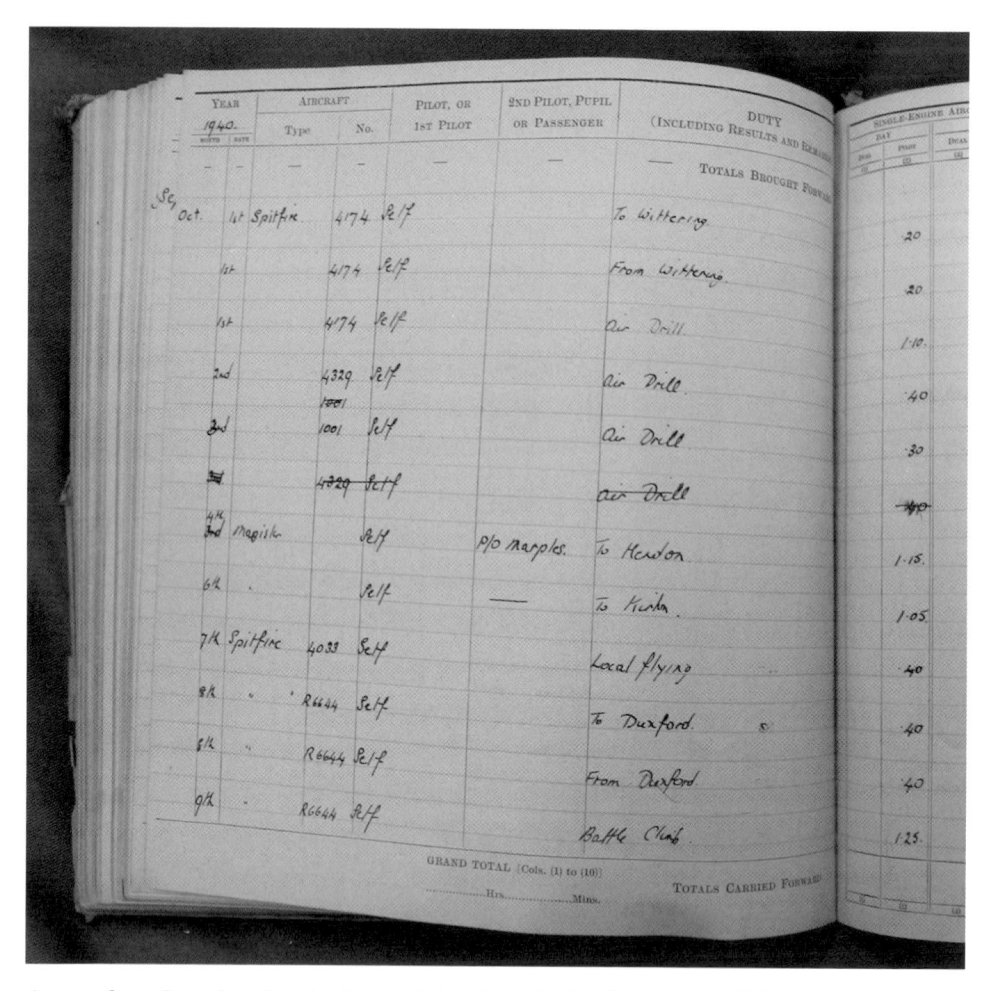

A page from Squadron Leader Burton's log book indicating several flights in R6644.

Howard Frizelle Burton – known universally as 'Billy' – was born in Letchworth Garden City, Hertfordshire on 21 June 1916, the youngest son of Major Louis Burton and his wife, Edith Jane Burton. Time would prove Billy to be an exceptional individual, no doubt destined for great things – but sadly it was not to be. War, however, had touched the Burton family very early on in young Billy's life – on 9 June 1917, Major Burton was killed in action on the Western Front.

Educated at Bedford, young Billy joined the Officer Training Corps, and in 1935 won a King's Cadetship with outstandingly high marks, meaning that the service met all fees for Billy to become a flight cadet at Cranwell. Without doubt, Billy thrived at Cranwell, playing in both the college's cricket, rugby and squash teams, serving as President of the Debating Society and sub-editor of the College Journal, in addition to being a member of the dramatic society.

Flight cadets gained initial flight experience on the two-seater Avro Tutor and de Havilland Tiger Moth biplanes, before progressing to more advanced single-engined biplane types including, as recorded in Billy's personal pilot's flying log book, the Hawker Hart light-bomber and its army cooperation derivative, the Hawker Audax, and the Hawker Fury fighter. On 7 October 1936, shortly before the end of his course, Flight Cadet Burton was flying Hawker Fury K5681, engaged on an air-firing exercise with Flight Lieutenant Roy James Oliphant Bartlett, but somehow the pair collided. Both pilots baled out, but Bartlett was killed when struck in mid-air by his aircraft, K5682, which crashed at Navenby, 8 miles south of Lincoln. Billy landed safely by parachute, and no blame was apportioned to either pilot by the subsequent Court of Inquiry.

Ultimately, Flight Cadet Burton passed out of Cranwell in December 1936 – having been awarded the highly prized 'Sword-of-Honour'. This great trophy, a Wilkinson's blade, was awarded by the Air Ministry to the flight cadet on each course having demonstrated 'outstanding ability, officer qualities and the potential to progress in the Service'. Billy's sword would prove unique, in fact, as the only blade inscribed 'Edward VIII', the sole such sword awarded during that somewhat controversial monarch's short reign. Clearly, Billy had lived up to all expectations of a King's Cadet and, as a commissioned pilot officer, was now on the second leg of his service career. Pilot Officer Burton's first posting was to a new squadron, 46, at Kenley, which had a proud First World War history and had recently re-formed, flying the Gloster Gauntlet.

In February 1939, Billy was an established member of 46 Squadron when its Gauntlets were replaced by the Hawker Hurricane. Flying Officer Burton first flew a Hawker Hurricane Mk I, L1792, on 20 February 1939, the flight comprising 'Local flying and circuits and landings'. By this time, he was commanding 'A' Flight, the Squadron being divided into two flights, 'A' and

'B', and so in addition to converting to and mastering the Hurricane himself, he also had to checkout his pilots on the Miles Magister monoplane trainer before authorising them to fly the new machine. In between these check-flights, Billy trained on the Hurricane, practising battle climbs, formation flying, mock interceptions, and night-flying, and was promoted to flight lieutenant in March 1939. On 20 June 1939, 46 Squadron's CO, Squadron Leader Barwell, assessed Flight Lieutenant Burton's ability as a fighter pilot and navigator as 'above the average' and in air gunnery 'exceptional'. The training for war, now on Hurricanes, continued relentlessly, with firing practice out to sea off the east coast, and squadron formation climbs to 25,000 feet. On 26 June 1939, however, Billy's time with 46 Squadron came to an end when he was posted to 12 Group HQ at Hucknall on 'operations staff duties'.

The declaration of war, however, returned Flight Lieutenant Burton to operational flying, when on 7 September 1939 he was posted to Duxford as commander of 66 Squadron's 'B' Flight. He first flew a Spitfire Mk I, K9988, on a thirty-five-minute familiarisation flight on 8 September 1939, and thereafter many more flights over the next few days whilst converting to type. It was a busy time, and in addition to operational commitments by day and night, the squadrons also continued training, practising attacks, cine-gun firing, and co-operation exercises with bombers and searchlights.

On 10 May 1940, Hitler attacked the West, achieving complete surprise and paralysing the Allied command system. Only Hurricanes would ever be sent to France, however, as Air Chief Marshal Dowding preserved his Spitfires for essential home defence. Nonetheless, Air Vice-Marshal Sir Trafford Leigh-Mallory, commanding 12 Group, moved the newly Spitfire-equipped 222 Squadron from Duxford to Digby, its place at the former station taken by the Defiants of 264 Squadron. 'L.M.' then lost no time in arranging an offensive patrol over the Dutch coast, involving both 66 and 264 Squadrons.

After practising tactics together, on 12 May 1940, Squadron Leader Leigh led six Spitfires of 66 Squadron up from Duxford to support five 264 Squadron Defiants on a patrol off the Dutch coast. Squadron Leader Leigh led Blue Section, whilst Flight Lieutenant Burton led the three Spitfires of Green Section. Passing close to RN destroyers off the Hague, a bomb was seen to splash into the sea nearby. Squadron Leader Hunter of 264 Squadron then sighted a Ju 88, and ordered his Defiants to attack. Chasing the raider to ground-level, the Defiants fired at the enemy machine from both sides. A Spitfire attacked from astern, sealing the enemy bomber's fate, which crashed into a field of cows, surrounded by water, 10 miles south-west of Rotterdam's Waalhaven airfield. According to the after-action report, 'The Ju 88 was deceived into thinking that he was dealing with Spitfires only. By turning and diving he actually played into the hands of the Defiants because their initial acceleration in the dive proved greater than the Ju 88. Turning only wasted the Ju 88's time and played into the Defiant's hands.'

Flight Lieutenant Burton's personal combat report:

> Took off with Blue Section for The Hague at 1320 hrs. At 1400 hrs crossed the Dutch coast. At 1403 hrs sighted enemy aircraft, probably a He 111 at 7,000 feet. Gave chase but enemy climbed into cloud and disappeared. Later noticed large explosion 400 yards to port of destroyers steaming south. Sighted enemy aircraft (E/A) with our machines chasing it. Dived down and carried out two deflection attacks from port quarter. Enemy eventually crashed 15 miles east of The Hague.

The Defiants were credited with the Ju 88 destroyed, whilst Squadron Leader Leigh, Flight Lieutenant Burton, Flying Officers Campbell-Colquhoun and Rimmer, and Pilot Officer Kennard, shared destruction of the He 111. The after-action reports concluded that 'The pilots of both squadrons are extremely enthusiastic about this scheme of patrolling as a composite flight or squadron and unanimous in their desire always to carry out patrols of this description in this formation'. It was certainly a significant day for Billy Burton – who had fired his guns in anger for the first time, but optimism would shortly prove unfounded.

Early the following morning, 'A' Flight of 66 Squadron escorted 264 Squadron's Defiants back to the Dutch coast, hoping for a similarly successful engagement whilst attacking enemy troop transports north of Den Haag. Inland, south-east of Rotterdam, a formation of Ju 87 Stuka dive-bombers was successfully engaged – then Me 109s rained down on the

RAF fighters. 66 Squadron lost Flying Officer Brown, who forced-landed in Belgium and evaded, but 264 Squadron was literally massacred: five out of six Defiants were shot down, during what was the Defiant's first encounter with Me 109s – proving the Defiant's total unsuitability as a day-fighter. There was also arguably no need for 12 Group to be prowling around the Dutch coast at this critical time, wasting resources for no apparent good purpose, and responsibility for the fiasco lay firmly with L.M.

On 14 May 1940, Flight Lieutenant Burton moved with 66 Squadron from Duxford to operate from the new airfield at Horsham St Faiths in Norfolk. There, life went on much the same as before, routinely patrolling and training – without any further offensive sorties across the North Sea. On the Continent, however, the Allies were facing disaster – and on 26 May 1940 the unthinkable decision was made to retire on and evacuate the BEF from the beaches of Dunkirk.

Air Vice-Marshal Park, commander of 11 Group, was in charge of the air component of Operation *Dynamo*, the Dunkirk evacuation, whose fighter squadrons operated from forward bases to extend their range. Even so, it was impossible, given the resources available to provide cover from dawn to dusk. Significantly, though, indicating the urgency of the hour, Spitfires were committed to battle across the Channel for the first time.

By 1 June 1940, certain Fighter Command squadrons had suffered sufficient losses to be pulled out of 11 Group, to rest and re-fit. On that day, 66 Squadron, fresh to the battle, therefore flew south, to Gravesend, from where Flight Lieutenant Burton participated in an uneventful patrol over Dunkirk. 'Clickety-Click' then returned to Duxford, and at dawn the following day was off to operate from Martlesham Heath. Flight Lieutenant Burton was in the 66 Squadron formation led by Squadron Leader Leigh across to Dunkirk's blazing oil tanks, 'Clickety-Click' arriving over the battered French port at 0745 hrs and patrolling at 29,000 feet. Billy, flying his usual Green 1 spot and leading Green Section, reported that at 0845 hrs:

> Sighted one Ju 88 at about 11,000 feet. Dived on him and got in a short burst, but could not observe results as windscreen misted up. Cleared this and then went through a lower bank of cloud.

> On coming out I found I was over Dunkirk. Enemy aircraft were everywhere. Attacked two Me 109s with short bursts but could see no results owing to ice on inside of my screen. Then carried out attack from dead astern on right-hand aircraft of formation of three He 111s. Broke sharply away to right and saw aircraft begin to lose height with smoke pouring from it. I was about to continue attack when noticed smoke pouring from the starboard side of my engine. Radiator temperature increased, so re-formed and landed at Manston.

Billy's attack on the He 111 was solo and therefore the result unconfirmed. This was, in fact, 66 Squadron's first major engagement of the Second World War, with all its pilots engaged, claiming three Me 109s and a Ju 88 destroyed. Sergeant Doug Hunt, however, was shot down and safely baled out, but Sergeant Hayman was reported missing. In his log book, Billy noted that during the combat the 'header tank' of his Spitfire (N3043) had been 'punctured', referring to the glycol coolant system.

By 3 June 1940, the evacuation was over, 338,226 Allied troops having been snatched from the jaws of defeat. The following day, 66 Squadron was sent to operate from Coltishall, where life continued much the same as it had before Dunkirk, with routine patrols and training, flying by day and night. On 17 June 1940, the French sued for peace.

After Dunkirk, the Luftwaffe's new-found access to airfields in the Pas-de-Calais, just over 20 miles across the English Channel from Dover, changed the whole strategic picture. This unexpected geographical shift put the entire British Isles within range of German bombers, which could now be escorted to London by the lethal Me 109 fighter. This unanticipated and, indeed, unprecedented military success was as big a surprise to Hitler as everyone else – the *Führer* now suddenly presented with an unexpected opportunity to mount a seaborne invasion of southern England. First, though, aerial supremacy, at least over the invasion area, was pre-requisite, and very soon the Battle of Britain would decide the issue.

For Flight Lieutenant Burton, action came on the evening of 19 June 1940, when he led Blue Section off from Coltishall, scrambled to intercept a suspected raider off the east coast. At 1930 hrs, 40 miles off Yarmouth, Billy sighted a Ju 88, flying south at 12,000 feet, which he engaged inconclusively. His last flight that month was on 27 June 1940, 'attack practice' in Spitfire N3032, bring his total solo flying hours to 731.55, 182.30 being on the Spitfire by day, 18.35 by night. Billy did not fly again until 5 July 1940, the reason being a happy occasion: Flight Lieutenant Burton got married, on 29 June 1940, to Miss Jean Ferelith Maxwell Robertson, only daughter of Air Commodore E.D.M. Robertson CB DFC, and Mrs Evelyn Jane Robertson.

From 2 July 1940, however, the *Luftwaffe* began attacking shipping in the Channel, probing British defences, and on 29 July 1940, Billy was in action again, damaging a He 111 over the North Sea, east of Hammond's Knoll.

August 1940 continued much the same for Coltishall's squadrons, chasing about after unescorted lone reconnaissance or nuisance bombers, whilst the Battle of Britain proper was being fought over the 10 and 11 Groups' areas. On 15 August 1940, 66 Squadron from Coltishall and 19 from Fowlmere, Duxford's satellite, were called upon to reinforce 11 Group and defend Martlesham Heath aerodrome, but the 12 Group Spitfires arrived too late to prevent Martlesham being bombed. Air Vice-Marshal Park was furious, but 12 Group countered that they had been requested too late, and considering time and distance, it was then impossible for L.M.'s Spitfires to arrive in time. It was the start of major friction between the two groups which would ultimately have far-reaching consequences for Fighter Command as whole.

On 3 September 1940, Billy Burton recorded in his log book, 'Promoted to Acting Squadron Leader and posted to command 616 (Fighter) Squadron'. Given the battering his new squadron had received at Kenley, and the low morale arising, Squadron Leader Burton had work to do; Pilot Officer Johnnie Johnson, however, was immediately impressed with his new CO: 'Billy Burton, being a regular officer who had won the Cranwell Sword-of-Honour in 1936, was an outstanding product of the Cranwell system. Exacting in his demands, he was always full of vitality and enthusiasm. I liked him at first sight and have never served under a better or more loyal officer.'

Half an hour after this initial interview, Johnnie was airborne for fifty minutes in Spitfire X4055, being put through his paces by Squadron Leader Burton. Afterwards, the CO concluded that Johnson's performance was 'Not bad', but emphasised the need to keep a constantly good look-out.

At Kirton, 616 Squadron began an intensive period of flying training, including interception practice with 264 Squadron's Defiants, and operational commitments such as scrambling after unidentified radar plots – 'bogeys', otherwise known as 'X-Raids'. It was all good experience. It was also to Squadron Leader Burton's enormous credit that on the morning of 19 September 1940, only a fortnight since 616 Squadron had been pulled out of Kenley, Billy led no less than fourteen Spitfires from Kirton to operate from Fowlmere, the Duxford satellite airfield, and participate in the operations of the Duxford Wing and relieve 611 Squadron. Between then and the end of the month, 616 would share the Wing commitment with Kirton's other Spitfire squadron, Squadron Leader 'Sailor' Malan's 74 'Tiger' Squadron. Billy would lead 616 Squadron on a number of largely uneventful Big Wing patrols, but on 27 September 1940 the Wing was engaged by Me 109s, 616 losing Pilot Officer Don Smith, its last casualty of the Battle of Britain. The following day, Billy led the Squadron on two more Wing patrols, after which it too was released from further Wing commitments.

Back at Kirton, 616 Squadron, now with operational experience over London and the south-east, continued training, whilst Squadron Leader Burton and his two excellent flight commanders, Flight Lieutenant Colin MacFie and C.A.T. 'Jerry' Jones, moulded the Squadron into the highly efficient fighting unit it became. Having relieved 65 Squadron at Tangmere on 26 February 1941, the following month 616, 610 and 145 Squadrons became the 'Tangmere Wing', commanded by the Wing Commander Douglas Bader. Fighter Command's new chiefs had decided on an aggressive stance for the forthcoming 'season', 'reaching out' and 'leaning into France', taking the war across the Channel to the Germans in north-west France, the objective being 'to establish air superiority over the enemy in his own country'. New operations were devised, including 'Rhubarbs', low-level nuisance raids which ultimately generated heavy losses and which the pilots hated, and the more complex 'Circus', involving a small number of bombers attacking a target such as an enemy airfield, transport and communications centre, port or factory, escorted by literally hundreds of Spitfires. Considering that less than a year before Fighter Command was on the back foot, fighting a critical defensive battle, it was optimistic indeed – but nonetheless inspiring, and the new wings eagerly looked forward to action, their morale high.

The pressure was relentless.

On the morning of 21 June 1941, the longest day of high summer 1941, the Tangmere Wing provided forward support, with the Hornchurch Wing, to Circus 16, attacking the airfield at St Omer – Longuenesse, where a big fire was started in a wood. *Oberfeldwebel* Luders of 6/JG 26 was attacked by Flying Officer Machacek of 145 Squadron, and Squadron Leader Burton, the latter reporting that:

Squadron Leader Burton walking in after a sweep, Westhampnett, summer 1941 – he is wearing a German *schwimmveste*, a far superior life jacket than the RAF's 'Mae West' and a highly prized trophy taken from a Me 109 pilot Burton had shot down over Kent.

Just after take-off my hood came adrift and I landed, had it fixed in about ten minutes and endeavoured to catch up the Wing. Climbed to 20,000 feet over Dungeness, could see no sign of Wing so dived and patrolled speedboat with two other Spitfires, about 10 miles east of Dover. About 1220 hrs our fighters started to come in and I suddenly noticed two Me 109s crossing the coast NE of Dover. I then saw one Spitfire attacking. I joined in and we cut off one Me 109; the other one quickly disappeared. We dived and zoomed for several minutes overland between Dover and Manston, alternately engaging E/A with quarter and beam attacks. Finally, E/A opened hood and baled out. His machine crashed into a railway embankment and blew up. Pilot landed safely and was made prisoner by a civilian. I personally cannot be sure which Spitfire pilot which responsible for destroying the E/A. It appeared that he was hardly damaged at all when he baled out. The other Spitfire attacking was of 145 Squadron, SO-D.

The enemy fighter was confirmed as destroyed and shared between the two Spitfire pilots.

Three days later, the Tangmere Wing participated in a Circus raid to Lille, Billy later commenting in his log book 'Odd squirt here and there at 109s which disappear downwards and fantastic speeds. Majority appear to be 109Fs'.

On the second operation of 23 July 1941, Squadron Leader Burton led the Tangmere Wing, escorting bombers attacking a tanker off Ostend. The II/JG 26 intercepted the 'beehive, Billy's log book recording 'Two squirts. Found 109 beating up a Spitfire. Sent 109 quickly back to France.'

By now, the pressure was beginning to tell, even on the Tangmere Wing's swashbuckling leader. Wing Commander Bader's wife, Thelma, and friends urged this human dynamo to take a break from operations but this he would not do. Inevitably, on 9 August 1941, it all went wrong. During another escort sortie, the Tangmere Wing was led into a trap and ambushed by a large force of Me 109s. In the ensuing combat, involving over seventy fighters at close-range, Wing Commander Bader was shot down (the evidence suggests accidentally by 616 Squadron's Flight Lieutenant 'Buck' Casson, of whom more later) and captured. It was a devastating blow to the Tangmere Wing and the war effort generally, given Bader's profile as a war hero.

On 5 September 1941, there was cause for celebration, though, when Squadron Leader Burton's DFC was gazetted, the citation for which read: 'This officer has led his squadron with commendable skill and coolness. He has participated in fifty-four sorties over enemy territory during which he has assisted in the destruction of two Messerschmitt 109's, probably destroyed a Heinkel in and damaged a further two enemy aircraft. Squadron Leader Burton has on all occasions proved an inspiration to his unit'.

It was a well-earned award, and due recognition for Billy's efforts in transforming 616 Squadron into one of the most confident and combat experienced squadrons in Fighter Command.

A spell as a staff officer and commanding RAF Hawkinge followed, then in March 1942, Squadron Leader Burton DFC was posted to HQ RAF Middle East in Cairo. The 'Middle East', so far as the military were concerned, stretched from the western Libyan desert to the Red Army's left-flank in Persia, north to the Balkans and south to Central Africa – and being oil-rich and providing shipping access via the Suez Canal from the Indian Ocean to the Mediterranean, was of great strategic importance. The war arrived in these lands when Mussolini's Italy entered the war as an Axis Power on 10 June 1940. Thereafter it became a matter of advance and retreat in the Libyan desert, as territory was gained but lost, and British forces were driven from Greece and Crete. The British, however, held the tiny island of Malta, between the North African coast and Sicily, providing a crucial base in the Mediterranean from which enemy supply routes could be harassed by sea and air. An Italian air force and army had been destroyed in Cyrenaica, another in Abyssinia, and the British controlled the Red Sea and, therefore, the vital Suez Canal. The region was the responsibility of HQ, RAF Middle East.

Squadron Leader Burton reached Cairo, via India, on 30 June 1942. The following month, serving on Air Vice-Marshal Coningham's staff as a liaison officer, Billy flew communications aircraft, including the Audax, Anson, Lysander, Proctor, and even a Blenheim Mk IV bomber, around the command. The pattern continued into September 1942, Billy flying a P-40 Kittyhawk for the first time (AL638) for an hour on 22nd, from Helwan to Ballah. On 7 October 1942, he spent another hour aloft in a Kittyhawk (AK741), during which 'Tried out two spins from which I had no trouble in recovering. Also tried out loop, but stalled on top'. On 22 October 1942, Billy flew a Hurricane Mk IIC, 'and fired cannons for practice'. That month, promoted to Acting Wing Commander, Billy had been posted to the recently formed 212 Group, commanded by Battle of Britain survivor Group Captain H.A. 'Jimmy' Fenton. In August 1942, Fenton had formed his new Group 'from scratch', comprised of two Hurricane-equipped wings, 243, a SAAF wing, and a Greek squadron, the intention being that the 212 Group would participate in the forthcoming British Eighth Army's break-out and advance from the Alamein Line.

In November 1942, Wing Commander Burton was posted to command of 243 Wing, based at Gambut. This formation comprised 1 Squadron SAAF, and 33, 213 and 238 Squadrons RAF, all equipped with the Hurricane Mk IIC, armed with four 20mm cannon – and focused on the ground-attack role. Having flown over Dunkirk, during the Battle of Britain and on the relentless offensive operations over France in 1941, this was beyond Wing Commander Burton's experience to date. Typically, he lost no time in familiarising himself with this new weapon and tactic, practising cannon-firing on 'an old car', 'a ship', and 'strafing practice with 213'. With 238 Squadron, the new Wing Leader practised 'flight formation', and practised 'jumping' these Hurricanes. Just one month later, however, Billy moved on again, succeeding Wing Commander G.D.L. Haysom DFC in command of 239 Wing, based at Marble Arch. This was 212 Group's other fighter wing, equipped with Kittyhawks, which had been heavily engaged in the desert campaign.

After the Second Battle of El Alamein (23 October – 11 November 1942), the siege of Tobruk was lifted and the Axis forces began a fighting retreat west to Tunisia. Amongst the battered enemy formations after Tobruk was the Italian 132nd Armoured Division *'Ariete'*, which had been all but destroyed, the name thereafter applying to a raggle-taggle task force. There was no respite, however, as on 9 January 1943, Wing Commander Burton recorded in his log book that he had flown a 'Kitty II' twice that day, 'Bombing Ariete Division with 500lbs', three more identical sorties following over the next three days. On 13 January 1943, 239 Wing, led by Billy, attacked a German landing ground in the desert, escorted Bostons the next day and flew an 'offensive sweep' on the next. Further sweeps followed, with Billy leading Kittyhawk fighters on 18 January 1943, covering the 'Kittybombers' of 250 and 260 Squadrons, which were 'bombing and strafing enemy motor transport concentrations near Tarhuna'. During that operation, Billy recorded in his log having destroyed an Me 109, the pilot of which was seen to bale out, and on 21 January 1943, whilst leading the wing on a sweep, attacked four Italian Macchi 202 Folgore fighters. Two days later, the Eighth Army entered Tripoli after an advance of over 1,400 miles, possibly the greatest single advance in military history – made possible through tactical air power. By 24 January 1943, 239 Wing was based at Castel Benito, from where Billy led the wing's 'first Kitty fighter-bomber raid on Tunisia', an attack on Ben Gardan airfield.

The pursuit, however, went on, as the Axis forces continued west, towards the Mareth Line, Billy leading his 239 Wing on numerous further 'bombing', 'strafing' and 'road attacks'. On 30 January 1943, for example, air support was called for by army units to deal with a German 88-mm gun located in a 'strong point', which Billy led 'Kittybombers' to successfully destroy. On 3 February 1943, Billy bombed barges and strafed a seaplane, attacking dispersed enemy vehicles two days later, on which sortie the Wing Leader 'Encountered one Me 109. No result'. On that day's second operation, 'Bombing Motor Transport in Ben Garden area, jumped by six 109s. No luck'. Such attacks, on retreating panzer formations, were a daily occurrence – and Billy led all of them – leading to a Bar for his existing DFC.

On 26 February 1943, Wing Commander Burton destroyed a 109 during another bombing commitment – which, according to the 239 Wing ORB, 'flew into a hill, in flames'. It would be Billy's final combat claim, bring his tally to two and four shared destroyed, one probable, one and one shared damaged. By now, Billy had substantial experience of air fighting and close air support, having led a flight, squadron, and a wing, in addition to having served tours on headquarters' staffs. This marked him out as one of the most experienced and able young officers in the service.

On 30 March 1943, *The Times* reported that:

> Two Western Desert fighter pilots have been awarded the DSO in recognition of brilliantly executed attacks on German tanks and armoured vehicles which were holding up the advance of troops attacking the Mareth Line. Both officers – Wing Commander HF Burton of Ashstead, Surrey, and Squadron Leader Weston Burt, of Southampton, are 26 years old and both were cadets at Cranwell in 1935.
>
> Wing Commander Burton led a flight of Spitfires against the Luftwaffe during the Dunkirk evacuation and again in the Battle of Britain. Later, he commanded a fighter squadron under Wing Commander Bader. He came to the Western Desert just before the battle of El Alamein, and in December took over the largest fighter wing in the desert. 'The most interesting feature of our work', he said, 'has been the ever closer and more direct support we are giving the army. What began as patrols over our forward troops and bombing targets well behind the enemy lines has gradually come to include similar attacks in the course of battle, when opposing ground forces are sometimes almost on top of each other. Our job is getting more specialised every day. We must be able to distinguish at a glance silhouettes of our own and enemy tanks and armoured cars. We must be familiar with military formations and tactics: we must be able to spot well dug-in enemy gun emplacements and then destroy them.'

In April 1943, the Allied air forces unleashed Operation *Flux*, which severed Rommel's supply line into North Africa. Wisely, the 'Desert Fox' believed that the remnants of his once much-vaunted Afrika Korps should now be evacuated to Italy, and make ready to fight again. Hitler, however, rejected this, and so, after the Allied ground offensives, Operations *Vulcan* and *Strike*, Axis forces in Tunisia finally surrendered, unconditionally, on 13 May 1943, bringing the fighting in North Africa to an end. Without doubt, the Allied air forces had been the primary factor in achieving that victory, preparing the way for what followed in Sicily, Italy and north-west Europe. With that kind of experience behind him, equally beyond question is the fact that Wing Commander Billy Burton could look forward to playing a key role in the continuing air war. Sadly, it was not to be.

After the Allied victory in Tunisia, on 18 May 1943, Wing Commander Burton left 239 Wing at El Adem, and with other officers, including Air Vice-Marshal Broadhurst and Squadron Leader Osgood 'Pedro' Hanbury DSO DFC, another Battle of Britain survivor and fighter ace, returned to England aboard an unarmed Lockheed Hudson transport aircraft, via Gibraltar. The journey was for a well-deserved home leave, during which Squadron Leader Hanbury and Wing Commander Burton attended a luncheon at RAF Kenley, now commanded by Group Captain Jimmy Fenton, formerly of WDAF 212 Group. The occasion was to celebrate the first DSO for Kenley's Wing Leader – none other than Wing Commander Johnnie Johnson, who had previously served under Billy as a lowly pilot officer in 616 Squadron. Afterwards, it was back to North Africa…

Early on 3 June 1943, Wing Commander Burton and the following officers, all returning from home leave, gathered at RAF Portreath, in Cornwall, ready for their return flight to North Africa:

> Wing Commander Paul Temple Cotton DFC, a reconnaissance pilot and staff officer attached to 216 Group.
>
> Wing Commander Jack Goodhead, an operations officer with 117 Squadron (27).
>
> Squadron Leader Osgood Villiers 'Pedro' Hanbury DSO DFC, also on the staff of 216 Group (25).
>
> Squadron Leader John Kenneth Young MBE, an Ops 'B' Controller with No. 1 Overseas Aircraft Delivery Unit (37).
>
> Squadron Leader Eric Paul of the RAAF, an Air Observer with 216 Group (33).
>
> Flight Lieutenant John Bowyer Buckley RCAF, a pilot in 216 Group (21).

The aircraft concerned, Hudson VI FK386 of No. 1 OADU, 44 Group, Transport Command, was to be flown by the CO of 117 Squadron, Group Captain Robert Gordon Yaxley (31) a pre-war officer who had been awarded the MC for his actions during the Arab revolt in Palestine during 1936. During the Second World War he had first commanded a squadron, then a wing, of Beaufighters engaged on anti-shipping strikes, earning a DFC, before receiving the first DSO awarded during the campaign in Libya. Yaxley's navigator was Flying Officer James McSherry (23), a New Zealander, his Wireless Operator/Air Gunner Pilot Officer Dennis Victor Edwards (23).

The problem, though, was that since 1 May 1943, there had been increased enemy fighter activity over the Bay of Biscay, as the Ju 88Cs of V/KG 40 provided cover for U-boats entering and leaving their bases on the French Atlantic coast – making the Bay dangerous airspace indeed. Especially in daylight. And for some unfathomable reason, Group Captain Yaxley decided to make the trip by day. The first leg was to re-fuel at Gibraltar, which meant passing over the Bay of Biscay in daylight, before continuing to 249 (Transport) Wing's base at Castel Benito, Tripoli. Wing Commander Burton DSO, DFC and Bar, and Croix de Guerre, was the most decorated officer aboard – but as he was officially an acting group captain, Yaxley was the senior officer.

Jean Allom, Billy's widow:

> I understand that Billy tried to do everything possible to dissuade Yaxley, but the latter, the more senior man, insisted upon doing so – with disastrous consequences. It is impossible to understand why such an experienced officer as Yaxley took such a foolhardy course of action.
>
> In retrospect, there seems to have been doom hanging over this flight as the Hudson should never have been flying that day – it was due to return several days earlier. The delay was caused by those servicing the aircraft discovering some desert insects therein, and so it had to be fumigated. Of course, the date on which the flight was to return to Gibraltar was then scheduled to take place, 3 June 1943, was one on which there was maximum *Luftwaffe* activity over the Bay of Biscay. Only two days before,

in fact, a Dakota had been shot down over the Bay – all aboard were lost, including the actor Leslie Howard.

Yaxley took off from Portreath at 0737 hrs on the day in question, and, perhaps inevitably, considering the high level of enemy air activity, was intercepted and shot down over the Bay of Biscay by a 14/KG 40 Ju 88C, flown by *Leutnant* Heinz Olbrecht. The defenceless and doomed Hudson crashed into the Atlantic – with the loss of all aboard: two fighter aces, one a wing leader, and officers between them decorated three DSOs, six DFCs, a MC, an MBE and a Croix de Guerre. It was a dreadful loss and blow to the WDAF. Perhaps saddest of all is the fact that Squadron Leader Hanbury, one of 'The Few' with over ten aerial victories, had got married whilst on leave – and would never meet his son, born nine months later.

It was not until 7 June 1943 that Jean received the official telegram notifying her that Billy was missing, although a subsequent letter from the Casualty Branch pointed out that 'This does not necessarily mean that he is killed or wounded, and if he is a prisoner of war he should be able to communicate with you in due course'. That was, however, a forlorn hope.

On 10 July 1943, Air Vice-Marshal Broadhurst wrote to 'My Dear Mrs Burton':

> I will report what little I know of this affair.
>
> First of all I would like to say how dreadfully sorry I am about the whole business and to offer you the deepest sympathy of all of us in the Desert Air Force.
>
> Billy had done a magnificent job of work with us and there is no doubt that he was cut out to be a 'Big Chief' in the RAF.
>
> I left in the first of the two aeroplanes to go … The other arrived at their departure aerodrome and from all the evidence I have it was Yaxley who decided to go through in daylight. Had I been with them I would never have allowed it. At first, I thought as you did, that they had been routed by day but I have been assured since that it was Yaxley's decision and I am not at all sure that he did not insist. It really is a deplorable business, and much as I would like

to tell you otherwise, I cannot hold out any hope of Billy being alive. It sounds a dreadful thing to say but I think it would be cruel to give you any hope when I have none myself.

I hope you will believe me when I say how sorry I am. I counted myself a friend of his and had a great admiration for him, as indeed the whole Force had. I'm so glad that you had that time at home with him – I know he had enjoyed every moment of it and by God he had earned it.

The Air Forces Memorial at Runnymede, commemorating those with no known grave, including Wing Commander Billy Burton DSO DFC.

In 1947, the authorities officially concluded that those reported missing aboard Group Captain Yaxley's Hudson had been 'lost at sea'. All are commemorated on the Air Forces Memorial at Runnymede. The loss of all aboard the Hudson was tragic – not least Billy Burton, who was, as Broadhurst said, destined to be a 'Big Chief' in the service, possibly even Chief of the Air Staff.

Pilot Officer Hugh 'Cocky' Dundas

On 9 October 1940, Pilot Officer Dundas first flew R6644 on a formation training exercise lasting thirty minutes, very helpfully recording in his log book both the Spitfire's serial number and individual code letter of 'R' – which is unusual because generally pilots recorded either one or the other, rarely both. This tiny detail – barely relevant at the time – is why we know

Flying Officer Hugh 'Cocky' Dundas at Tangmere, 1941.

A page from Dundas's log book, recording the 'triangular dogfight', during which he flew R6644, with his brother, Flying Officer John Dundas DFC, and Flight Lieutenant Colin MacFie.

that Spitfire R6644 was coded QJ-R whilst with 616 Squadron. In total, between 9 October 1940 and 20 November 1940, 'Cocky' – so-called owing to his penchant for cocktails – flew R6644 thirteen times on the usual training flights, standing and interception patrols.

Hugh Spencer Lisle Dundas was born at Barnburgh Hall, near Doncaster in Yorkshire, on 22 July 1920, into a wealthy family with aristocratic connections, the second son of his colliery director father, Frederick, and his wife, Silvia. Having attended Aysgarth and Stowe, Dundas became a trainee solicitor. His elder brother, John, born on 19 August 1915, having achieved a first in history at Oxford, was a *Yorkshire Post* journalist who, having covered the Munich Crisis over Czechoslovakia in September 1938, immediately joined 609 'West Riding' Squadron. Inspired by John, but to his parents' dismay, in May 1939, Hugh also joined the socially elite AAF, after failing the medical three times, and was commissioned into 616 'South Yorkshire' Squadron, then based at Doncaster.

Having been mobilised upon outbreak of war, Pilot Officer Dundas successfully completed his service flying training at Brize Norton between 10 October 1939 and 17 February 1940, before re-joining 616 Squadron, which moved to Leconfield on 2 March 1940. On 27 May 1940, 616 Squadron flew to and operated from Rochford, participating in the Dunkirk air fighting. Returning to Leconfield on 6 June 1940, the Squadron continued patrolling the north-east and North Sea, occasionally engaging lone German nuisance raiders or reconnaissance aircraft, and on 3 July 1940, Dundas fired his guns in angler for the first time, receiving a third share in a Do 17 destroyed east of Withernsea. Two days later a half share of a Do 17 probable followed, and on 15 August 1940, that unprecedented day of fighting which saw *Luftflotte* 5 attack the north-east, came a half share in a Ju 88 destroyed off Flamborough Head, and half of another claimed as a probable.

Pilot Officer Dundas flew south to Kenley with 616 Squadron on 19 August 1940, but had a traumatic experience three days later. At 1845 hrs on 22 August 1940, fourteen Spitfires of 616 Squadron were scrambled from Kenley to patrol base at 5,000 feet but, with action over the Channel and Manston in mind, were soon vectored to patrol Hawkinge at 15,000 feet. No enemy aircraft were sighted, however, and so, flying in sections line astern, the Squadron was ordered back to base. Over Dover, though, high-flying Me 109s ambushed Green Section; Pilot Officer Lionel 'Buck' Casson's Spitfire was hit in the wing by a 20mm cannon round but he regained Kenley safely; Pilot Officer Hugh 'Cocky' Dundas:

> Suddenly my aircraft was hit so hard that I assumed a heavy anti-aircraft shell was responsible. Thick white smoke filled the cockpit. I could see nothing, and as the Spitfire went into a spin, I was pressed, hard, against the side of my cockpit.

I was terrified and just sat there thinking that this was the end, until a voice in my head told me to open the hood and get out, which I did. Centrifugal force still pressed me into the cockpit and I got stuck, half in, half out. With the ground perilously close I managed to fall clear. My parachute opened and I watched as my Spitfire exploded in a field. I landed a couple of hundreds away from my burning aircraft, my left leg was bleeding and my left shoulder was dislocated.

The following day I discovered the humiliating truth: I had not been shot down by our own ack ack, as I thought, but by an Me 109 none of us had even seen.

Dundas had probably been ambushed and shot down by *Unteroffizier* Schildknecht of 8/JG 54. It was not a good start to 616 Squadron's Battle of Britain proper, but this scenario was not uncommon for squadrons new to the south-east as Pilot Officer Peter 'Sneezy' Brown of 611 Squadron explained: 'Chasing lone or unescorted formations of bombers about East Anglia or the North was entirely different to the pace of combat in the South. This was entirely due to the presence of Me 109s – and many squadrons found the transition traumatic.'

In this melee, Sergeant Phillip Wareing claimed a Me 109 destroyed, which was confirmed by Flight Lieutenant Denys Gillam, the commander of 616 Squadron's 'B' Flight.

Dundas was admitted to Kent and Canterbury Hospital, returning to 616 Squadron on 12 September 1940, by which time the battered remnants had been withdrawn from Kenley to Kirton. Dundas was unimpressed, commenting that the Squadron 'had deteriorated into a FTS, or at best an OTU'. More to his liking was 616 Squadron's contribution to Duxford Wing operations, Pilot Officer Dundas flying to Fowlmere daily between 19 and 28 September 1940. There the impressionable young pilot officer came into contact with Douglas Bader for the first time – which would later prove significant.

On 10 October 1940, Hugh's brother, Flying Officer John Dundas, 'turned up', being on 'sick leave after being mildly peppered by a Me 110.

A SPITFIRE'S STORY: THE INVISIBLE THREAD

As usual, when he visits the Squadron, the evening developed into a party'. At 0800 hrs the following day, the two brothers, Hugh flying R6644, took-off and engaged in a 'triangular dogfight' with the commander of 'B' Flight, Flight Lieutenant Colin MacFie, which 'started at 10,000 feet and ended up between the hangars; the troops were impressed, the CO wasn't. It was colossal fun', wrote Hugh in his diary.

John Dundas was, in fact, a highly successful and respected member of 609 Squadron, which was heavily engaged throughout the Battle of Britain, flying from the 10 Group bases of Middle Wallop, near Winchester, and Warmwell, inland of Weymouth. During the early part of the Battle of Britain, the fighting had been intense over Weymouth Bay, the Channel and Portland, John Dundas recording many successes, leading to his DFC being gazetted on 22 October 1940. On 28 November 1940, elements of JG 2 – led the *Kommodore*, *Major* Helmut Wick, with fifty-six victories the highest scoring German ace at the time – clashed with 609 Squadron over the Isle of Wight; Flying Officer Dundas shot Wick down over the Solent, his last radio transmission being 'Whoopee, I've got a 109!' – before he too was shot down, by Wick's *Rottenhundt*, *Oberleutnant* Rudi Pflanz. Like Wick, John Dundas was never seen again and remains missing to this day. It was a devastating blow to Hugh: 'I suppose it had to happen', he wrote, 'I suppose that we were inordinately lucky to have survived intact as long as we did… It was the last encounter of the year, at squadron strength, between Spitfires and Messerschmitts. It certainly contributed nothing, one way or the other, to the course or outcome of the war. But it affected my life deeply. I think that hardly a day has gone by since then when I have not thought of John.' The show, however, and the killing, had to go on, regardless of personal loss – as every fighter pilot knew full well.

Having flown to Tangmere with 616 Squadron on 26 February 1941, the weather remained poor, curtailing flying – but with the appointment of the first Wing Leaders and the arrival of Wing Commander Douglas Bader at Tangmere on 18 March 1941, it was clear that something big was in the offing. It was: the start of Fighter Command's Non-Stop Offensive, the objective of which was 'to establish air superiority over the enemy in his own country'. Bader immediately identified with Squadron Leader Burton, a fellow

Cranwellian, who he knew from 616 Squadron's contribution to the Duxford Wing in September 1940 – whereas Bader did not know his Wing's other squadrons, namely 145 and 610 Squadrons. Consequently, Bader exclusively led the Wing at the head of 616, and specifically with 'Dogsbody Section', comprising Flying Officer Dundas, Pilot Officer Johnson, and variously either Sergeant Alan Smith or the New Zealander Sergeant Jeff West. This became an 'inner sanctum' in the air, and on the ground Bader gathered his favourite officers about him to enthusiastically discuss tactics – as Dundas recalled:

> We expressed our dissatisfaction with formations adopted in the past… the half pints went down again and again whilst we argued the toss. Dundas suggested that four aircraft flying in line abreast, some 50 yards apart, could never be bounced from behind. Those on the right would cover the tails of the Spitfires on the left and *vice versa*. No enemy could therefore approach unseen, but if attacked the formation could break upwards, one pair to port, the other to starboard. This was identical, of course, to the German *Schwärm*. It is difficult to understand why Fighter Command took so long to imitate the enemy. The vic had rapidly been found virtually suicidal, and individual squadrons had been experimenting with their own tactical formations for some time. These generally seem to have involved some kind of line astern formation – not abreast, like the *Schwärm*, comprising two pairs, leader and wingman. Nursing a hangover at breakfast the following morning, Dundas regretted his inspirational suggestion: 'Not being a drinker, "DB" strode into the Mess with his buccaneering gait and was clearly in rude health. He told me that he had considered my idea and had decided to try it out. I nodded in weak agreement but was somewhat startled when he added "This morning"!'

Wing Commander Bader then led Dogsbody Section, comprising two pairs: Dundas and himself, and 610 Squadron's Squadron Leader Woodhouse and Sergeant Maine. The Section climbed to 26,500 feet over mid-Channel and prowled up and down, just south of Dover – deliberately inviting trouble.

A SPITFIRE'S STORY: THE INVISIBLE THREAD

Six Me 109s of *Stab*/JG 51 – coincidentally led by *Major* Werner Mölders, who had invented the *Schwärm* in Spain – soon appeared, tailing the Spitfires and at the same height. At what he guessed to be the optimum moment, Bader warned 'OK boys, get ready for it… BREAK!' – and broke both pairs around to reverse the situation. The Spitfires immediately whipped round, the four pilots almost blacking out, so tight was the turn. As Dundas levelled out, resuming the Section's original course, there was no sign of the enemy – but then rounds raked his machine. Thick smoke engulfed his cockpit. Dundas opened his hood and limped back to crash-land at Hawkinge, covered by Squadron Leader Woodhouse. During the break, tracer had also flashed past Maine, who shook off his assailant before firing at an Me 109 and hitting its fuselage. Maine was then hit by anti-aircraft fire but broke again and attacked another 109 at point blank range – which crashed into the sea. On this occasion, only one Spitfire was shot down in combat, but the Germans overclaimed; whilst *Major* Mölders filed his sixtieth *Abschuss*, *Oberleutnant* Horst Geyer claimed two.

After Flight Lieutenant Holden had collected Flying Officer Dundas and returned him to Westhampnett in the Station's Magister communications aircraft, Wing Commander Bader held a de-brief. Despite Dundas having been shot down, the benefits of the line abreast formation in preventing a surprise attack were evident. The fault laid with Bader, who had mis-timed the break, leading to several of the 109s remaining behind the Spitfires as they levelled out. Moreover, instead of breaking in opposite directions, the two pairs should have turned in the same direction. Once the correct timing could be achieved, all involved agreed that this new formation, the aircraft occupying similar positions to the fingers of an outstretched hand, was the future. Over the years, it has frequently been written that Wing Commander Bader was entirely responsible for the so-called 'Finger Four' – which was soon adopted not just by the Tangmere Wing but throughout Fighter Command.

Pilot Officer Johnnie Johnson:

> The 'Finger Four' was really Cocky Dundas's idea. We had all seen the Germans flying in these loose formations of fighters, lean and hungry looking, with plenty of room between them, like a pack of hunting dogs. Prior to going to Tangmere, we of

616 Squadron were not flying vics but pairs. Then Bader arrived. At first, we flew in three fours, these being loose fours and in line astern, and then Dundas suggested that we should fly fours in line abreast. Consequently, after a little experimentation, we adopted this in May 1941.

The 'season' of 1941 was bitterly contested over northern France, during which time Dundas destroyed three Me 109s and damaged others, leading to his DFC being gazetted on 5 August 1941. Promoted to flight lieutenant, the following month he was posted to command a flight of 610 Squadron, and in December 1941 was given command of 56 Squadron, flying the new but initially problematic Haw Typhoon Mk IA fighter-bomber. By November 1942, Dundas was a Wing Commander, leading the first Typhoon wing. January 1943, however, saw a return to Spitfires, this time leading 324 Wing in Tunisia, further successes following over Malta and Sicily. In January 1944, Dundas was rested, joining the staff of Air Vice-Marshal Harry Broadhurst, commanding the Desert Air Force in Italy, his DSO gazetted in March 1944. Six months later it was back to operations, leading 244 Wing, and in October 1944 Dundas became one of the service's youngest group captains – a Bar to the DSO followed.

Having been permanently commissioned, Group Captain Dundas returned to England in 1946, retiring from the service in 1947, to become air correspondent for Beaverbrook Newspapers. Flying was in the blood, though, and after re-joining what was now the Royal Auxiliary Air Force, he commanded 601 'County of London' Squadron until 1950. After various editorial and managerial posts on newspapers, he became managing director of the television company Redifusion in 1970, served as chairman from 1978–1985, and was also a director of Thames Television from 1968, and chairman 1981–1987. Heavily involved in charitable work for the RAF Benevolent Fund and the Cancer Relief MacMillan Fund, after the death of Group Captain Sir Douglas Bader in 1982, together with Air Marshal Sir Denis Crowley-Milling and Air Vice-Marshal Johnnie Johnson, Dundas was a founding trustee of The Douglas Bader Foundation, a charity established as a living memorial to Sir Douglas, assisting the amputee community. Having been made a CBE in 1977, Dundas was knighted in 1987, for services to business, and, having been a Deputy Lieutenant of Surrey since 1969, became High Sherriff in 1989.

On 10 July 1994, Group Captain Sir Hugh Dundas passed away, aged 74, highly distinguished in both war and peace.

Flight Lieutenant Colin MacFie

When taken on charge by 616 Squadron, R6644 was allocated to 'B' Flight – commanded by the mercurial Flight Lieutenant Colin Hamilton MacFie, already an experienced pilot and veteran of many air battles at twenty. 'Mac' first flew R644 for an hour's formation practice on 18 October 1940, and for thirty minutes the following day, investigating an 'X-Raid'; his final flight

The mercurial Flight Lieutenant Colin 'Mac' MacFie, commander of 'B' Flight.

in the machine would be a thirty-minute air test on 20 December 1940 (by sheer coincidence I write this on 20 December 2024).

Born in Cheltenham on 12 June 1920, MacFie was educated at Cheltenham and Epsom Colleges before studying at the Liverpool School of Architecture. With another war with Germany looming large, on 12 March 1939, MacFie was commissioned as an Acting Pilot Officer in the AAF, joining 611 'West Lancashire' Squadron at Speke, this unit having initially been formed as a bomber squadron at Hendon on 10 February 1936, moving to Speke, its peacetime station, five months later, then being re-designated a fighter squadron on 1 January 1939. Having previously operated the Hawker Hind, on 19 May 1939, 611 Squadron re-equipped with Spitfires. During the last days of peace, on 13 August 1939, the Squadron moved to Duxford for its annual camp, and three days later Pilot Officer MacFie was awarded his coveted flying badge, his training complete. On 26 August 1939, 611 Squadron was 'embodied', which is to say called out to full-time service, mobilizing on 1 September 1939 – the day Germany invaded Poland. In the event of war, 611 was to move to its wartime station of Duxford, where it had actually remained after summer camp, moving to Digby a month later. From there, the Squadron flew numerous routine patrols and shepherded convoys off the east coast.

The winter of 1939/1940 was a harsh one, with much snow, rain and generally poor flying weather. On 28 February 1940, visibility over East Anglia was down to just one mile, and was so bad that 611 Squadron's dawn patrol failed to even find the coast. All four of the Squadron's sections then went forward to operate from North Coates, and at 1310 hrs, Green Section, comprising Flying Officer Harry Hamilton, a Canadian (Green 1), and Pilot Officer MacFie (Green 2), took-off to patrol over a convoy. Upon taxiing out, Sergeant Alfred Bruce's Spitfire (Green 3), however, became stuck in mud up to the axles, forcing him to fly the sortie in another aircraft. Given the deteriorating visibility, at 1328 hrs, Flying Officer Hamilton, when informed of Bruce's predicament, ordered him not to take-off – too late: Green 3 was airborne by 1325 hrs and hurrying to find his Section, the two pilots of which had sighted the convoy of forty ships heading north. During this patrol, the visibility closed in from a mile to just 75 yards, and at 1334 and 1338 hrs, Bruce was ordered by Digby Control to 'pancake'. There was no response from Green 3, whose 'pip squeak' radio homing signal ceased at 1402 hrs, the last fix being midway between the Otter Dowsing and East Dudgeon lightships. With the weather clamping down, Hamilton led MacFie back to the coast:

> Landfall was made north of Spurn Head but appeared so quickly that Flying Officer Hamilton had not time to turn. He climbed with No 2 to 1,000 feet over Caistor, and before deciding to abandon his aircraft by parachute made a further effort to return to North Coates by descending over the sea with flaps down and airscrew in fine pitch. At 50 feet he came out of the cloud and returned to base, sometimes being as low as 10 feet, and generally below the masts of shipping. The weather was described by Flying Officer Hamilton as being 'a bit rough'. [ORB]

Fortunately, following his leader, Pilot Officer MacFie also landed safely – but 23-year-old Sergeant Alfred Eric Andrew Bruce was never seen again.

The following day, 611 Squadron was signalled by 12 Group's AOC, Air Vice-Marshal Sir Trafford Leigh-Mallory:

> Very much regret to hear that Sergeant Bruce is missing on what was a gallant effort to carry out a difficult duty. At the same time, I wish to congratulate Green 1 and 2 on carrying out this convoy patrol in the face of great difficulties.

It was, indeed, a gallant effort.

For Fighter Command's Spitfire squadrons, going into the spring of 1940, the routine nature of operations continued – and for a while even after Hitler attacked the West on 10 May 1940. This was because, wisely, Air Chief Marshal Dowding only sent Hurricanes to what he knew was a lost battle in France, determinedly resisting pressure to send superior Spitfires, which would be crucial to the defence of Britain ahead. However, after the unthinkable decision was made for the BEF to withdraw to and be evacuated from Dunkirk, Spitfire squadrons were committed to battle over the French coast – meeting the Me 109 for the first time – amongst them 611 Squadron.

With Operation *Dynamo*, the Dunkirk evacuation, entering its penultimate day, shortly after 0100 hrs on 2 June 1940, Squadron Leader James McComb, commanding 611 Squadron, received orders to fly from Digby to Martlesham Heath airfield, there to re-fuel and join four other squadrons for a patrol over Dunkirk. At dawn, McComb led his pilots south, and having re-fuelled, at 0705 hrs 611 Squadron left Martlesham with 32 Squadron flying top cover, then 66, 266, 611 and 92 below. The German fighters had been operating over the French coast in strength, and Air Vice-Marshal Park had responded in kind – although it is important to appreciate that this was more a convoy of squadrons arriving over the combat area in strength, rather than a cohesive wing formation. Over Dunkirk, at 0905 hrs, 92 Squadron attacked a formation of German bombers, whilst 611 Squadron 'mixed it' with the enemy fighter escort. For twenty minutes McComb's men so effectively occupied the Me 109s that 92 Squadron was able to attack the He 111s and Ju 87s without loss, claiming seventeen of the enemy destroyed. No. 611 Squadron's pilots claimed three Ju 87s, four Me 109s and a 110 – Pilot Officer MacFie being amongst the successful claimants:

> I lost the rest of 611 while over Dunkirk and continued to patrol the town, 14,000 feet. While on the seaward side I observed AA fire out to sea and on approaching same I spotted six Ju 87s approaching land with escort of Me 109s just above them. I attacked rear Ju 87 who broke formation and I followed him … spotted him again attacking shipping off the town and got him on his pull-out, firing a long burst dead astern, then a deflection burst when he did a climbing turn to right. He continued turn, nose dropped and he hit the water, breaking up.

This hapless *Stuka* is believed to have been a machine of 1/StG 2: *Unteroffizier* W. Bierfreund was killed, *Unteroffizier* H. Schlöffel reported missing.

A SPITFIRE'S STORY: THE INVISIBLE THREAD

The following day, *Dynamo* concluded, 611 Squadron resuming its normal duties at Digby, and it would be on yet another monotonous convoy patrol, on 21 August 1940, that Pilot Officer MacFie next fired his guns in anger. At 1630 hrs, Green 3 of 611 Squadron 'Tally Ho'd' a He 111 east of Spurn Head, which, after a cat and mouse chase in and out of cloud, MacFie, Green 2, expended all his ammunition at, the bomber finally disappearing into cloud; it was claimed as damaged.

On 7 September 1940, MacFie was promoted to Acting Flight Lieutenant and posted to command 'B' Flight of 616 Squadron, which, as we have seen, was re-building to strength at Coltishall, having previously been roughly handled at Kenley (more of which later). No. 616 Squadron was also engaged on similar operational duties to 611 Squadron, and on Monday, 16 September 1940, Flight Lieutenant MacFie damaged a lone Ju 88 'snooper' east of Donna Nook.

After 616 Squadron relieved 65 at Tangmere on 26 February 1941, Flight Lieutenant MacFie next saw action on 27 March 1941, having scrambled with Blue Section at 1436 hrs. Finding a Me 110 reconnaissance machine over Littlehampton, MacFie, Blue 1, attacked it from astern, noting 'flashes from port engine and oil was splashed over his engine' [ORB], also claiming this as damaged.

This was the beginning of Fighter Command's Non-Stop Offensive (again, of which more later), taking the war across the Channel to the Germans in north-west France. In March 1941, it was decided that all sector stations would host a three-squadron-strong wing of Spitfires, which was now the RAF's primary daylight fighter in theatre, and that month saw the first 'Wing Leaders' appointed. To Tangmere went the legless Wing Commander Douglas Bader on 18 March 1941, and almost immediately the tempo of battle became relentless.

On 24 April 1941, certain Tangmere Spitfires flew 'Rhubarbs', crossing the Channel at wave-top height, thereby avoiding radar detection, and attacking targets of opportunity. No. 616 Squadron contributed two pairs of 'B' Flight aircraft to the operation: Flying Officer Hugh Dundas and Sergeant Sydney Mabbett prowling uneventfully over Abeville, whilst Flight Lieutenant MacFie and Sergeant Thomas McDevette crossed the sea to attack Maupertus airfield, near Cherbourg. There, MacFie strafed seven I/JG 2 Me 109s on the ground, but McDevette was hit by flak, never to be seen again. 19 June 1941 saw the Tangmere Wing participate in Operation *Derby*, during which Bader's Spitfires, with Northolt's 303 (Polish) Squadron providing top cover, was supposed to rendezvous over base with thirty-six bombers for a raid on Le Havre. In the event, just two bomber squadrons arrived, and the only reaction from the *Luftwaffe* was when 616 Squadron fended off a handful of Me 109s near the target: Flight Lieutenant MacFie claimed one as damaged, which forced-landed at Octeville and probably belonged to JG 2's training unit; it would be his last combat claim.

The afternoon of 5 July 1941 saw the Tangmere Wing orbiting Lille on Circus 33, watching three Stirlings accurately bomb the Lille-Fives steel works. The Wing then weaved behind the bombers, shepherding them out of France over Gravelines. No. 610 Squadron's Flight Lieutenant Lee-Knight escorted a Spitfire out of France which had a 'dead propeller', but approaching Margate the pilot baled out. Lee-Knight broadcast a fix on the downed airman's position, some ten to 15 miles east-south-east of Manston, covering and guiding a Lysander to that location, which was then able to direct ASR operations. Thanks to Lee-Knight, the Polish pilot, Sergeant S. Kryzyzagórski of 308 Squadron, was rescued safely. Over the target area, 610 Squadron's Sergeant Mains destroyed an Me 109E, the pilot of which baled out, but then the Spitfire pilot noted with some alarm that his oil temperature was 97°, forcing him to retire and land at Hawkinge. 616 Squadron, however, suffered a significant loss: on the return trip, Flight Lieutenant MacFie was shot down in Spitfire Mk IIB P8651 near Dunkirk. In addition to Kryzyzagórski and MacFie, 54 Squadron lost Pilot Officer Kenward Knox, who was killed, and on this occasion German combat claims were entirely accurate: *Oberleutnant* Josef Priller, *Leutnants* Horst Ullenberg and Robert Unzeitig, all of I/JG 26, claiming Spitfires destroyed in this action.

The 616 Squadron ORB recorded that 'We are all very sad at his loss as he had been with the Squadron since the beginning of September 1940, and had endeared himself to everyone despite his taciturnity'. Fortunately, Flight

Lieutenant MacFie had baled out over France and was later reported to be a prisoner.

Whilst behind the wire, on 8 August 1941, Flight Lieutenant MacFie's DFC was gazetted; it would be a long war: he would not be liberated until May 1945.

Remaining in the post-war service, MacFie commanded both 1 and 3 Squadrons, flying Gloster Meteor and de Havilland Vampire jet fighters, before eventually retiring as a Squadron Leader in October 1963. Perhaps surprisingly, for such a man of action, or, indeed, perhaps not, having left the service Squadron Leader MacFie settled in Attadale in Wester Ross, in the north-west Scottish Highlands, where he worked as a gardener; he died, aged 61, on 7 December 1981.

Pilot Officer Lionel 'Buck' Casson

Between 27 October 1940 and 20 December 1940, Pilot Officer Casson flew R6644 on five occasions, concluding with a battle climb to 31,000 feet.

Lionel Harwood Casson – known to all as 'Buck' – was born in Sheffield on 6 January 1915, and after Birkdale and King's School, Ely, joined his father working in the local steel industry. Although a reserved occupation, this did not prevent the air-minded Casson joining the AAF.

Pilot Officer Lionel 'Buck' Casson.

'Buck' Casson:

On 23 July 1939, I was commissioned as an Acting Pilot Officer in 616 'South Yorkshire' Squadron of the AAF, based at Doncaster. Our annual summer camp at Manston commenced on 24 August 1939, and there I flew the Avro 504N and Tiger Moth. We were there when war was declared on 3 September 1939. Between 7 October 1939, and 23 March 1940, I undertook my service flying training at No 2 FTS at Brize Norton. There we flew the Harvard and Oxford aircraft and I passed second on course, being assessed as 'above average' overall. On 6 April 1940, I reported back to 616 Squadron, by then based at Leconfield. There I served as Duty Pilot, Orderly Officer, and Operations Officer. On 29 April 1940, however, I was posted to 6 OTU at Sutton Bridge, for operational training. First, we had dual testing and instrument flying on Harvards before going solo on Hurricanes. Then we practised Fighter Command Attacks, 1 and 2, then 3 and 4.

At this time, some Hurricane squadrons had already been sent to France, and when the shooting started on 10 May 1940, they immediately suffered losses. We had been trained as replacements, so on 15 May 1940 I was posted to Arras to join the BEF's Advanced Air Striking Force (AASF). I set off at 1500 hrs and left my car at Peterborough. Got train to London by 1900 hrs. No transport, so train to Uxbridge by 1230 hrs. Reported in, signed forms and collected equipment.

Pilot Officer Casson kept a diary, recorded daily, capturing the unfolding drama as it affected him personally:

<u>16 May 1940</u>
Got to bed 0330 hrs. Up at 0600 hrs. Paraded 0730 hrs and left Uxbridge 0900 hrs. Boarded steamship with kit at Southampton and departed at 1430 hrs but had to wait off Portsmouth for tide.

A SPITFIRE'S STORY: THE INVISIBLE THREAD

<u>17 May 1940</u>

Docked at Le Havre 0600 hrs. Changed money and enjoyed seeing the town. 2230 hrs entrained for Arras.

<u>18 May 1940</u>

Train left 0300 hrs and arrived Amiens 1415 hrs. Bridge and line ahead blown up. More air raids. Night at YMCA.

<u>19 May 1940</u>

Left kit behind and caught a train leaving south. Reached St Roche marshalling yards where we were heavily bombed for 1 hour 20 mins by Ju 87 and Ju 88. Engine and first carriage OK, but rest of train smashed up. After being terrified by the bombing, managed to return across the lines and scramble up the bank onto the road. Walked by roads to Aumale and Gournay with little sleep or rest. Got mixed up with lots of refugees, some dead and some wounded, dead horses, etc. Finally got to Rouen and given meal by Scottish Highland Division. Departed early and luckily was able to halt a long low-loader with two aero-engines on board from Glisy airfield.

<u>22 May 1940</u>

Climbed aboard and relaxed all the way to Cherbourg. Next morning in *Duke of Argyle*, escorted by two destroyers, left in a hurry and arrived Southampton 1530 hrs. Then posted to 79 Squadron at Biggin Hill. Took train and taxi to Uxbridge but no room available, so I joined (Pilot Officer) Tom Murray (also previously of 616 Squadron), and we booked a room at the Charing Cross Hotel, then went without cash to the Paradise Restaurant where we were very well looked after.

<u>23 May 1940</u>

Reported Uxbridge 1045 hrs. Changed French money and bought toilet requisites, socks, shirt, underwear, etc. Had first bath since 14 May! Left Charing Cross Hotel without payment being requested!

<u>24 May 1940</u>
Drove in Tom's 5S to Biggin Hill and CO [Squadron Leader J.D.C. Joslin, who also arrived that day, to take over from Squadron Leader R.V. Alexander] of 79 Squadron gave us 48 hours leave. Got new uniform etc at Moss Bros. Caught train home and arrived 1840 hrs.

When the German offensive began on 10 May 1940, 79 Squadron, which was based at Biggin Hill for home defence, was deployed across the Channel, to operate from Mons-en-Chausee, in support of the AASF. From the following day, the Squadron was heavily engaged, moving first to Norrent Fontes, thence to Merville. By 20 May 1940, 79 Squadron was informed by Wing Commander Harry Broadhurst DFC that the 'situation was critical', and at 1400 hrs that day orders were received to evacuate Merville and return to England via Boulogne. During its ten-day period in France, 79 Squadron had lost seven Hurricanes destroyed, and several others damaged, with two pilots killed, two more wounded, and another captured. It was, therefore, a squadron re-building to strength that Pilot Officer Casson joined at Biggin Hill. Returning on 26 May 1940 – the very day that the decision was reluctantly made for the BEF to retire on and evacuate from Dunkirk. On that day, Buck wrote in his diary 'Drove south in my car (my sister had collected it from Peterborough) and arrived Biggin Hill 1825 hrs'. Refreshed by leave following his brief but exhausting time in France, two days later 79 Squadron flew to Digby, in 12 Group, for practice flying, returning to Biggin Hill on 5 June 1940. Two days previously, the Dunkirk evacuation had successfully concluded, but on this day the Germans launched 'Fall Rot' (Case Red), the final offensive to smash remaining Allied resistance on the continent. That afternoon, Squadron Leader Joslin led eleven Hurricanes, including Pilot Officer Casson, to re-fuel at the forward coastal base of Hawkinge, just inland of Folkestone, before joining 32 Squadron to escort Blenheims attacking the German-held airfield at Abbeville. In his diary, Buck wrote:

My first operational sortie with 79 Squadron as bomber escort. Attacked by some Me 109s and the squadron split up. I was alone and luckily a single Me 109 passed about 1,000 feet below me and I opened fire on it; it turned over and dived towards Cherbourg leaving a stream of black smoke. I must have hit it, but how badly damaged it was I could not tell so I did not make a combat report. I returned escorting the Blenheim bombers and found our Squadron at Biggin Hill all refuelled.

Buck did, however, complete a combat report, in fact, according to which his first 'squirt' at the enemy comprised two bursts of two – three seconds, at 1345 hrs between 10,000 feet and 13,000 feet west of Abbeville. Flying Green 3 and approaching Abbeville, a dozen Me 109s appeared, approaching the RAF formation from the south: 'The formation broke up and a dogfight ensued. As my Leader dived to attack, I turned steeply and saw two Me 109s approaching from the coast. I climbed about 1,000 feet above them and dived upon the tail of one and fired two short bursts. After this I broke away below as three more 109s came into attack.'

<u>6/7 June 1940</u>
Escort and patrol Abbeville/Amiens from Manston.

<u>8 June 1940</u>
On offensive patrol Le Treport/Aumale and again our Squadron split up when attacked by more Me 109 aircraft. I was alone and seeing a flight of He 111s made two quarter attacks on the leading aircraft then being short of fuel I broke off. I was able to locate a small grass airfield at St Andre de l'Eure and landed there. Fortunately a French officer was on the scene; he took me quite some distance in his car to breakfast, having instructed the groundcrew to re-fuel my aircraft. He drove me back and we exchanged the top button of our uniforms! He left me assuming everything was OK for take-off, but there were no ground staff about. I found it impossible to start the engine and had to call over a labourer who was digging a trench round the airfield.

I got out the starter handle from under the fuselage and inserted it on the starboard side of the engine. I showed the labourer what I wanted him to do and climbed back into the cockpit. Then I gave 'thumbs up' and pressed the starter while he wound the handle, and luckily the engine fired OK. I replaced the handle, taxied to the end of the field then opened up at full bore. I was not airborne before reaching the boundary trench, but striking the mound of earth was just sufficient to enable me to keep the plane up and then climb away. I flew to Dreux where the Squadron had been instructed to go originally, but I found only three of 79 Squadron there. The Engineering Officer told me that my plane had been refuelled with 90 Octane and would have to be altered. Finally, because the rest of the unit had returned to Biggin Hill, we four were released eventually and luckily got back to base without mishap.

9 June 1940

At dusk I was a pilot at 'readiness' in 'A' Flight of 79 Squadron when we were scrambled from Biggin Hill to intercept a plotted X Raid over the English Channel. This was most unexpected for as day fighters we were on the point of being released, and in fact our dispersed Hurricanes were undergoing their Daily Inspections, one-by-one, ready for the morrow.

As luck would have it I found my aircraft being serviced when I reached it and so was directed to another. Parachutes had not been moved and I was happy to use the one in situ, but there was no helmet and the ground staff couldn't find mine which I had left in my own aircraft.

The CO and the other four pilots were by now at the end of the airfield ready for take-off and in my eagerness not to let the side down I raced up to join them but without a helmet. This mad, misguided enthusiasm which could have had disastrous consequences taught me a lesson I shall not easily forget.

We took-off and climbed up over the sea into the last rays of the setting sun; I without oxygen and no R/T. Without radio reception and relying on observation only, my reactions to changes of formation, direction, etc were necessarily slow and the CO, after several efforts to contact me by R/T, realised the situation and waved me to break away.

I turned homeward and descending found myself over London in darkness. I could pick out the Thames but could not find Biggin Hill. Eventually I stumbled upon Kenley although I didn't recognise it at the time, and it was only as I made a low run across the area that a floodlight briefly turned on then off again and gave me a clue, that I was just able to discern the hooded runway lights. I prepared to land and as I made my final approach with the aircraft landing lights on the ground floodlight was turned on again and I touched down.

Quite unaware that Kenley was a bit like an inverted saucer, I found myself rapidly reaching the end of the runway and had to swing to starboard to avoid overshooting. This resulted in a burst port-tyre and I was admonished by the Station CO for the incident. Shortly afterwards, however, after getting in touch with my unit and learning that not only was I an AAF pilot but that my night flying experience was limited to only two hours dual and 2.10 hours solo on Harvards at FTS, he was kind enough to tell me, over a drink, that I had actually put up a good show – whilst, naturally enough, warning me against such a foolhardy exploit in the future.

According to my log book, that flight lasted 1.10 hours and brought my grand total on the Hurricane to a mere 18.50 hours, plus 12 hours carried out at Sutton Bridge OTU.

<u>10 June–3 July 1940</u>
Patrols Hawkinge, Dungeness. Escort and patrol Calais/Merville.

<u>4 July 1940</u>
Able to drive north as at last posted back to 616 Squadron at Leconfield, and to fly Spitfire Mk Is. CO was Squadron Leader Marcus Robinson.

7–31 July 1940
Formation and cloud flying. Air drill. No 3 fighter attacks. Gun co-operation – Saxton. Air to air firing at Acklington. Aerobatics, X Raids. Dusk and night flying.

1–11 August 1940
Dusk and night flying. X Raids 25,000 feet and 27,000 feet. On 11th, crashed on take-off but survived – some story!!

That day, Buck was flying Spitfire R6686, somehow hitting a stationary aircraft on take-off, the collision breaking his port undercarriage leg, from which wheel and tyre parted company. Instructed to land by the Duty Pilot, there was no option but to make a wheels-up crash-landing on the airfield; Buck's Spitfire was damaged but repairable.

The diary continues:

15 August 1940
Two X-Raids to east coast – Ju 88 aircraft from Norway attacked Driffield but many got shot down.

That day, 616 Squadron claimed eight Ju 88s destroyed, four probables and two damaged, for no loss. The day's outcome was undoubtedly a fillip for the northern-based squadrons, which were all confident and keen to head south, to the main combat area. The difference between the fighting up north and that over the south was one thing: there were no Me 109s beyond London. The tempo of combat, therefore, was completely different – as 616 would soon discover.

19 August 1940
The Squadron with fifteen aircraft moved to Kenley and I followed with a replacement on the 24th.

Three days later the Squadron experienced its first clash with the enemy whilst operating from Kenley: Green Section was bounced over Dover by a *Staffel* of JG 51's Me 109s. Within seconds Pilot Officer Hugh 'Cocky'

Dundas was taking to his parachute, his Spitfire in flames, and a cannon shell damaged Pilot Officer Casson's fighter. Sergeant Wareing, however, claimed a 109 destroyed in the resulting skirmish.

28 August 1940
We had five hours flying on X Raids at 20,000 feet over Thames estuary, Manston and Hawkinge.

2–31 August 1940
I flew on nine X raids and claimed He 111 bombers – 1 probable and 1 damaged.

1 September 1940
I flew five sorties and claimed one Me 109 probable and one Do 17 confirmed. Hole blown in my port wing.

2 September 1940
Airborne four times patrolling base – no action because raiders retreated.

3 September 1940
Got my kit packed by 0900 hrs. About 1100 hrs, scrambled to 15,000 feet – no action. 1415 hrs, flew to Coltishall as Squadron withdrawn from 11 Group due to heavy losses. Billy Burton was promoted as our CO. I went with him and Wing Commander Biesegel to Wroxham for evening.

4 September 1940
Given 48 hours leave from mid-day. 0930 hrs my car arrived, so I drove home, taking Dick Hellyer to Doncaster.

6 September 1940
Arrived at Coltishall and flew sector recce. Only Holden, Brewster, two NCOs and myself left to fly.

7–8 September 1940
Airborne for X-Raids and practice formation attacks. Colin MacFie joined us as Flight Lieutenant.

616 'SOUTH YORKSHIRE' SQUADRON

<u>9 September 1940</u>
Moved up to Kirton-in-Lindsey.

<u>10–30 September 1940</u>
X-Raids. Training new pilots (including Johnnie Johnson, later to become the RAF's official top-scoring fighter pilot of the war, and 'Nip' Hepple). Repeated trips to Duxford G1 (Fowlmere). To Ringway.

<u>1–4 October 1940</u>
At Ringway as air support for troops embarking at Liverpool, but too foggy to give air cover.

<u>5 October 1940</u>
Bought my fox terrier 'Mac'. Flew sector recce then returned to Kirton.

<u>6–31 October 1940</u>
X-Raids. Air drill.

<u>1–11 November 1940</u>
X-Raids. Flight formation. Army co-op. Low flying practice and aerobatics.

<u>13–20 November 1940</u>
To and from Ringway – X raids and sector recces.

<u>21 30 November 1940</u>
X-Raids. Formation practice. Attacks 1, 3 beam. Tom Murray left to go as test pilot.

<u>6–24 December 1940</u>
After German air raids on Sheffield, I had flights at 21,000 feet over the city on the 16th, and followed with a 'goodwill' formation over Doncaster, Sheffield, Wortley etc. on the 24th. On other days practised attacks 1 and 3, cloud and formation, battle climb to 31,000'.

<u>1–12 January 1941</u>
Battle climb to 32,000 feet. Cloud flying. Beam attacks.

A SPITFIRE'S STORY: THE INVISIBLE THREAD

13–16 January 1940
I had bad cold – danger of sinus.

17–18 January 1941
Beam attacks. X-Raid and flew to 25,000 feet after a Ju 88 but lost it in cloud – landed back in a snowstorm.

9–31 January 1940
Fog, mist and deep snow. I had seven days leave. Operated on Link trainer. Did compass checks.

1–16 February 1940
Air drill. Cloud flying. 1, 3 and beam attacks. Battle climb 28,000 feet. Night flying twice. Convoy patrol.

17 February 1941
Fog and very low cloud. More snow and sleet. Lecture on RDF, IFF, CHL, GCI, AI etc., guns.

22–25 February 1941
X-Raids 20,000 feet. To Wittering, then with 266 Squadron on sweep over French coast at 29,000 feet. Landed Duxford then to base.

26 February 1941
To Tangmere. Changed our aircraft with Spitfire IIs of 65 Squadron. Did a sector recce (Branscombe).

28 February 1941
Billeted in Rushman's house by Oving Village. Very low cloud and heavy rain – no flying, my Spitfire I (X4184) changed to Spitfire II (P7753).

March 1941
Wing Commander Douglas Bader, 'Dogs Body', always flying from 616 Squadron dispersal. He and 616 Squadron would lead the Wing. We also flew Channel sweeps 35,000 feet, patrols of Dungeness, Selsey Bill, St Catherine's Point and Boulogne/Calais at 15,000/35,000 feet. We also practised air drill, cloud

flying, dusk and night patrols. Tangmere was bombed by Ju 88s on 12/13 March 1941 and buildings and vehicles hit. Played golf at Goodwood with Douglas Bader and Ken Holden.

April 1941

I flew into Gatwick to give an army General and others details and demonstration with Spitfire. Six other aircraft types there also. More patrols from I.O.W. [Isle of Wight] and Dungeness. Slept at dispersal for night flying. Cloud flying. Escorting eighteen Blenheims to Cherbourg and return. Then escorting seventeen Blenheims to Le Havre and return – lost Sergeant Sellars. Formation and line astern aerobatics. At 0550 hrs, more Ju 88 bombing – six killed and fifteen injured.

May 1941

Often up for readiness at 0425 hrs for dawn patrols. Also on night flying duty. Air drill. Channel patrol. Moved to Westhampnett airfield. Tangmere badly bombed, but Hampden and Whitley bombers landed on return from raids. On 5th I intercepted a reconnaissance Ju 88 at 15,000 feet over Portsmouth; it dived south to 100 feet over the sea – I shot the rear gunner, but got hit and my glycol leaked. I had to return, and just crossing the coast at 950 feet with cockpit full of smoke, turned the aircraft over and baled out near Littlchampton. On 30th played golf with Douglas Bader and Ken Holden, then I collected Douglas Bader's wife, Thelma, and sister Jill. We all went to Brighton for evening.

June 1941

Formation aerobatics. Flick rolls and spins. Escorted eighteen Blenheims to Le Havre. Sweeps – Straits of Dover, Boulogne, Dunkirk. Wing Circus, Straits, 20,000 feet. Wing Circus Dungeness, Boulogne, Gravelines. Wing to Hastings, Berck, St. Omer, Gravelines. Wing to Dungeness, Berck, Hazebrouck, Dunkirk. Other wing sorties to Mardyck, Lille, St Omer – Le Touquet, Hucoueliers, Desvres, Gris Nez, etc.

A SPITFIRE'S STORY: THE INVISIBLE THREAD

<u>July 1941</u>
On 3 July 1941, I borrowed Douglas Bader's black night-flying Hurricane II and flew via Kirton-in-Lindsey to Doncaster, then got bus to Sheffield and home at 2200 hrs. On 6th, the family saw me off from Doncaster and I arrived Tangmere 2000 hrs. Escorting Stirling bombers on several raids over France. More Wing sweeps over France. Tested Spitfire VB cannons on height test. Air drill. Convoy patrols. Colin MacFie confirmed as POW. Orde made good sketch of me and some others. 145 Squadron left for Catterick and replaced by 41.

Then came that fateful day, 9 August 1941, and Circus 68, a raid on the power station at Gosnay, by five 226 Squadron Blenheims. As ever, an impressive array of Spitfires supported this effort, the North Weald Wing providing the Escort Wing, Hornchurch the Escort Cover, whilst Target Support, clearing the way ahead to the target and covering the Beehive's withdrawal, involved two Wings: Kenley and Tangmere – some forty-eight fighters in total.

For this now routine offensive operation, Dogsbody Section of 616 Squadron comprised Wing Commander Bader, with Sergeant Jeff West No. 2, Flight Lieutenant Hugh Dundas No. 3, and leader of the second pair in the 'finger four', and No. 4, Pilot Officer Johnnie Johnson. Also leading sections of four within the Squadron formation would be Squadron Leader Billy Burton (Yellow Section) and Flight Lieutenant Buck Casson (Blue Section).

Westhampnett's Spitfire squadrons, 610 and 616, the latter, as ever, leading, took off at 1040 hrs. High above Chichester, Squadron Leader Holden slid 610 Squadron into its usual position, above and slightly to port of 616. As the two squadrons left Chichester, bound for Beachy Head, there was no sign of Squadron Leader Elmer Gaunce's Merston-based 41 Squadron, and so 610 and 616 Squadrons set course for France. Still climbing, maintaining radio silence, Wing Commander Bader waggled his wings insistently, indicating that 'Dogsbody 3', Flight Lieutenant Dundas, should take the lead. Dundas slid across, tucking his wing tip just 2 or 3 feet from Bader's. From this close proximity, Dundas saw the Wing Leader mouth three words: 'Air Speed

Indicator', meaning that this crucial instrument on Spitfire Mk VA W3185 was unserviceable. The Wing had to climb at the right speed to ensure pre-planned timings were met, but if the formation leader was unable to measure his air speed, this was impossible. Without doubt, Wing Commander Bader should have handed over to either Dundas or Burton, and gone home, as per standing orders. This, however, was not even a consideration, Bader handing the lead over to Dundas until the target area was reached. Fortunately, Dundas had written on the back of his hand the time at which the Wing was due over the French coast, in addition to the speed to be maintained. The 21-year-old Flight Commander then 'settled down to concentrate on the job', climbing the formation to 28,000 feet.

Dundas led the Wing over the French coast right on cue. This crucial timing observed, Bader accelerated ahead and informed 'Dogsbody 3' over the RT that he was resuming the lead. The Spitfires' arrival over the coastal flak belt was greeted by dangerous little puff-balls of black smoke which made the formation twist and turn. 'Beetle' (Group Captain Woodhall, Tangmere

Wing Commander Douglas Bader DSO DFC, in Spitfire P7666 at Tangmere, April 1941.

Control) then informed the Wing Leader that the Beehive itself was 'on time and engaged'. As the Tangmere Spitfires forged inland, therefore, some distance behind them the bombers and various cover wings were now also bound for France.

Soon, 616 and 610 Squadrons had progressed into a very dangerous French sky indeed, 'Beetle' – Tangmere Control – having already reported some seventy-two bandits, representing odds outnumbering the Spitfires by nearly 3:1. As the 'beehive' left England, *Jafü* 2 scrambled *Stab*/JG 26 and all three *Schlageter Gruppen*, but kept JG 2 on the ground, in reserve. Clearly this was not to be an uneventful sortie. Tension mounting, the Spitfire pilots switched on their gunsight reflectors and gun buttons to 'fire'. Anxiously they searched the sky, an ever-watchful eye kept on the 109s positioned 1,000 feet above the Wing, waiting to pounce. Bader himself dipped each wing in turn, searching the sky below for some Me 109s reported by Squadron Leader Holden, the CO of 610 Squadron; the radio messages arising were recorded by the listening station at Beachy Head:

DB   I can't see them. Will you tell me where to look?
KH   Underneath Bill's section now. Shall I come down?
DB   No, I have them. Get into formation. Going down. Ken, are you with us?
KH   Just above you.

As Dogsbody Section dived on the enemy, Flight Lieutenant Casson followed with three other aircraft of 'B' Flight. Dogsbody 3, Flight Lieutenant Dundas, had 'smelt a rat' in respect of the *Schwärm* of I/JG 26 109s that Dogsbody Section was now rapidly diving towards. By this time, the whole of Dogsbody Section was firing, although Dundas, still uneasy and suspecting a trap, had a compelling urge to look behind. Suddenly Pilot Officer 'Nip' Hepple shouted over the R/T: 'Blue 2 here. Some buggers coming down behind, astern. Break left!'

It was, as Dundas had suspected, a trap. Wing Commander Bader had been deceived into diving upon the outnumbered 109s below, which were bait – high above lurked more German fighters, hoping that their enemy would fall for the oldest trick in the book. Hoping for an easy victory, Bader had taken the bait. Now, as the Spitfire pilots were in turn ambushed, they hauled their aircraft around in steep turns. The sky behind Dogsbody Section was full of Me 109s, all firing – without Hepple's warning the Spitfires would have been nailed. As the high 109s crashed into 616 Squadron, Squadron Leader Holden decided that it was time for his Section to join the fray and reduce the odds. Informing Flight Lieutenant Denis Crowley-Milling of this decision, Holden led his Spitfires down to assist. Flight Lieutenant Casson, following Bader's Section, was well throttled back to keep his flight together. Also attacking from the rear, Casson managed a squirt at a *Rotte* of 109s. Flying Officer Marples, No. 3 in Casson's Section, then shouted a warning of even more 109s diving upon the Wing – whilst Squadron Leader Billy Burton urged the Spitfires to 'Keep turning', thus preventing the 109s (which could not out-turn a Spitfire), getting in a shot. Suddenly the organised chaos became a maelstrom of twisting, turning fighters.

More radio messages:

> 'Are we all here?'
> 'Two short.'
> 'Dogsbody from Beetle. Do you require any assistance?'
> 'Beetle from Elfin Leader. We are OK and withdrawing.'
> 'Thank you, Billy. Douglas, do you require any assistance? Steer three-four-zero to the coast.'

The silence from 'Dogsbody' was ominous. Flight Lieutenant Casson, Blue 1, remembered:

> I watched Wing Commander Bader and 'A' Flight attack and break to port as I was coming in. I was well throttled back in the dive, as the other three had started to fall behind and I wanted to keep the flight together. I attacked from the rear, and after having a squirt at two 109s flying together, left them for a single one which was flying inland alone. I finished nearly all of my cannon ammunition up on this boy, who finally baled out at

6,000 feet, having lost most of his tail unit. The other three 'B' flight machines were in my rear and probably one of the lads saw this.

I climbed to 13,000 feet and fell in with Billy Burton and three other aircraft, all from 'A' Flight. We chased around in a circle for some time, gaining height all the while, and more 109s were directly above us. Eventually we formed up in line abreast and set off after the Wing.

Billy's section flew in pairs abreast, so I flew abreast but at about 200 yards to starboard. We were repeatedly attacked by two Me 109s which had followed us and were flying above and behind. Each time they started diving I called out and we all turned and re-formed, the 109s giving up their attack and climbing each time.

About 15 miles from the coastline I saw another Spitfire well below us and about half-a-mile to starboard. This machine was alone and traveling [*sic*] very slowly. I called up Billy on the R/T and suggested that we cross over to surround him and help the pilot back as he looked like a sitting duck. I broke off to starboard and made for the solitary Spitfire, but then, on looking back for Billy and the others, was amazed to see them diving away hard to the south-west for a low layer of cloud into which they soon disappeared. I realised then that my message had either been misunderstood or not received. Like a greenhorn, I had been so intent upon watching Billy's extraordinary disappearance to the left, and the lone Spitfire to my right, I lost sight of the Me 109s that had been worrying us. I remember looking for them but upon not discovering their position assumed that they had chased Billy instead. I was soon proved wrong, however, when I received three hits in both fuselage and wing. This occurred just broke for some cloud at 5,000 feet, which I reached but found too thin for cover, and was pursued by the 109s.

I then picked out two more 109s flying above me and so decided to drop to zero feet, fly north and cross the Channel at a narrow point as I was unsure of the damage sustained and the engine was not running smoothly. I pressed the teat and tried to run for it, but the two Me 109s behind had more speed and were rapidly within range, whilst the other two flew 1,500 feet above and dived from port to starboard and back, delivering quick bursts. Needless to say I was not flying straight and level all this time!

In the event I received a good one from behind, which passed between the stick and my right leg. taking off some of the rudder on its way. It passed into the petrol tank but whether the round continued into the engine I do not know. Petrol began leaking into the cockpit, oil pressure was dropping low, and with the radiator wide open I could smell the glycol overheating.

As the next attack came, I pulled straight up from the deck in a loop and on my way down, as I was changing direction towards the sea, my engine became extremely rough and seized up as white glycol fumes poured forth. There was no option but to crash-land the aircraft. I tried to send 'Dogsbody' a hurried message, then blew up the wireless and made a belly landing in a field some 10 miles south of Calais. The 'Goons', having seen the glycol, were decent enough not to shoot me up as I was landing, but circled about for a time and gave my position away to a German cavalry unit in a wood in a corner of the field. One of the pilots waved to me as he flew overhead, and I waved back just before setting fire to the aircraft. Due to the petrol in the cockpit, and because I was carrying a port-fire issued for this purpose, igniting the aircraft was easy. No sooner had I done this than a party of shrieking Goons armed with rifles came chasing over and that was the end of me!

What eventually happened to the lone Spitfire which I went to help out I have no idea. As the 109s followed me, I assume that he got away okay, I certainly hope so.

I will never forget that day, one which I have gone over so often in my daydreams.

A SPITFIRE'S STORY: THE INVISIBLE THREAD

Flight Lieutenant Casson had been shot down by *Hauptmann* Gerhard Schöpfel, *Gruppenkommandeur* of III/JG 26.

Wing Commander Bader was also missing from the engagement, also later reported to be a prisoner. How he had been brought down remained a mystery, however. The Wing Leader's impression, having lost his tail, was that he had collided with a German fighter, but no such collision occurred, however, and the Germans were unable to produce, with certainty, any pilot responsible for shooting down the famous legless fighter ace. In 1995, whilst researching *Bader's Tangmere Spitfires* with the cooperation of all known surviving Tangmere Wing pilots, I made the startling discovery, reading Buck's account of that day's events, that, considering the other losses that day and nature of Bader's demise, that Buck had not shot down a 109 that day but his Wing Leader. Such accidental incidents of so-called 'friendly fire' were not uncommon in the heat and confusion of battle, and the new Me 109F, lacking the angular appearance and tail-struts of the 'E', was curvaceous and similar in appearance to a Spitfire.

In a letter dated 6 September 1995, Buck commented that 'I didn't see DB bale out … I had no idea he had been shot down or had collided with a Me 109'. And on 10 April 1996, 'When I met up with DB at *Dulag Luft* there was no question whatsoever of us colliding with each other over France, nor was there the slightest mention of it when we saw each other at Warburg. You will appreciate that I well-knew the difference between a Me 109 and a Spitfire in the heat of a dogfight. I was nowhere near DB when he was shot down or apparently collided with a 109. As a matter of interest, I saw the pilot of the Me 109 I shot down bale out, but did not see his parachute open.' In a subsequent telephone conversation, Buck was adamant: 'I was an experienced fighter pilot and well knew what a 109 looked like. I shot down a 109 that day.'

No enemy aircraft, however, were involved in a collision, and the tail unit of the only 109 to fall was not shot away, confirmed by a more recent excavation of the crash site concerned. These are inescapable facts arising from a chaotic air battle – in which mistakes easily happen.

So ended Buck Casson's war, the remainder of which was spent behind barbed wire, until liberated and repatriated in May 1945. During his career as an operational fighter pilot, Buck had destroyed 3½ enemy aircraft, probably destroyed four, and damaged four more. His DFC was gazetted the week after he was shot down and captured, the citation acknowledging that:

> This officer has been engaged on operations over a long period and has destroyed two, probably destroyed four and damaged a further two enemy aircraft. Flight Lieutenant Casson carried out many offensive patrols following the Dunkirk evacuation and later fought in the Battle of Britain. This year he has participated in a large number of offensive patrols over Northern France. His efficiency, leadership and courage have set an excellent example.

It was undoubtedly a well-deserved award.

In May 1947, Buck was re-commissioned into 616 Squadron at Finningley, at that time operating Mosquitos as a bomber squadron of the AAF. In 1949, the Squadron re-equipped with Meteor jet fighters, having been, in fact, the RAF's first jet fighter squadron on that type in 1944. In 1950, Squadron Leader Casson became 616 Squadron's CO, his service as such honoured with the AFC on 1 June 1953. In 1954, Squadron Leader L.H. 'Buck' Casson DFC AFC, left finally left the service; he died on 8 October 2003.

Sergeant Bob 'Butch' Morton

The next pilot known to have flown R6644 with 616 Squadron was Sergeant Bob 'Butch' Morton, on 8 November 1940, recording twenty-four routine sorties in Spitfire 'R' between then and 15 February 1940.

Born Robert Alexander Morton in London during 1920 to a couple who had achieved success as a comedy duo and successfully toured overseas. Aged 3, 'Bob' was uprooted when the family moved to Hull, where he developed an interest in aviation, becoming the local font of aviation knowledge amongst his young friends. Upon leaving school, he became an apprentice at the Blackburn Aeroplane and Motor Company at Brough, but the only enjoyable thing about the job, he later recalled, was watching aircraft in the circuit during his lunch break. Unsurprisingly, a true aviation

A SPITFIRE'S STORY: THE INVISIBLE THREAD

Left: A sketch of Sergeant Robert 'Bob' Morton by a fellow PoW.

Below: A page from Bob Morton's log book indicating flights in R6644, QJ-R.

enthusiast, Bob joined the RAFVR as a trainee pilot, and after just two lectures and a drill parade, war broke out. Having been mobilised, from ITW Hastings, Bob returned to Brough for elementary flying training, then completed service flying training at Cranwell. Although selected for a 'provisional commission', this never came through, and so Bob reported to 7 OTU at Hawarden as a sergeant-pilot in September 1940, where he converted to Spitfires. During his first Spitfire flight, Bob felt someone should have warned him of the aircraft's tendency to perform a vicious flick roll as flaps were lowered – it later transpired the cause to have been only one flap working. Two days later, Bob slow-rolled a Spitfire, 'only for the Perspex canopy to explode, probably due to an invisible hairline crack'.

On 29 September 1940, with 9.50 hours on Spitfires, Sergeant Morton, together with a Pilot Officer Peace, reported to 74 Squadron at Coltishall. Re-building to strength and receiving replacements, there were more pilots than Spitfires, and the newcomers found themselves with nothing to fly:

> Twice in three weeks I was at readiness, helmet draped over the control column and parachute ready on a wing, but on both occasions, before the scramble order was received, some friend or other of the flight commander turned up at dispersal and instantly offered a flight in my aeroplane. Enough was enough and Peace and I presented ourselves to the CO, the South African 'Sailor' Malan, requesting flying or a posting. Malan chose the latter, and so I was posted to 616 Squadron at Kirton.
>
> The atmosphere of 616 Squadron was like sunshine breaking through the clouds. Everyone was relaxed and I was immediately accepted as one of the crowd. It was still customary for a sergeant to salute upon entering the pilots' dispersal hut, and I never resented showing this mark of respect to any officer present – they were worth respecting: Billy Burton, the CO, modest, almost self-effacing, except when firm leadership was called for; 'Cocky' Dundas, always planning some practical joke, which often recoiled upon himself; Colin MacFie, 'B' Flight Commander, a boyish 20-year-old who always wore a red silk scarf instead of a collar and

tie – and destined to be shot down and captured a few days before I was. Amongst the sergeants my closest friend was Alec McCairns, also shot down but who made a 'Home Run' from Stalag IXC at Bad Sulza. I quickly acquired the nickname of 'Butch', because of my five-feet-three height, and this stuck throughout my Squadron life, even becoming an unofficial radio call sign.

It was November 1940, when I joined 616 at Kirton and the winter was a hard one. It seemed to be spent repeatedly digging Spitfires out of the deep snow in their sand bagged bays, whilst teams of 'Erks' shovelled snow onto high tractor hauled trailers. One joyful incident stands out: tired of inactivity, MacFie decided to try and take off for a weather test. The aerodrome at Kirton was unusual in being a few feet higher in the centre than at the boundary, with the result that an aeroplane at the far side was out of sight from the dispersal hut. It was customary when the wing was right to taxi to the far side of the field, appear over the rise with the undercarriage already raised, hold the machine well down, and graze over the roof of the hut with an explosion of sound. On this occasion we were having a tea-break from snow clearing, and so were all in the dispersal hut. We watched MacFie taxi out of sight, and waited expectantly for his reappearance. He breasted the rise with wheels up, sending a spectacular bow-wave of snow from his radiator as it ploughed through the surface! Cups of tea went flying as everyone dived for the floor, realising what must have happened to MacFie's propeller – everyone but me, who stood staring gormlessly in disbelief! Fortunately his Spitfire was fitted with a wooden, jablo covered, ROTOL propeller, which tended to dissolve into powder upon high-speed contact with the ground or water, instead of the alloy-bladed de Havilland airscrew. As a result, with each blade shorn to the same length, the aircraft remained more or less flyable and MacFie managed to heave his Spitfire over the dispersal hut and complete a shaky circuit landing – he walked back to the hut with a very red face!

Sergeant Morton went to Tangmere with 616 Squadron on 26 February 1940:

> At this time, I had a coat of arms painted on my Mae West: argent, on a pale azure, three crowns for Hull, on a chief of the second the tail of a Spitfire diving into a cloud; the motto was 'Spotto, Squirto, Scrammo', or 'I spot, I shoot, I remove myself'. It was highly commended by Wing Commander Bader. Outside our 'A' Flight hut soon appeared a notice: 'Bader's Bus Company: Daily Trips to the Continent. Return Tickets Only!' The 'trip' turned out to usually take place twice daily, although as it turned out my season pass abruptly expired in July 1941. The 'Bus Company' bit derived from the Wing's radio call sign of 'Greenline Bus'.

Many adventures followed that fateful summer of 1941, the following being selected from Bob's unpublished memoir.

Sergeant Bob Morton: 'My mother asked me to have a studio photograph taken – so I did!'

A SPITFIRE'S STORY: THE INVISIBLE THREAD

17 May 1941

Sergeant Morton was practising dogfighting over Brighton with two new pilots:

> At about 10,000 feet I put the other two into line-astern prior to beginning the exercise. At that moment I saw two aircraft approaching us, about 1,000 feet above and slightly to one side. They were not Spitfires. I might have thought them 109s except they had rounded wingtips, the well-known distinguishing mark of the 109 being is square wingtips. As this pair of aircraft came abreast of us they turned onto their backs and dived vertically for the ground. This gave me sight of the engine cowlings – bright yellow! At that time everyone had heard of the yellow-nosed 109s, which we believed were from a crack unit. Forgetting al about the accepted procedure of shouting 'Tally Ho!', I simply yelled 'Come on, chaps, it's the real thing!' We gave chase! The 109s levelled out at about 1,000 feet, heading back across the Channel with me in hot pursuit. Although we believed that the Spitfire 'had the legs' of a 109, I lost ground. By the time they reached the French coast I was at least 300 yards behind. Although I knew that they were out of range, I gave them a parting squirt before turning for home.
>
> That was the first time I thought about the other two Spitfire pilots. There was no sign of them. I later learned that the first had tried to follow me down, but his eardrums had perforated as he had not yet learned the art of swallowing or yawning in a steep dive. The other pilot heard my shout, but then found himself alone in the sky. Unable to locate us, he returned to base and reported the mystery.
>
> As I neared the English coast, however, I became aware that I was not alone. The 109s, or perhaps another pair, were sneaking up behind. Then began a real Biggles-style dogfight. I had first read the Biggles stories in the *Modern Boy* comic and was greatly impressed by one of Captain W.E. Johns' footnotes. He stated that

in a head-on attack it was not done for a British pilot to break away; if the German also refused to break then he should be rammed. This I thought magnificent at the time, but now knew that I did not possess courage of that magnitude! This fight began with a head-on attack. Only the previous day I had heard Wing Commander Bader say that every pilot, in his first fight opened fire whilst still out of range. I determined that I would not fire until I saw smoke coming out of the enemy's gun muzzles. At the instant I did, I thumbed the firing button only to discover that the 109 was no longer there! It was not courage which had prevented me from breaking away, just my inability to think about more than one thing at a time! Fortunately for both of us my opponent was no less dim! The fight ended inconclusively shortly afterwards, how long it lasted I had no idea. For the first time it occurred to me that I had not informed the Ground Controller of the affair, so did so. 'Are you all right?', asked the Controller.

'Fine thanks', I answered, 'How are you?'

After examining my Spitfire the Flight Sergeant told me that he could only find one bullet hole. This seemed astonishing. This single bullet had whistled in all directions within the tailplane, clearing out all the internal structure so that the whole unit had to be replaced!

A week or two later, in one of our regular intelligence bulletins, we were warmed to look out for the new Me 109F, which had better performance than the old Me 109E and could, in fact, outdistance a Spitfire. Apparently, it could be recognised by its rounded wingtips…!

26 June 1941

Sergeant Morton found himself in trouble again:

It grieves me to have to report an incident worthy of the notorious 'Pilot Officer Prune', who at the time had yet to appear in the

> pages of our training publication *Tee-Em*. Whilst returning alone across the Channel from the morning sweep, I kept the sun over my right shoulder, saving continuous study of my compass. In the afternoon we carried out another sweep. Again, I became separated from my companions, though no action came my way, and again I set out for home – with the sun again over my right shoulder! Consequently, it seemed to take longer to reach the eastern end of the Isle of Wight. What in fact I eventually reached was the Naze, near Clacton, but this, like my intended point, had a sunken ship with masts and a funnel showing above water. I was satisfied, so struck inland for the aerodrome having not looked at my compass.
>
> When my fuel began to run low, I selected a suitable field for a precautionary landing. It looked like a grass field. In fact, it was ploughed and full of growing wheat. The first touch sheared off my undercarriage legs. The Spitfire dug its nose into the ground, rotated laterally through 180°, smashed down travelling tail first, reared up on its tail and turned through another 90° before coming to rest. Sometime during this performance, the fuselage snapped in half. As a few hundred (or perhaps just a dozen!) soldiers came running up, I turned my attention to the panel over the radio set in the fuselage, mainly to hide my red face.
>
> 'Are you all right?', asked one of the soldiers.
>
> 'No!', I replied savagely, 'I've swallowed my chewing gum!'

As the 616 Squadron diary noted, Bob had 'mistaken the northern part of the Thames Estuary for the south coast near the Isle of Wight'. His Spitfire was a write-off – but fortunately the pilot walked away.

9 July 1941

Sergeant Bob Morton:

> On 8 July 1941, our first Spitfire Mk VB was delivered, with two cannon instead of eight machine-guns. To my delight the

CO asked me to take it out over the sea and test the cannon. Why I was chosen was a mystery; none of our officers, except Wing Commander Bader, had ever used cannon and all would have liked the chance. I went straight down to the hangar and sought out the Flight Sergeant. 'I know what you've come for', he said. 'We're having a bit of trouble lining up the cannon. Can you come back after lunch?' I said that I would, but during lunch an afternoon sweep was ordered. I flew with my heart in my mouth, fearful that someone else would be testing the new Spitfire. Immediately we landed I went straight to the hangar but the work was still not finished, nor was it after tea, when I was asked to return in the morning. Again a sweep intervened, and after lunch another. On that occasion I flew as No. 2 to a new pilot, Flying Officer Gill. As soon as we got over France he commenced imitating the Blackpool Big Dipper. My maps kept being flung from their storage pocket, and it was all I could do to remain in contact with him. Looking behind was out of the question. The result was inevitable: again the golden rain, again the explosions within my Spitfire.

This time, as I levelled out, the whole aircraft was vibrating. I discovered later that a shell inside my port tailplane had opened it up like a baked potato. As before, I made for the coast, but this time the engine stopped completely, one propeller blade sticking up in front of me in silent immobility. I tried to call up the other aircraft, as MacFie had done a few days before, when he too was shot down, but I knew that nothing was getting through. I also knew that I had five engine starter cartridges left. With great concentration, I went through the whole starting procedure with each one. Each time the propeller kicked over but stopped again. I looked at my altimeter; all prisoners of war begin to go 'round the bend' eventually, but I started early: the altimeter read 3,000 feet, the minimum safe height for baling out being 300 feet. For some reason I decided that it was already too late. However, the aircraft was still under control and I had no sure knowledge that my parachute was undamaged following the cannon shells exploding within the fuselage. Fortunately there was a huge expanse of ripening wheat below, near St Omer, with a large house in the middle of it. I steered away from the house, not wishing to give the occupants the danger of sheltering me or the embarrassment of refusing, and landed gently with wheels up. Some German soldiers then captured me and took me to St Omer in a lorry which only had one tyre.

I never returned to Tangmere, but I would like to think that if ever I do, I shall find a new Spitfire Mk VB awaiting my test flight.

As it happened, in Sergeant Morton's enforced absence, his CO, Squadron Leader Burton, test-flew the new Spitfire, recording in his log book, 'Cannon firing, P8707. Nearly hit a boatload of fishermen!'

During captivity, Bob was promoted to Warrant Officer, but never did get that commission, which had eluded him in 1940. After repatriation he was de-mobbed and became a teacher, still living in Hull. A character, in 1996, he accompanied myself and friends on our search for the Spitfire Wing Commander Bader baled out of over France on 9 August 1941, and enthusiastically participated in our successful excavation of a Spitfire Mk IX near St Omer (which has never been satisfactorily identified, despite initial confidence that it was a particular aircraft lost by the Kenley Wing in 1943).

Bob Morton died peacefully on 25 September 2007, aged 86.

Chapter Four

65 'East India' Squadron

On 26 February 1941, having handed over their Spitfire Mk IIAs to 616 Squadron, the pilots of 65 Squadron flew the latter's Mk IAs to Kirton, there to re-fit and re-build, in 65 Squadron colours R6644 becoming YT-R.

No. 65 Squadron was disbanded after the First World War, re-forming at Hornchurch in 1934, flying a succession of biplane fighter types until re-equipping with the Spitfire in March 1939. By the declaration of war, 65 Squadron was fully operational on the Spitfire, by day and night, going on to participate in the Dunkirk fighting. In July 1940, the unit took the name 'East India' when the East India Fund donated the money for six Spitfires, which were allocated to 65 Squadron. The legend 'East India Squadron' was painted in bright yellow on the Spitfires' fuselages, which, according to the ORB, 'looks wizard'. During the first half of the Battle of Britain, 65 Squadron was heavily engaged, flying from Hornchurch and forward bases such as Rochford and Manston, adding claims for thirty-two and a half enemy aircraft destroyed, losing eight pilots killed in the process – amongst them Flying Officer Franciszek Gruska, reported missing on 18 August 1940, the first Polish Spitfire pilot to die in the Battle of Britain. Withdrawn to Turnhouse on 27 August 1940, 65 Squadron returned to 11 Group on 29 November 1940, remaining at Tangmere until relieved by 616 Squadron.

At Kirton, 65 Squadron also became an extension of the OTU process, receiving and training new pilots, who flew the typical training flights of the period, in addition to such sorties as a low-level 'attack' in aid of Barton's 'War Weapons Week', anti-aircraft cooperation, and routine patrols of Sheffield, the Humber, Hull and North Sea off Donna Nook. Wing formation exercises were also flown, in company with 266 'Rhodesia' and 401 'Ram' Squadrons, the latter of the RCAF.

Fortunately, in the case of 65 Squadron records were well-kept, and so we have a good, if not entirely comprehensive, record of which pilots flew R6644 between 26 February and 10 April 1941, when this Spitfire moved on again.

Above: On 4 February 1941, the weather at Tangmere was unsuitable for flying, releasing the pilots who donned their best uniforms ready for a night out in Brighton. Just before leaving the station, however, press photographers arrived, so the pilots had to pose for the cameras – and hence why they are so smartly dressed! From left: Sergeants Peter Mitchell, Harold Orchard and Hugh Chalmers, Flying Officers Brendan 'Paddy' Finucane and the New Zealander Ron Wigg, and Sergeant Peter Rose. Orchard was killed in action the following day, shot down over France in Spitfire P7733; Rose was killed 3 May 1941, flying photographic reconnaissance Spitfires; Mitchell was killed on 26 July 1942 in a flying accident at Dum Dum, Calcutta; and Finucane, who became a highly decorated wing leader, was reported missing on 15 July 1942.

Opposite above left: From left: Sergeants Hugh Chalmers, Peter Mitchell and Sergeant Peter Rose (on wing); anonymous intelligence officer with Flying Officers Brendan 'Paddy' Finucane and Ron Wigg, and Sergeant Harold Orchard.

Opposite above right: Sergeant Peter Mitchell would be killed in a flying accident near Dum Dum, aerodrome, Kolkata, and is buried in the Indian city's Bhowanipore Cemetery. (Pooja Das Choudhury)

65 'EAST INDIA' SQUADRON

No. 65 Squadron pilots at Kirton-in-Lindsey, March 1941; from left, standing: Pilot Officer Rathie; Sergeants Hewlett, Johnson and Mitchell, and Pilot Officer MacPherson. Sitting, from left: Flight Lieutenant Grant; Sergeants Rose, Oldnall, Stillwell and Foulger.

Pilot Officer Robert Strang

Who flew R6644 from Tangmere to Kirton is unknown, but after application of 65 Squadron's livery, the first 65 Squadron pilot recorded as having flown R6644 was a New Zealander, Pilot Officer Robert Harold Strang – known to all as 'Jack'. This first sortie was on 'War Ops', a patrol of 1.10 hrs, as was the second, of 1.05 hrs, both on 2 March 1941. Strang flew the Spitfire six more times, all on training flights, actually making the aircraft's last recorded flight with 65 Squadron, dogfighting practice, on 9 April 1941.

Pilot Officer Jack Strang, a New Zealander.

65 'EAST INDIA' SQUADRON

'Jack' Strang was born in Invercargill on 16 May 1918, the youngest son of Robert Matthew Strang, a leading figure in the manufacturing, timber and banking industries; he was also chair of Southland High School's board of governors, and a respected sports administrator. An elder brother, Winston, was a gifted athlete, but Jack preferred spending time on fast motor cycles and sports cars. Remembered as being 'very self-confident' and 'an average scholar' by his fellows, Jack attended the local primary and Southland Boys' High School, leaving school in 1934 and joining the family coffee and spice trading business. Air-minded, he also joined Southland Aero Club, of which his parents were enthusiastic supporters, becoming a Civil Reserve Scheme pilot, promising to go to war if required in return for forty free flying hours. As a student pilot, Jack proved to be 'above average', flying DH82s and DH60s, excelling at aerobatics.

On 21 November 1939, Jack was commissioned into the RNZAF as an acting pilot officer, and after successfully completing his service flying training at Taieri and Wigram, he received his wings in January 1940. Then, along with another eleven 'Kiwi' pilots, he left his homeland on the *Akaora*, bound for England and to fight with the RAF – seven of these men would subsequently be killed on active service, and two would become prisoners of war.

Having arrived in England during May 1940, Jack trained at various flying training schools before converting to Spitfires at 7 OTU, Hawarden. On 2 September 1940, he was posted to 65 Squadron at Turnhouse – where his cousin, John, also a fighter pilot and also known as 'Jack', was expected, causing a certain amount of confusion.

After 65 Squadron's move to Tangmere in November 1940, Pilot Officer Strang had a lucky escape on 1 December 1940: whilst patrolling Mayfield, the Merlin engine of Spitfire P9545 inexplicably burst into flame, forcing the pilot to take to his parachute – fortunately safely.

On 9 May 1941, Strang was promoted to flying officer and transferred to 485 Squadron, the first all-New Zealand fighter squadron in Europe, formed in March 1941. By October 1941, 485 Squadron was based at Redhill, equipped with the Spitfire Mk VB, contributing to the Non-Stop Offensive. On 2 October 1941, 485 Squadron was sweeping over France, north of Calais, when Strang became separated from the formation due to bright sun. Four Me 109s pounced on the lone Spitfire, Strang turning to meet the enemy and blowing the tail off one of his assailants in a running battle back across the Channel, the Spitfire out-turning the Me 109s, which eventually gave up the chase off Dover.

Later in October 1941, Strang was promoted to flight lieutenant and became a flight commander on 485 Squadron, which was the subject of a morale-boosting public relations exercise when pilots were photographed with their presentation Spitfires, Flight Lieutenant Strang's being 'Southland 1', W3578.

By 25 January 1942, 485 Squadron was based at Kenley, by then Strang had made 104 flights, a total of 500 flying hours in 18 months. This included sixty-seven operational flights (eighteen sweeps over France, three scrambles, thirty bomber escorts, five ASR patrols, and eight convoy protection sorties). That day, 485 and 452 Squadrons, the latter an Australian squadron, took-off from Kenley at 1130 hrs, aiming to rendezvous with the Northolt Polish Spitfire Wing over Hastings for a fighter sweep over France. The Kenley Spitfires arrived at the rendezvous at 1149 hrs, but there being no sign of the Poles, set course for Le Touquet. From there, flying 5 miles out to sea, the Spitfires flew up the French coast to Cap Gris-Nez and returned south of Dover – where Flight Lieutenant Strang was last seen out of control, hurtling towards the sea. There were no enemy aircraft in the vicinity, and so the consensus of opinion was oxygen system failure and anoxia was the cause. A heavy sea was running at the time, driven by high winds, and despite a search by a section of the Squadron, Strang and Spitfire AB788 were never seen again.

Left behind was Marguerite, Jack Strang's English widow, who would never re-marry. After her husband's death, Mrs Strang travelled to New Zealand, remaining with her parents-in-law until the war ended. It was particularly tragic that the week Flight Lieutenant Strang was reported missing, a propaganda film about a day in the life of a Spitfire pilot was released in New Zealand – the pilot concerned being Jack Strang, causing his family further, unfortunate, distress.

Jack Strang was one of 12,000 New Zealanders to die in the Second World War – 4,000 of them airmen.

65 'EAST INDIA' SQUADRON

Sergeant Ron Stillwell

According to 65 Squadron records, Sergeant Stillwell flew R6644 on three occasions, 'War Ops' on 6 and 12 March 1941, and 'low-flying practice' on 24 March 1941; Squadron Leader (as he became) Stillwell's pilot's flying log book disagrees, recording just two flights, the first on 6 March 1941, as Blue 1 in cloud formation practice, and a cine-gun camera exercise on 27 March 1941 – perfectly illustrating that official records, or indeed any records, cannot be taken as gospel. Either way, at least we have confirmation that Stillwell did fly R6644, and it was this log book that confirmed the Spitfire's individual letter of 'R' with 65 Squadron.

Ronald Leslie Stillwell was born on 31 January 1920, joining the RAFVR on 8 February 1939, and undertaking his elementary flying at White Waltham. Following mobilisation and completion of advanced service flying training, Sergeant Stillwell converted to Spitfires at 5 OTU, Aston Down, before a posting to 65 Squadron at Hornchurch on 19 August 1940. Ten days later,

Sergeant Ron Stillwell with presentation Spitfire Mk VB AA734 'Calcutta'.

A SPITFIRE'S STORY: THE INVISIBLE THREAD

Sergeant Stillwell about to scramble in YT-X.

Stillwell flew to Turnhouse with 65 Squadron, for its rest period having been heavily engaged in the Battle of Britain to date. Afterwards, Stillwell went south with the Squadron to Tangmere, thence to Kirton. During the summer of 1941, although still based at Kirton in 12 Group, 65 Squadron flew south to operate from 11 Group stations such as Redhill and West Malling, participating in the Non-Stop Offensive, and in August 1941, Sergeant Stillwell recorded some success, destroying a Me 109 on 18 August 1941, and damaging others on 12 and 22.

The operation of 12 August 1941, was noteworthy: Circus 77, 65 Squadron flying to Duxford the previous evening to spend the night there before forming a wing with 266 and 19 Squadrons, patrolling the Dutch coast Schouwen and Walcheren. As the Spitfires separated into sections of four, searching out the enemy, Me 109s attacked. Stillwell fired at one inconclusively, then fired head-on at another, which was:

Evidently damaged, as I saw something fall off from under his tail as a result of my burst. About ten minutes after we had been flying back (at a height of 100 feet) I saw a rubber dinghy of the 'K' type just to my left with a man sitting in it. He was waving to attract attention. I accordingly broke off on company with another Spitfire, orbited the dinghy and climbed to 9,500 feet. I called up on Group Guard 1 and 2 (Channels B and C) for a fix, but could get no answer. I called up the other Spitfire to ask about his petrol and he replied that he had plenty. I therefore told him to continue orbiting and calling up whilst I returned on a set course of 290° at 200 mph, and I passed over Martlesham twenty-five minutes after passing the dinghy. When I landed at Martlesham I at once informed the ASR Officer and gave him the position of the dinghy.

The airman was saved.

In October 1941, 65 Squadron returned to the Tangmere Sector, based at the Westhampnett satellite, claiming a probable Ju 88 off Worthing on 31 October 1941. Promoted to warrant officer on 1 May 1942, Stillwell was commissioned in June 1942, in which month his DFM was gazetted, the citation referencing the life-saving incident of 12 August 1941. In April 1942, a similar incident arose whilst Stillwell was returning from a sweep: sighting an airman in the sea, although short of fuel himself, Stillwell managed, in the tight confines of his cockpit, to remove his own dinghy and drop it to the man, splashing down just a few yards away. This airman was also picked up, but was sadly already dead.

On 15 October 1942, Flying Officer Stillwell left 65 Squadron after what was a very long time, over two years, spending a month flying the twin-tailed P-38 Lightning with the 97th USAAF Squadron at Maydown, then, after a spell instructing, re-joined 65 Squadron on 7 June 1943, then based at Selsey, an advance landing ground on the south coast, and operating the Spitfire Mk IX. It was during this time that fighter squadrons began a nomadic existence, operating from these temporary fields, often with just tented accommodation, in preparation for the Allied invasion of Normandy. When that happened, the fighter and fighter-bomber squadrons would be keeping on the move, supporting the advancing Allied armies, and so this was an important dress rehearsal. In October 1943, Ron was promoted to flight lieutenant and given command of 'B' Flight.

In December 1943, 65 Squadron re-equipped with the North American P-51 Mustang III – possibly the best fighter of the war. In 1940, the British Purchasing Commission had approached North American Aviation to build Curtiss P-40s – but rather than manufacture an already obsolete design, NAA's James H. Kindelberger designed a new aircraft, intended as a single-engined, single-seater, long-range fighter and fighter-bomber. Called the 'Mustang' by the RAF, the new fighter was initially powered by the Allison V-1710 engine, which provided for only limited high-altitude performance. Nonetheless, the RAF successfully operated the machine in the tactical reconnaissance and fighter-bomber roles – but the Mustang came into its own when in mid-1942, the Allison engine was replaced by the Rolls-Royce 65, two-stage inter-cooled engine. This dramatically increased the Mustang's performance over 15,000 feet without sacrificing range, and entered service as the P-51B, or Mustang III. The next stage of development was the P-51D, the ultimate Mustang, the maximum speed of which was 440 mph, range 1,650 miles, ad a service ceiling of a staggering 41,900 feet. The Mustang was armed with six .50 calibre Browning machine guns, and could carry six or ten 5-inch rockets, or a 500lb bomb beneath each wing.

Ron Stillwell:

> We lost our Spitfires for the then very new Mustang III. We had just been informed 'To you will go the honour of being the first single-engined fighter unit to fly to Berlin in daylight'. A voice from the back of the room quickly pointed out, ominously, that the words 'And back' had been omitted!

After years of planning, on 6 June 1944, the Allied liberation of enemy occupied Europe went ahead, the greatest combined operation ever seen. With masses of Allied shipping in the Channel, great battleships unleashing a devastating bombardment of enemy positions, and the Allied air forces dominating the skies, a Norwegian Wing Leader patrolling the Normandy

Ron Stillwell DFM pictured when a flight lieutenant and commanding a flight of 65 Squadron.

beaches on D-Day described the scene as 'like looking down into hell'. A part of 122 Wing, with 19 and 122 Squadrons, 65 Squadron was naturally involved. On D-Day + 4, 10 June 1944, Flight Lieutenant Stillwell was in action over Caen at 1045 hrs, flying the Mustang III:

> I had just finished bombing and was orbiting over Presto 3 and 4, and 5 and 6, who were strafing, when I saw four aircraft coming in from the port, which I took to be Mustangs, as they had black and white stripes on the mainplanes and red, white and blue roundels on the fuselage and upper wing surfaces. I think one had a yellow outline around a roundel on the fuselage. The wingtips were painted to give a square appearance and the remainder of the camouflage was a dark green and brown. As Tonic Squadron (19) were operating nearby and had just turned in that direction, I assumed them to be Tonic aircraft. The leading aircraft opened fire from 150 yards in a quarter attack and I immediately saw that

they were Me 109s, with one gun firing through the spinner. I broke hard to port and up, reporting them on the R/T. Presto 2 (Flight Lieutenant Milton) broke starboard and half-rolled – I saw no more of him. By this time 12+ E/A had arrived and were carrying out determined attacks in pairs. I finally got behind one and gave several bursts from 300 yards, quarter to astern, but observed no strikes. He pulled straight up and rolled onto his back. I followed and rolled with him, firing whilst inverted. As he dived down, his undercarriage dropped and he continued straight on down. I then saw tracer passing over me, and saw four Me 109s behind. I pulled up hard to the left, blacking out. I saw no E/A after that. Throughout the combat my gunsight was unserviceable due to oil from the defroster. I claim one Me 109F damaged.

From what was clearly a confusing engagement, as *Luftwaffe* aircraft were not painted to represent RAF fighters, Flight Lieutenant Milton and Flying Officer Driscoll were missing.

On 9 July 1944, the Normandy campaign still ongoing, Stillwell was promoted to squadron leader and given command of 122 Squadron, thereby remaining with 122 Wing. The Allied armies were victorious in Normandy by late summer 1944, battering the retreating Germans in the Falaise pocket, as the enemy desperately tried to reach and cross the Seine, and in October 1944, Squadron Leader Stillwell was rested once more and sent to Aston Down as Chief Gunnery Instructor. Credited with three enemy aircraft destroyed and various others damaged, his DFC was gazetted on 7 November 1944. The war in Europe having ended on 8 May 1945, Squadron Leader Stillwell went to Hutton Cranswick as a senior administration officer, but during the process of being permanently commissioned in November 1945, a medical flagged up tuberculosis in both lungs. Consequently, he was medically discharged from the service on 15 September 1947, and in civilian life rose to be a council chief executive.

Squadron Leader Ron Stillwell DFC DFM AE, a modest man who would talk of others being heroes, but never himself, died in Middlesex during February 1993.

Sergeant Vic Lowson

Sergeant Lowson practised flying in R6644 on 12 and 15 March 1941, and on the evening of 21 March 1941, flew the Spitfire on an operational dusk patrol.

Victor Lowson was born on 22 January 1920, at 3 Cardean Street, Dundee, the son of John, an engineer employed at the local gas works, and Helen Lowson. Victor was educated at Glebelands Primary School and the Morgan Academy, both in Dundee; he was a brilliant scholar and committed member of the local Boys' Brigade. A keen sportsman, in adult life this clean living and Christian Scot never touched either tobacco or alcohol. After leaving school he joined the office staff of Jute Industries, and on 27 May 1939 joined the RAFVR.

Having been called up for full time service upon the outbreak of war, Sergeant Lowson completed his service flying training before learning to fly Spitfires at 7 OTU Hawarden, starting his course there on 22 September 1940. On 6 October 1940 he reported to 54 Squadron at Catterick, but was

Sergeant Victor Lowson, a Scot, in presentation Spitfire AD268, 'Bengal – Nagpur Railway No II'.

posted again, five days later, to 65 Squadron at Turnhouse. Whilst there, Victor became a member of the 'Caterpillar Club', membership of which was open to airmen whose lives had been saved by Irvin parachutes. This adventure occurred on 26 November 1940: Sergeant Lowson was patrolling over the Firth of Forth, between May Island and North Berwick, with the Irish Pilot Officer Finucane and Polish Flying Officer Szulkowski. The Section patrolled the estuary for some 20 minutes, crossing from north to south, returning before flying up-river towards the bridge and back. Sergeant Lowson later reported that:

> The order was received to patrol Crail, and immediately afterwards the Ground Controller contacted with a 'pip-squeak-zero', so I then switched on the Contactor. When the Section reached Crail we were ordered to 4,000 feet, which entailed flying through a layer of cloud. From the conversation on the R/T I understood that we were trying to intercept an enemy aircraft. As instructions came through we changed course and height frequently, never flying one course for very long.
>
> After some time the order to 'pancake' was received, and immediately we started losing height through cloud down to 500 feet. When we emerged from the cloud bank I saw that we were over water. I could see no land in any direction. Immediately the Section Leader requested a homing bearing but got no response except the order to 'pancake' being repeated. The Section Leader continually tried to obtain a homing from Ground Control but without success.
>
> In the meantime I noticed that we were flying due west and did so for about 10 minutes before a coastline was sighted, although I was unable to identify our position. We then followed the coastline in a northerly direction whilst still trying to contact the Ground Station. By this time it was quite dark and ground detail was invisible, except for the coastline. The Section Leader then asked me to try and contact the Controller, but I was likewise unable to get a reply.

65 'EAST INDIA' SQUADRON

At this point I dropped behind the formation, and the Leader, seeing this, and taking into consideration our shortage of petrol, ordered me to climb to 4,000 feet and bale out. I left the formation and climbed through cloud until I reached 5,000 feet, when I turned and flew south before turning west, the idea being to get over land before I jumped. On seeing a break in the clouds below me I went down to find a landmark, but although I could confirm being over land I was unable to identify my position. Thereupon I climbed to 8,000 feet, still heading approximately west, and abandoned the aircraft.

Sergeant Lowson made a safe parachute descent; his Spitfire, X4233, which had seen action flying from Hornchurch in the Battle of Britain, was destroyed.

Squadron Leader Gerald 'Sammy' Saunders, commanding 65 Squadron, at Tangmere in January 1941, with, from left: Sergeants Lowson and Stillwell, Flying Officer Smart, Pilot Officer Norwood and Flying Officer Finucane – the significance of the 'For Sale' sign is unknown!

On 29 November 1940, 65 Squadron flew south to Tangmere and another tour of duty in 11 Group. Shortly afterwards, Sergeant Lowson saw the enemy for the first time when he came close to a Ju 88, although the intruder disappeared into cloud.

Having withdrawn to Kirton on 26 February 1941, during the summer, 65 Squadron would frequently fly to Redhill or West Malling, operating from there with other 12 Group squadrons as a wing, contributing to the Non-Stop Offensive. On 24 July 1941, 65 Squadron joined 257 and 401 (RCAF) Squadrons at West Malling, to fly Circus 61, Sergeant Lowson subsequently damaging an Me 109 at 20,000 feet over St Omer. In October 1941, the Squadron returned to the Tangmere Sector, Lowson being commissioned the following month, remaining with the Squadron when the next move came, to Debden in December 1941.

By May 1942, 65 Squadron was commanded by Squadron Leader Tony Bartley DFC, a Battle of Britain veteran (who later married the actress Deborah Kerr). On 23 May 1942, Bartley led twelve 65 Squadron Spitfires on a sweep over France, as part of the Debden Wing. Between Lumbres and Calais, Red Section, led by Pilot Officer Lowson, attacked three Fw 190s: Victor fired at and damaged one of them with an eight second burst of machine-gun fire, watching his bullets strike home before the 190 dived away, out of control; he was the only RAF pilot to successfully engage the enemy on that day.

On 21 July 1942, 65 Squadron was in action again, as the Squadron diary records:

> During the afternoon, 65 Squadron participated in a Debden Wing mass Rhubarb. 12 Spitfires, led by Squadron Leader DAP McMullen DFC took off from Great Stamford at 1616 hours and, together with other Debden squadrons, set course for Blankenberg. 65 flew directly over Blankenberg and turned left, re-crossing the coast in the vicinity of Zeebrugge. Very intense light flak was experienced almost continually whilst over enemy territory. Targets attacked included numerous gun posts, a military car park, a light rail way engine, a factory building opposite Zeebrugge

Pilot Officer Vic Lowson at Debden in 1942.

railway station, two searchlight posts, two barges, two aircraft (believed to be dummies) on an aerodrome, and a light bridge over a canal. 11 pilots returned safely to Great Stamford by 1750 hours, all having attacked ground targets. Eight of our aircraft had been hit by light flak. The machines of Squadron Leader McMullen and Sergeant Hearne were write-offs, and Sergeant Tinsey's Category 'B'. The other five were all Category 'A'.

Pilot Officer Victor Lowson, flying as Red One, was seen to be hit by machine-gun fire shortly after crossing the enemy coast. He succeeded in getting back across the enemy coast but, about 2 miles out to sea, prepared to bale out by climbing from sea level to approximately 1,500 feet and turning on his back. The machine then plunged vertically into the sea and the pilot was unable to fall clear. Warrant Officer R.L. Stillwell circled the spot several times where Pilot Officer Lowson had crashed but nothing more was seen of him. Pilot Officer Lowson was one of the Squadron's most senior members and his loss is deeply felt.

The loss was no doubt particularly 'deeply felt' by Vic Lowson's friend Ron Stillwell. The pair had been sergeants together in 65 Squadron, and had lived and flown with each other for what was, in those days, a very long time. The next day, Squadron Leader McMullen wrote to the missing pilot's parents:

> It is with the greatest regret that I have to write and tell you that your son, Pilot Officer Victor Lowson, is missing as a result of operations yesterday afternoon. I am allowed to tell you in confidence that he was taking part in a low flying attack against enemy troops and gun positions on the coast of Belgium, near Zeebrugge. Whilst shooting up gun positions his Spitfire was hit and crashed into the sea about 2 miles off the Belgian coast. I am very much afraid that there is little chance that he survived.
>
> He was one of our best pilots, a Section Leader and potential Flight Commander. In fact, during this flight he was leading a Flight into attack. He always showed exceptional promise as a pilot, an officer and a leader. It has come as a great blow to me personally that he is now missing.
>
> Vicky was the best loved lad on our Squadron, his quiet steadiness of purpose and gentle wit having endeared him to us all during the long time that he has been with us. He will always remain in the hearts of the rest of the Squadron as one of the very best.

Another letter followed on 8 August 1942, this time from 65 Squadron's Intelligence Officer, Flight Lieutenant Hugh Tarrant:

> I regret that we have received no news of Victor. Should we hear anything at all in the future I will notify you immediately. I hope you will accept my personal sympathy. As an Intelligence Officer I am naturally older and more experienced than the pilots in my Squadron; I would like to assure you now that Victor was quite the finest boy that I ever met in the Service. I am happy to think that he liked me and looked upon me as a friend. I miss his companionship in this Squadron very deeply.

65 'EAST INDIA' SQUADRON

On 14 February 1943, the Air Ministry confirmed that as nothing further had been heard of Pilot Officer Lowson since the day he crashed in Spitfire W3697, he must be 'presumed dead for official purposes'.

Whilst researching Victor Lowson's story, I traced Jack Lowson, still living in Dundee and who still felt his elder brother's loss deeply. Amongst the family's treasured artefacts were Victor's Caterpillar Club badge, made into a brooch and worn proudly by his sister-in-law. Most poignant of all was Victor's diary, a four-leaf clover still pressed into the pages.

Pilot Officer Victor Lowson is commemorated on Panel 170 of the Runnymede Memorial.

A four-leafed clover pressed into the pages of Vic Lowson's diary; sadly his luck ran out when reported missing on 21 July 1942.

A SPITFIRE'S STORY: THE INVISIBLE THREAD

Sergeant Arthur Johnson

According to 65 Squadron records, Sergeant 900452 A.H. Johnson flew R6644 on 12, 13, 27 and 31 March 1941 – although his log book indicates a flight on 29, not 27, a dusk patrol of forty-five minutes.

Born in Warrington on 26 February 1916, Arthur Johnson was another pre-war reservist, who joined 'B' Flight of 65 Squadron as a replacement pilot shortly after the Battle of Britain. Whilst the Squadron rested at Kirton

Sergeant Arthur Johnson (right) at Kirton in January 1941, with Spitfire Mk IA YT-B.

65 'EAST INDIA' SQUADRON

and participated in offensive operations with the 12 Group Wing during the summer of 1941, Johnson demonstrated the makings of becoming a successful fighter pilot.

On 8 July 1941, Sergeant Johnson destroyed a Me 109 2 miles south of Mardycke, the cockpit of which he saw 'disintegrate', and claimed a probable; another Me 109 destroyed followed on 24 July 1941, 10 miles west of Audruicq, which 'burst into flames … a bright flash was visible when it hit the ground'; then, on 12 August 1941, Johnson claimed a 109 probable, which turned over onto its back and was last seen spinning into cloud.

On 21 October 1941, Fighter Command sent five wings to sweep the Pas-de-Calais, 41, 65 and 129 Squadrons sweeping St Omer. With 65 Squadron occupying the centre position, the formation crossed the coast at Le Touquet, proceeding towards St Omer at 19,000 feet. Then, six Me 109Fs and six of the new Fw 190s attacked, 'the Wing', according to the 65 Squadron ORB, 'on withdrawing south of Boulogne, continually harassed'. The CO, Squadron Leader 'Pancho' Villa ordered the Squadron to break, and the Spitfires scattered, engaging individually. In the ensuing action, Sergeant Oldnall claimed a 109 destroyed, as did Pilot Officer Mitchell, whose engine failed, causing him to bale out over the sea and take to his dinghy, from which he was rescued two hours later by a naval MTB. Sergeant Johnson, however, was missing, as was Sergeant Tucker of 129 Squadron. The 12 Group Wing had been hit by the JG 26 *Geschwaderstab* and elements of I/JG 26 – the 1/JG 26 *Staffelkapitän*, *Hauptmann* Josef 'Pips' Priller claiming Spitfires destroyed 4km west of Etaples and 15km NNW of Le Touquet. It is possible that the latter was Sergeant Johnson, in Spitfire AD267, who was attacked over the French seaside resort, claiming two 109s destroyed before shot down himself, his Spitfire erupting into flame. Baling out badly burned and landing safely by parachute, Johnson was captured by a unit of the Waffen-SS, spending the remainder of the war as a prisoner, mostly in the infamous Stalag Luft III.

During his time behind the wire, Sergeant Johnson made two unsuccessful escape attempts, nearly reaching the American lines before being re-captured on the second. Repatriated in April 1945, Arthur Johnson became area manager of a major insurance company in southern England – but, sadly, deeply affected by his wartime experiences, took his own life in 1967.

Pilot Officer Robin Norwood

Pilot Officer Norwood made the first of five training flights in R6644 on 13 March 1941.

Born in Chelsea on 21 October 1910, Robin Keith Collen Norwood had much to live up to: his father was descended from Norse kings – and had won a VC during the Boer War, having rescued a wounded private soldier under heavy fire. Sadly, Captain John Norwood VC would be the first VC holder to be killed during the First World War, whilst serving with the 5th Dragoon Guards in France, on 8 September 1914 – his thirty-sixth birthday.

After school, Robin Norwood first went into the wine business, learning to fly privately at the Southern Aero Club and achieving his pilot's licence on 27 May 1934. On 8 January 1938, he joined the RAFVR, and by 1939 was working as a patent agent. Mobilised on 2 September 1939, he reported to the London Transit Centre, was sent home to await further orders and eventually began his service flying training on 6 May 1940, at 6 FTS, Montrose. Commissioned as a pilot officer on 17 August 1940, on that day Norwood arrived at 5 OTU,

Pilot Officer Robin Norwood.

65 'EAST INDIA' SQUADRON

Aston Down, to convert to Spitfires, two days later being posted for conversion at 7 OTU, Hawarden. That process complete. On 2 September 1940, Pilot Officer Norwood reported to 65 Squadron at Turnhouse.

In November 1940, 65 Squadron moved to Tangmere, and on 30 December 1940, Pilot Officer Norwood, in company with Pilot Officer David Glaser, caught his first glimpse of the enemy whilst patrolling Beachy Head: a Ju 88, at which both pilots fired before the raider escaped into cloud.

On 12 August 1941, 65 Squadron flew to Wittering to patrol the Dutch coast on Circus 77, in company with 19 and 266 Squadrons. Flying in sections of four, Pilot Officer Norwood occupied the Blue 3 position in the section led by 65's CO, Squadron Leader John 'Pancho' Villa DFC. Arriving over the patrol area, the stretch of water between Schouwen and Walcheren, at 1210 hrs 65 Squadron descended to below 1,000 feet. Almost immediately the Spitfires were attacked by Me 109s, which operated individually, diving to attack before disappearing into cloud. An Me 109 was seen to dive into the sea, and as Pilot Officer Norwood and Sergeant Stillwell followed their leader as he engaged a 109, they were both attacked and forced to break away; afterwards, Norwood watched a Blenheim crash into the sea, 12 miles off the Dutch coast. Al of 65 Squadron returned safely to base.

Later that month, Norwood was promoted to flying officer and became an instructor at 57 OTU, Hawarden. On 12 February 1942, he joined 54 Squadron at Castletown, being promoted to flight lieutenant the following month. The Squadron was bound for service overseas, leaving England on 18 June 1942, travelling by ship to the Middle East. Whilst awaiting an east-bound convoy in Freetown, South Africa, the ship was diverted to Australia, crossing the equator on 1 July 1942 and arriving in Melbourne on 13 August 1942.

From September 1942, 54, with 452 and 457 (Australian) Squadrons formed No. 1 Fighter Wing RAAF, based at Richmond, New South Wales, commanded by Australia's greatest ace, Wing Commander Clive 'Killer' Caldwell DSO DFC.

On 19 September 1942, the engine of Flight Lieutenant Norwood's Spitfire failed, forcing him to make a dead stick landing on the airfield, one he walked away from. 2 December 1942, saw the Wing declared fully operational, providing defence against Japanese air attack, and on 7 July

1943, 54 Squadron intercepted a heavy Japanese raid on Fenton, Flight Lieutenant Norwood inconclusively engaging enemy bombers. In November 1943, Norwood was rested, but returned to 54 Squadron just a fortnight later, remaining with the unit in Australia until returning to England in February 1945, serving as a gunnery instructor. In 1946, Norwood left the service, but nothing is known of his post-war life, except that he died on 2 April 1970.

Sergeant Humphrey Baxter

Sergeant Humphrey Baxter made just one flight in R6644:

> A short, one-hour, familiarization jaunt, on sector reconnaissance, from Kirton, just three days after I had joined 65 Squadron. I can only hope that my handling of her on that occasion (or perhaps I should say mishandling?!) didn't contribute to the engine fire R6644 ultimately suffered! Writing this in September 1993, what a very long time ago it all seems in retrospect, and yet the memories of those distant days is brought into sharp focus, poring over faded log book entries.

Another replacement pilot joining 65 Squadron at Kirton, on 12 March 1941, Baxter also saw action when the 12 Group Wing participated in offensive operations over France during the summer of 1941. On 12 August 1941, Baxter flew with 65 Squadron in a Wing with 19 and 266 Squadrons, sweeping the Dutch coast. Over Haamstede, Baxter watched Sergeant Arthur Johnson open fire at a

Sergeant Humphrey 'Red' Baxter, another Scot.

Me 109E, then, sighting another 109 in front and to starboard, fired himself, out of range, losing the rest of Green Section in the process. Travelling west at 1220 hrs, a cannon shell hit Baxter's Spitfire in the fuselage, his attacker overtaking him and receiving a burst of fire, causing 'a considerable amount of white and black smoke' to 'issue from the port side of the E/A', which 'immediately appeared to fall out of the sky to the right of me'. The 109 was claimed as a probable, and, escorted by Sergeant Hugh Chalmers back across the North Sea, Baxter returned safely to Ipswich. This success, however, would be short-lived.

Humphrey Baxter:

> One of those you mention was Sergeant Robert MacPherson. Hereby hangs a wry tale. On the day I was eventually shot down, I had made use of Mac's 'chute, as my own was in for inspection and re-pack that day, 21 August 1941. I think Mac was on leave for a couple of days. He was fairly tall, knocking on the 6 feet

Squadron Leader Saunders, fifth right, standing, outside Kirton's dispersal hut with, Pilot Officers MacPherson (second left, standing) and Norwood (fourth left, standing), and kneeling, from left, Sergeants Baxter, Chalmers, Lowson and Stillwell; the rest are unknown.

mark, whereas I'm a short-arse. Needless to say, I entirely forgot to adjust the harness from his own setting….

On 21 August 1941, 65, 121 and 401 Squadrons operated from West Malling, sweeping south of Gravelines at 23,000 feet. Me 109s were all around, periodically diving to attack the Spitfires, Sergeant R.H.A. Williams of 65 Squadron recording the 12 Group Wing's only claim, a probable Me 109F over St Omer. Two Spitfire pilots were missing, however: Sergeant W. Kay, who was shot down and killed over the Dunkirk area – and Sergeant Baxter:

> My active span ceased abruptly on a beautiful summer day, at 26,000 feet over the Pas-de-Calais. I fell for the old, old, trick – a 109 abeam, and just getting him in the gunsight, when, of course, I was jumped up the backside by his cobber! Cannon fire made a very sorry mess of Spitfire Mk IIA P8160, YT-J for 'Jessie'. And I had to bale out hastily. I suffered various bits of canon-shell splinters etc, plus a fractured skull, but otherwise nothing fatal.
>
> When I baled out, I still retained a bit of lucidity and decided that it would be best to drop a fair distance away from the rarified air at that level. I probably plummeted some 12,000 feet before finally pulling the ring. My old school-time physics seems to remind me that normal acceleration is about 122 feet per second in free-fall, so you will gather that a ring-pull I was doing a fair belter, to say the least! The result was catastrophic, far outdoing any minor cannon-shell splinters, fractured skull etc: the full breaking strain being taken up between my crotch! I was speaking in a rather high-pitched squeak for several weeks, and am convinced Jerry believed he had captured a eunuch!!
>
> Jerry was, of course, awaiting me when I finally grounded. I was then hospitalized in St Omer for several weeks. Thereafter I became a guest of the Reich, sojourning in various POW camps, including the well-known Stalag Luft III, until finally effecting an escape, with a couple of pals, during the concluding stages of

the war. We made our way westward, through the chaos of the time, to eventually link up with the advancing Allied forces on Luneburg Heath. It all seems a helluva long time ago, from the days of a callow 21-year-old to a now ageing OAP!

After the war, Humphrey Baxter went into crofting in the Scottish Highlands. We corresponded in 1992–1993, but his current status is unknown.

Sergeant Peter Rose

Sergeant Rose flew R6644 twice on 21 March 1941, first on 'flying practice', then from Wittering to Kirton, and the following day practising 'low-level attacks'.

Peter Garratt Rose was born to John and Ida Rose on 17 May 1916, at Burton-on-Trent in Staffordshire. Peter's father had served in the local county regiment during the First World War, after which his services were retained to assist with administration on the continent. Major Rose was joined there by his family, which remained with him in France until he left the army in 1920. Back in England, Peter became a pupil at Burton Grammar School, where he became an accomplished member of the school rowing club. In 1930, Peter was coxswain and steered the school crew, in which his elder brother, John, rowed at stroke, to

Sergeant Peter Rose, Tangmere, 4 February 1941.

victory in the Burton Regatta, winning the Leander Challenge Vase. In 1932, Peter rowed at bow and was again in the winning team. That year he left school, joining both his father and elder brother at the local brewing company Bass, Ratcliff & Gretton Ltd. Major Rose was the company accountant, and spent fifty years of his life working there. His brother John worked in the Engineering Department whilst Peter was a clerk in the Bottling Department. Peter, though, had always wanted to fly, and so, much against his mother's wishes, he joined the RAFVR in 1936, learning to fly at Burnaston, near Derby. Unfortunately, this meant that the close rowing relationship John and Peter had so enjoyed ended, so much did Peter's flying training interfere with practice on the River Trent. Life went on otherwise much the same, however, until 13 June 1939, when Peter was called up for full time service.

After 'square bashing' and ground schooling at 3 Initial Training Wing, Sergeant Rose's service flying training was successfully completed

Sergeants Chalmers and Rose, Tangmere, 4 February 1941.

65 'EAST INDIA' SQUADRON

before he reported to 7 OTU, Hawarden, for conversion to Spitfires. By this time the Battle of Britain was drawing to a close; when Sergeant Rose reported to his first fighter squadron, 65, the unit was resting at Turnhouse after being heavily engaged whilst previously flying from Hornchurch. He then flew with 65 Squadron at Tangmere, moving with the Squadron to Kirton-in-Lindsey on 26 February 1941. Such was the monotony of mundane flying at Kirton, however, that Peter transferred to 1 Photographic Reconnaissance Unit, based at Benson, 'to escape the boredom of patrolling the east coast'.

In warfare, intelligence is key, accurate information regarding the enemy's strength and deployment being essential to formulating effective strategy and tactics. As in the First World War, aircraft were essential to this process, observing and photographing enemy troop movements, installations and shipping – and RAF photographic reconnaissance owed its creation to a most colourful character: Sidney Cotton. An Australian, Cotton had flown in the First World War with the RNAS and was an inventor, responsible for,

Sergeant Chalmers – note his privately purchased sheepskin gloves.

amongst other things, the Sidcot flying suit. A maverick, in 1917, following disagreements with senior officers, Cotton resigned his commission and went into the civilian aviation business. Before the Second World War broke out, however, Cotton was recruited by MI6 to use his businesses as a clandestine means of taking aerial photographs of German naval and troop movements. After war was declared he was commissioned into the RAF as a squadron leader and given command of the new 1 Photographic Development Unit (PDU) at Heston, soon replacing the unit's original Blenheims with Spitfires. With wing mounted cameras fitted, the first Spitfire photographic reconnaissance flight was made to the German city of Aachen on 18 November 1939. During the Battle of France in May and June 1940, PDU Spitfire pilots flew 557 sorties, losing 12 aircraft. After Dunkirk the unit re-formed at Heston as 1 PRU, having found the Spitfire a superb aerial reconnaissance machine when fitted with long focal length oblique cameras. With 1 PDU, Cotton pioneered high-altitude photography, his aircraft returning with essential data, but, yet again he clashed with authority – after returning from France with a high-profile passenger whom he charged a personal fee for the flight, Cotton was removed from post in June 1940 and never reinstated. Nonetheless, his early work laid the foundations of photographic reconnaissance, and 1 PDU morphed first into the Photographic Reconnaissance Unit, then, on 14 November 1940, became 1 PRU.

The weight of camera equipment and full fuel tanks, however, dictated that 1 PRU's Spitfires were unarmed, relying upon height and speed for protection. All equipment deemed superfluous was stripped out, empty gun ports blanked off and panel join lines even filled with plaster, thus ensuring a completely smooth finish – these tweaks increasing the Spitfire's speed from around 362 to 390 mph. Indeed, the Spitfire would remain in service as a photographic reconnaissance mount until long after the cessation of hostilities in 1945, by which time it had undergone numerous adaptations throughout the spectrum of marques. When Sergeant Rose joined 1 PRU, the unit, commanded by Wing Commander G.W. Tuttle, had been based at Benson, in South Oxfordshire, since December 1940, and was a part of 16 Group, Coastal Command. Clearly, the PRU pilots' role was a very dangerous, not to mention unsung, one – flying unarmed aircraft deep over enemy territory and returning with essential intelligence. Indeed, the longest such sortie from Benson was to the Polish port of Gdansk, a round trip of 1,500 miles. Sergeant Rose had certainly found an exciting alternative to monotonous convoy patrols.

Saturday, 3 May 1941 dawned cloudless, remaining fair with good visibility. Throughout the day, 1 PRU carried out a number of sorties to photograph the industrial Ruhr Valley. On that day, Sergeant Rose was making only his second trip since having joined 1 PRU less than three weeks previously. At 1300 hrs that day, his Spitfire, R6805, was seen in difficulties over the village of Soumagne, near Liège in Belgium. The aircraft's Merlin engine was heard by eyewitnesses on the ground to be running very roughly. The Spitfire was then seen spinning, out of control and the pilot baled out.

The village policeman, Leonard Melon, rapidly donned his uniform, stepping outside his front door and watching a parachute drifting south-west. In that direction he could see smoke billowing up from the Spitfire's crash site. Melon immediately set off on push bike, pedalling furiously to the scene. En route, the policeman was stopped by excited villagers confirming that the aircraft had crashed near the hamlet of Maireux, in a field owned by the Demollin-Spronck family, where a crowd had already gathered. Upon arrival, Melon noted that a single-engined aircraft had buried itself deep into the sloping field. In an orchard, some distance from the blazing wreckage, he found the body of the young pilot. Eyewitnesses told him that as the parachute descended, both wings had suddenly been torn from the aircraft, one of these scything through the parachute's shroud lines. The hapless pilot then plunged to earth, his descent unchecked.

Dr Robert Berlemont was also at the scene and pronounced life extinct. Beside the body lay a collection of keys and two identification tags: one stated 'RAF No. 748692 P. Rose', the other 'Do Not Remove. No. 58849'. German troops soon appeared and seized the items as Melon covered the corpse with a blanket. The Germans ordered Melon to remain at and guard the crash site, whilst they examined the body and picked through the smouldering debris of Sergeant Rose's Spitfire. Later, Melon was joined by his colleague from the nearby village of Melen, and with the help of German soldiers the two

Belgian police officers loaded the pilot's body onto a cart and went to the mortuary. Melon then returned to the crash site and mounted an overnight guard with other policemen from neighbouring Olne.

On Monday, 5 May 1941, Sergeant Rose's funeral took place in the village church at Fecher. For some reason the Germans refused permission for burial in the local cemetery, so some 2,000 patriotic Belgian mourners accompanied the cortege to the crash site. Some 300 students from Liège University were in the congregation, carrying wreaths in both Belgian and British national colours. The coffin was draped in a Union Jack, and covered in floral tributes. Truckloads of German soldiers then suddenly appeared, breaking up the gathering and confiscating the coffin. After the mourners were dispersed, the Germans returned the pilot's body to Leonard Melon for burial. Instead of doing so at the crash site, as instructed by the Germans, the policeman interred Sergeant Rose, by cover of darkness and in secret,

The wreckage of Sergeant Rose's Spitfire at Soumagne, illicitly photographed by a Belgian civilian.

A more peaceful scene today.

in vault 295 at Soumagne Cemetery, belonging to Mme. Cleriux, of Liège. For the Rose family in Burton-upon-Trent, however, an agonising time ensued as Peter was simply reported 'missing'. Eventually, information was received from Germany by the International Red Cross Committee (IRCC) on 17 December 1942 confirming that Sergeant Rose had been killed at Soumagne on 3 May 1941 – thus ending any speculation that he may still be alive, perhaps a prisoner – and stating that he was buried in grave 295 of Soumagne Cemetery. And therein lies another tale.

By the cessation of hostilities in Europe, 42,000 aircrew remained missing, and scant information was available regarding the actual fates of countless others, even though buried by the Germans. Families, understandably, were anxious for news of what fate had befallen their missing or lost loved ones. Consequently the Missing Research & Enquiry Service (MRES) was set up to scour the battlefields for the missing, and collate what facts could be gleaned from local people and other sources. In August 1945, this grim work in Belgium and Holland became the responsibility of Wing Commander

A SPITFIRE'S STORY: THE INVISIBLE THREAD

Angus MacLean's 2 MRES, based in Brussels. The case of Sergeant Rose was examined by this unit, which confirmed that the Spitfire pilot was not resting in grave 295 – but in the shared Cleriux vault 295. This, however, was not an acceptable scenario to the authorities – or to Peter's father, John. On 20 September 1945, Mr Rose wrote to the Imperial War Graves Commission (IWGC):

> I have been reliably informed that the body of my son… killed on 3 May 1941, was interred on 5 May 1941, in a coffin provided by the inhabitants of the commune, in a private family vault (295) in the Municipal Cemetery at Soumagne, near Liège, as a temporary measure.
>
> I presume that in the normal course of events, the coffin will be transferred to a British Military Cemetery, but I shall be grateful if you will inform me whether an application to have the body brought over to a cemetery here in Burton would be favorably considered.

The IWGC (since 1960 the Commonwealth War Graves Commission) policy, however, was to concentrate British and Commonwealth war dead in military cemeteries, not send remains home, and, in the interests of equality, all casualties, regardless of rank or status, were to have uniform headstones and, wherever possible, individual graves. In the case of 25-year-old Sergeant Rose, the inhabitants of Soumagne protested when it was announced that the pilot's remains would be completely removed from the local cemetery and interred at a concentrated military cemetery some miles away. A compromise was reached when the British authorities agreed to the young Sergeant-Pilot remaining at the Municipal Cemetery – but in his own grave. This was duly done, and so Sergeant Rose became the only British casualty buried at that place, where his grave can be found today.

In 1948, Major and Mrs Rose visited Soumagne and were told the full story of their son's death and crash by M. Spronck, on whose land the Spitfire crashed, who presented the grieving parents with Peter's leather flying helmet. The villagers then erected a memorial to their own war dead, near Sergeant

Rose's grave, a kerbstone surround to which being funded by the villagers. Ultimately the original metal cross was replaced by a Portland headstone, the simple epitaph on which was chosen by the Rose family. As Peter's elder brother, John, commented, 'How well they chose their words; how adequately they describe a most I lovable brother'. Forty years after his parents visited his brother's grave, John and his family arrived unannounced in Soumagne – and were moved to discover fresh flowers on Peter's immaculately kept grave. Indeed, each successive generation of children in Soumagne are told the story of 'their' young pilot, whose courage and sacrifice represented hope in those terrible days of occupation, thus maintaining the currency of Peter's memory in a very real and personal way.

Sergeant Rose's grave in Soumagne Cemetery, Belgium.

The inscription on Sergeant Peter Garratt Rose's headstone comes from Shakespeare's Julius Caesar, Act V, and is indeed a poignant and moving epitaph:

> His life was gentle; and the element so
> Mixed in him that nature might stand up and
> Say to the entire world: 'This was a Man.'

Flying Officer Brendan Finucane

Flying Officer Finucane first flew R6644 on 'War Ops', 22 March 1941, and again during a wing formation practice on 6 April 1941. With 29½ aerial victories, Finucane was the most famous pilot known to have flown this Spitfire.

A SPITFIRE'S STORY: THE INVISIBLE THREAD

Flying Officer Brendan 'Paddy' Finucane (H.H.J. Brendan Finucane KC).

Brendan Eamonn Fergus Finucane – universally known as 'Paddy' – was born in Dublin on 16 October 1920, the eldest of five children, and attended the Christian Brothers' O'Connell School. In 1936, Finucane's parents, Thomas and Florence, moved the family to Richmond, Surrey, where after leaving school Finucane, who had a natural aptitude for mathematics, became

65 'EAST INDIA' SQUADRON

an accounts clerk. Air-minded, in 1938 Finucane successfully applied for a SSC, his elementary flying training being completed at 6 EFTS Sywell – a course the 17-year-old nearly failed. Eventually, his service flying training was passed at 8 FTS Montrose, 8 Advanced Flying School Evanton and 3 FTS South Cerney before conversion to Spitfires at 7 OTU, Hawarden on 28 June 1940. On 13 July 1940, Pilot Officer Finucane was posted to Hornchurch and 65 Squadron, joining 'B' Flight, commanded by Flight Lieutenant G.A.W. 'Sammy' Saunders (later to become Squadron Commander).

Between 1 and 18 August 1940, Finucane flew fifty-two sorties, claiming the destruction of two Me 109s, two probables and another damaged. On 3 September 1940, after the Squadron had withdrawn to Turnhouse, Finucane was promoted to flying officer – and remembered by a comrade, the Polish Squadron Leader Bolesław 'Gandy' Drobinski, as 'a very quiet sort of man, totally dedicated to being a fighter pilot; he spent little time in the bar'. At Turnhouse, the Pole engaged his Irish friend in dogfight practice – ending far below the specified minimum height. On 28 November 1940, 65 Squadron returned south, to Tangmere, Finucane claiming the destruction of an Me 110 and two Me 109s, and sharing in the demise of a Ju 88. On 26 February 1941, Flying Officer Finucane flew to Kirton with 65 Squadron, where he flew R6644, and on 15 April 1941, destroyed a 109 south of Dover.

At Kirton, on 8 April 1941, the first Australian fighter squadron in Britain was formed, 452, commanded by a British Battle of Britain veteran, Squadron Leader Roy Dutton. Finucane was promoted to flight lieutenant and posted to 452 Squadron as a flight commander on 14 April 1941. Soon afterwards, whilst providing a display of air drill over Scunthorpe, Dutton and Finucane collided, the latter's airscrew nearly severing his CO's tail. Miraculously, Squadron Leader Dutton managed to crash-land in a turnip field, smashing through a dry-stone wall, and survived – a close call indeed.

On 13 May 1941, Flight Lieutenant Finucane's first DFC was gazetted, and on 11 July 1941, still based at Kirton and flying with the 12 Group Wing, he claimed 452 Squadron's first aerial victory, a Me 109 destroyed near Lille. Ten days later, 452 Squadron went south, to Kenley in 11 Group.

On 3 August 1941, Finucane resumed his combat success, destroying a Me 109F and claiming a probable near St Omer. By this time, his exploits

A SPITFIRE'S STORY: THE INVISIBLE THREAD

65 Squadron pilots at Kirton, April 1941, including two pilots of R6644: Flying Officer Finucane (third left) and Sergeant Lowson (second right). (H.H.J. Brendan Finucane KC). By this time the colour scheme had changed – whilst the black port wing remained, the remainder of the under-surface was 'sky', as was the spinner, and day-fighter band around the tail root. (H.H.J. Brendan Finucane KC)

had captured the public's imagination to the extent that the press, having previously described him as an anonymous Irish flight lieutenant, could withhold his name no longer. On 9 August 1941, the legless Wing Commander Douglas Bader was captured – leading to the press dubbing Finucane 'Bader's successor'. The propaganda machine had lost one hero but found another; on 9 September 1941, a Bar to Finucane's DFC was gazetted; another followed on 26 September 1941.

Three weeks before Finucane's 21st birthday, an Air Ministry bulletin declared that as his score stood at twenty, he required one more victory before his birthday – and on 13 October 1941 he claimed two Me 109Fs destroyed and another damaged over the Pas-de-Calais. Shortly after claiming the destruction of that twenty-first enemy aircraft, and soon after receiving the

65 'EAST INDIA' SQUADRON

The same 65 Squadron pilots with the same Spitfire Mk IA – exasperatingly the code letter and serial are invisible, although what can be seen of the serial's last digit appears to be a 4. There were, however, several Spitfires with serials ending in 4 on charge with 65 Squadron at this time, so we will never know if this is R6644. (H.H.J. Brendan Finucane KC)

Bar to his DFC, Flight Lieutenant Finucane spoke on the radio about his experiences of flying sweeps over France. At that time he was commanding a flight of the Australian 452 Squadron, the Irish ace opining that 'Australia must be a grand country if it's anything like its pilots, and after the war I'm going to see it. I like a job with figures – accountancy or auditing'. Having related various tales of derring-do, Finucane concluded by saying that his post-war ambition was 'to go to Australia – and audit books'.

Those victories, however, were his last flying with 452 Squadron, having claimed, between 3 August 1941 and 13 October 1941, eighteen Me 109s destroyed, two probables and two damaged. On 21 October 1941, Finucane's DSO was gazetted, but he broke an ankle during the blackout, resulting in him being hospitalised at RAF Halton in November 1941, and recuperating in Torquay until 18 January 1942. The following day he returned to 452 Squadron at Kenley, a week later being promoted to squadron leader and given command of 602 Squadron at Redhill.

A SPITFIRE'S STORY: THE INVISIBLE THREAD

On 20 February 1942, Squadron Leader Finucane and Pilot Officer Lewis took-off at 1055 hrs on a 'Rhubarb', as the latter reported:

> Crossed English coast at Manston, made French coast north of Dunkirk. Flew at 0 feet SW down coast about 3 miles out. Squadron Leader Finucane fired at a small boat. Just south of Dunkirk saw two E/A take-off from Mardyck. We turned hard starboard and climbed to meet them. Met in head-on attack which developed into a general dogfight, during which I fired one very short burst. Squadron Leader Finucane then ordered 'Home, flat out' and reported he'd been hit. He flew at 0 feet and I at 500 feet behind him, weaving violently. The Fw 190s kept catching me up, necessitating my turning to engage them several times, Squadron Leader Finucane turning to give a hand when things got too warm. During one attack I fired a burst approximately two seconds at a 190 and bits appeared to fly off his tailplane. I kept turning and saw one E/A landing on the water. The other E/A followed and did two more attacks but did not fire.

It was the only time Finucane was wounded in aerial combat. His Spitfire, Mk VB BL548, was hit in the wings, fuselage and tail. One round entered the fuselage, shrapnel hitting the ace pilot. According to the 602 Squadron ORB, Squadron Leader Finucane returned to Kenley 'with difficulty... suffering from shock, and fainted just after landing. MO reports superficial flesh wounds and will be OK in a week'.

By 13 March 1942, Squadron Leader Finucane was back in action, destroying a Fw 190 off Cap Gris-Nez. Between that date and 8 June 1942, he would destroy a total of three and a half German fighters, probably destroy four and damage four, and be awarded a third of a Ju 88 probable. On 21 June 1942, by which time his personal score stood at twenty-six and six shared destroyed, eight and one shared probable and eight damaged, Finucane was promoted to wing commander and appointed to lead the Hornchurch Wing. There would, however, be no more victories.

65 'EAST INDIA' SQUADRON

'Paddy' Finucane pictured whilst commanding 452 (Australian) Squadron, congratulating a successful pilot. It was Finucane's expressed intention to practice as an auditor in Australia after the war but he never made it, being reported missing on 15 July 1942.

On 15 July 1942, Wing Commander Finucane briefed his pilots for a 'Ramrod' operation against a German army camp near Le Touquet. The Hornchurch Wing flew east, across the Thames, then over the Channel at zero feet, avoiding detection by German radar. The attack was timed for the Spitfires to arrive over their target whilst enemy soldiers queued for lunch. At 1222 hrs the French coast was crossed at Le Touquet – when a German machine-gunner opened fire from the dunes below. A single bullet damaged the 'Wingco's' radiator – of which he was unaware. His wingman, Pilot Officer Aikman, informed his leader of the damage, causing Wing Commander Finucane to turn hard right, taking a course that would take him back over the coast and home. As the two Spitfires re-crossed the coast, Alan Aikman let fly, destroying a German machine-gun position. Streaming white glycol fumes, his leader had no choice but to ditch in the sea, Finucane's last radio transmission being 'This is it, chaps'. Spitfire BM308 then gently alighted on the waves – but instead of momentarily remaining afloat, giving the pilot time to exit the aircraft, the shamrock emblazoned aircraft plunged vertically into the depths. Aikman circled the spot, directing ASR launches to the spot, but only an oil slick marked the grave of the great Paddy Finucane.

The Spitfire was actually most vulnerable to ground fire, the coolant system beneath the engine protected only by thin aluminium sheet – easily punctured by a single rifle-calibre bullet. And a single, lucky, round was all it took to hole the system, meaning that with an overheating engine the aircraft was only going in one direction – down. Indeed, another great ace, Flight Lieutenant Eric Lock DSO DFC had already been lost in almost identical circumstances the previous year. This latest loss of Wing Commander Finucane was another tragedy and a futile waste of life – his log book poignantly endorsed 'A most gallant and able officer'; he had accumulated 548.20 hours on Spitfires, 304.30 of which were operational.

The free world mourned 'Spitfire Paddy' – who was still only 21. Three thousand people crowded into Winchester Cathedral for his Requiem Mass, and in his adoptive Richmond, the mayor launched an appeal for a 'Finucane Memorial'; the Finucane family received a plethora of sympathetic messages, including telegrams from officers of air rank and even two Soviet aces. Although the war continued for another three years, Finucane's name remained fifth on the list of the RAF's top-scoring aces.

Wing Commander Brendan E.F. 'Paddy' Finucane DSO, DFC & two Bars remains missing to this day. Remembered on the Runnymede Memorial, sadly Paddy Finucane never got to audit books in Australia.

Sergeant D. Foulger

Sergeant Dennis Foulger first flew R6644 on 30 March 1941, shortly after arriving on 65 Squadron fresh from 7 OTU. He flew this Spitfire fourteen times, more than any other pilot, all training sorties, but little of him is known. Indeed, to squadron mates he was 'Reg', but in the 65 Squadron ORB Sergeant D. Foulger is reported as having arrived at Kirton, together with Sergeant H. Baxter, on 12 March 1940.

65 'EAST INDIA' SQUADRON

On 15 April 1941, 65 Squadron flew to operate from Wittering and carry out an offensive sweep with 266 and 402 Squadrons. The route taken was via Dungeness, around Boulogne, returning via Hornchurch and Dover, with 402 Squadron at 20,000 feet, 65 at 22,000 feet, and 266 at 24,000 feet. There was no aerial opposition or AA fire seen over France, but as the 12 Group Wing headed towards Dover, Flying Officer Brendan Finucane heard an R/T warning by another pilot of Me 109s behind. Turning into the sun, Finucane saw Sergeant Hewlett being stalked by a Me 109, at which Finucane opened fire, claiming that the enemy fighter 'went into a steep dive, straight into the sea'. Elsewhere, Sergeant Lowson observed a 109 attacking Sergeant Foulger, but

Sergeant Dennis 'Reg' Foulger – about whom so little is known.

before he could attack it the enemy fighter broke away. Foulger's Spitfire, P8179, was damaged by cannon fire in the fuselage and tailplane, the engine and undercarriage also being damaged when the pilot crash-landed at Hawkinge.

That particular day was the birthday of *Generalmajor* Theo Osterkamp, the *Jafü* of *Luftflotte* 2, and that afternoon *Major* Adolf Galland, *Kommodore* of JG 26, left Wissant for Le Touquet in his Me 109F with *Oberleutnant* Hans-Jürgen Westphal flying Rottenhund, the purpose of the sortie being to deliver champagne and lobster to 'Oncle Theo'. Galland, however, was unable to resist sweeping the Channel, and ambushed the Wittering Wing, shooting down two Spitfires of 266 Squadron and, very likely, Sergeant Foulger being the third Spitfire the ace claimed 30km west of Dover. Foulger was lucky to escape with his life. Official records again contradict each other: the casualty file states that he was injured, the 65 Squadron combat report stating that he was not. That he was injured, however, appears more likely, given that Sergeant Foulger did not fly again for five days.

We know from the 65 Squadron ORB that Foulger remained with 65 Squadron for the rest of April and early May 1941, making his last recorded flight with the unit, a dusk patrol, on 3 May 1941. Thereafter, Foulger disappears from the record, with no further recorded flights or even a posting out of 65 Squadron. We do know that on 20 August 1944, having been commissioned, Flying Officer Foulger arrived at Peruglia, Italy, joining 92 Squadron and flying Spitfire Mk VIIIs on dangerous ground-attack sorties in support of the advancing Allied armies. It is understood that he remained with 92 until the war in Europe ended, and survived. According to one 65 Squadron survivor, Foulger came from Sussex and may have died in 1967 – and any further information welcome by this author.

On 2 April 1941, 308 'City of Krakow' Squadron, based at Baginton, near Coventry, in 12 Group, received orders to exchange its Hurricanes for Spitfires. The following day, Flying Officer Byszyinski and six mechanics left for RAF Northolt, returning with copious notes and translations on the workings of the Spitfire. On 4 April 1941, 308 Squadron's CO, Squadron Leader Jan Orzechowski, together with Flight Lieutenant Younghusband and Sergeant Muchowski, flew to Kirton-in-Lindsey and collected three of 65 Squadron's Mk IAs. Three more Spitfires were collected the next day, and on 6 April 1941 the Polish pilots familiarised themselves with the Spitfire in the air, which they considered 'very manoeuvrable and lighter to handle than the Hurricane'. [ORB] On 10 April 1941, R6644 was collected by an unknown Polish pilot and flown to Baginton, the aircraft's association with the 'East India' Squadron now over.

Between 26 February 1941 and 10 April 1941, nine young men had flown R6644: four would be killed in action, the remains of three of them never found, and three would be captured – statistics well illustrating the uncertainties faced by wartime fighter pilots.

The Polish connection now added a whole new dimension to the story.

Chapter Five

308 'City of Krakow' (Polish) Squadron

The Krakow fighter squadron of the Polish Air Force was formed in 1929, consisting of two flights, or 'Eskadry' in Polish, 121 and 122, each equipped with twelve aircraft, based at Rokowice, near the city of Krakow. Upon formation, the unit operated Spad biplanes, re-equipping during the early 1930s with Czech made Avia BH33s. In 1933, came the Polish P.7 fighter, replaced three years later by the P.11c, a high-winged monoplane powered by a radial engine but with an open cockpit, fixed undercarriage and a fixed-pitch airscrew. At that time, a third flight, 123, was also formed. Between the wars, the Krakow Squadron trained and participated in numerous rallies and practice camps at home and abroad, Flight Lieutenant Bajan's trio of aerobatic pilots becoming legendary, not least in 1934, when Bajan won the International Challenge Cup against strong German entries. Peace, though, was not to last.

On the night of 31 August 1939, Nazi Germany invaded Poland in an undeclared act of war. Simultaneously, German troops crossed the frontier along its entire length, attacking guards and forward defensive positions. At dawn, the *Luftwaffe* bombed

The winged arrow crest of 308 'City of Krakow' Squadron.

aerodromes and major strategic assets throughout Poland. In spite of all the diplomatic unrest that summer, the German attack achieved complete surprise.

31 August 1939, was, however, the first day of mobilisation in Poland, reservists reporting to their units and operational squadrons dispersing to various airfields. Few, though, believed that war would actually break out, the reservists expecting little but an inconveniently long stay with the colours ahead of them. The Poles trusted that Britain and France would honour its pledge to support Poland in the event of Nazi aggression, and mistakenly believed that would be sufficient to deter *Herr* Hitler. Many expected the Soviets to side with the Western Allies, unaware of the secret Non-Aggression Pact signed by the foreign ministers of Germany and Russia on 23 August. On that day, Poland's fate was sealed. Although at 1100 hrs on Sunday. 3 September 1939, Britain and France declared war on Nazi Germany following Hitler ignoring their ultimatum to withdraw from Poland, in reality the Western powers were not geographically positioned to provide military support. In real terms, therefore, Poland was on her own.

Sixty-three German divisions attacked Poland, facing fifty-six Polish. The German attack was spearheaded by fifteen mechanised *panzer* divisions, whereas the Poles only fielded two motorised formations (although, what is perhaps not widely appreciated is that the German army remained largely horse-drawn throughout the war). Indeed, the enemy's superiority of arms was considered 8:1. Moreover, the German *Wehrmacht* was a modern force, equipped and armed to current standards, whereas Poland went to war with the equipment of 1925. Importantly, Germany's diplomatic successes of 1938 and 1939 had secured strategic advantages in that Poland's northern frontier and most of the southern was controlled by Germany, and the attack was made simultaneously from north, south, east and west. Offensives on both flanks and steady pressure in the centre provided for envelopment. Nonetheless, by the campaign's ninth day, German losses were such that it was clear that the Poles' determined fighting spirit had been overlooked – a factor emphasised by the propaganda machine preparing German public opinion for news of heavy casualties. This fighting spirit, in fact, would define the Polish contribution to the Allied cause throughout the hard-fought Second World War.

In 1939, Poland, even more than Britain and France, was ill-prepared for a war in which air power played a crucial role. The immense capital investment required to create and maintain a modern air force was quite simply beyond the means of a newly independent country. The technical inferiority of its air force made Poland vulnerable – but the bravery of her aircrews was beyond doubt. The first German aircraft to be destroyed during the Second World War were two Do 17s shot down over Olkusz by Lieutenant Wladyslaw Gnys of 131 Flight, the Krakow Squadron's three Flights, 121, 122 and 123, fighting over the southern front, losing its CO, Flight Lieutenant Wiorkiewski, killed in action, and the famous Flight Lieutenant Bajan seriously wounded, never re-gaining use of an arm; over Warsaw, Lieutenant Felix Szyska was shot down and baled out, but badly wounded when fired upon by German soldiers during his descent; Lieutenant Styanislaw Skalski, of The Torun Squadron's 142 Flight, attacked a Hs 126 reconnaissance machine, which was ultimately shot down by Lieutenant Marian Pisarek of 141 Flight – the gallant Skalski, however, landed alongside the downed German, giving first aid to both wounded crew members before arranging their admission to a military hospital.

The Pursuit Brigade's Henryk Szczesny became the PAF's top-scorer by the campaign's conclusion, with ten victories, by which time the Krakow Squadron's 121 and 123 Flights had recorded nine aerial victories, 122 Flight ten; in total the Polish fighter pilots claimed the destruction of 126 enemy aircraft during the campaign. The Polish fighter squadrons, including the Fighter Brigade and Army Co-operation units, lost fifty pilots and 114 aircraft, whilst the bomber force suffered 90% casualties in aircrew and aircraft. With the end result of Germany's invasion being obvious, on 5 September 1939, the PAF devised a plan to evacuate the service flying training schools, experimental establishments and workshops, and by 14 September 1939, losses were such that the Polish Air Force was unable to continue operations. Some squadrons lost their last aircraft on that day, others, threatened with being overrun, destroyed their remaining machines. On 17 September 1939, fittingly in a violent thunderstorm, the few remaining Polish aircraft crossed the Romanian border, ending the air fighting over Poland. On the same day, in another undeclared act of war, Russia invaded eastern Poland.

On 1 October 1939, German troops entered Warsaw. Six says later, Polish resistance finally ceased – although the Polish Home Army would continue fighting a partisan war until the Germans were finally defeated five years later. From a Polish viewpoint the short, tragic, campaign was a consequence of unpreparedness, the outcome, against ruthless and efficient violence, inevitable. Nonetheless, Poland's defiant spirit, refusing to surrender without a fight, no matter what the odds, set a benchmark of courage that would resonate throughout the Second World War. It is important to understand the Polish character, fundamental to which is a powerful sense of duty and love of country; for 500 years, Poland fought two or three defensive wars every generation. Poles know full-well, therefore, that material possessions, even the family home, can be lost – instantly. Anything that the enemy can use must be destroyed, so therefore not valued highly. Polish soil, though, cannot be destroyed, and neither can national solidarity. Consequently, the Polish nation has survived even when forced into exile. It is this long history of suffering and its profound effect on the Polish psyche which, more than anything, explains why, when Poland had fallen, the Polish Armed Forces trekked west, determined to continue the fight. It also explains why, when the call was made for the PAF to reassemble in France and later Britain, only the dead, those who were prisoners or ordered to remain in Poland, did not respond – for others, not continuing the fight and ultimately liberating Poland was unthinkable.

On 25 October 1939, British, Polish and French delegates met at the French Air Ministry. The Poles argued that their air force should be re-formed in Britain, given their familiarity with British aero-engines but ignorance of French equipment. The French countered that the Poles should be equally divided between Britain and France, believing that Polish squadrons could be quickly formed and would be welcome reinforcements on both sides of the Channel. Finally, it was decided that 300 Polish aircrew and 2,000 ground staff would be stationed in Britain, the rest in France. Crossing into such neighbouring and neutral states as Romania,

Hungary, Latvia and Lithuania, the Poles were at first interned, so this now meant that a mass evacuation of Polish personnel had to be organised. In Rumania, where the majority of air force personnel were interned, officers and 'other ranks' were immediately segregated. Unsurprisingly, Romania was unprepared for this influx of personnel, and things were chaotic. Interned there was a certain Bolesław Henryk Drobinski, a fighter pilot, who obtained a pass to visit the local dentist, upon production of which to the Romanian guard, the Pole was told that the pass was for three men, Bolesław, Henryk and Drobinski, so where were the other two? Thinking quickly, Drobinski grabbed two of his comrades, the threesome setting off on a long trek through clearing depots and internment camps, ultimately reaching England to fly with the RAF. When the news was received that General Wladyslaw Sikorski had joined the Polish government in exile and taken command of Polish forces in France, many more Polish airmen staged individual escapes, the majority travelling by sea via Constanza, Beirut, Malta and Marseilles.

In France, Lyon became the main collecting area, and from March 1940, Polish pilots began joining French squadrons. Unfortunately, as in Poland, after Hitler's surprise attack on the West of 10 May 1940, the Poles once more fought back with obsolete aircraft, this time with inadequate French aircraft. Again, the outcome of the campaign was never in doubt, and by 3 June 1940, the BEF had been evacuated from Dunkirk, France surrendering formally on 22 June 1940. Thereafter the Poles made for England, on occasion having to use force against the French to effect their evacuation: ships were requisitioned at gunpoint and sailed first to Gibraltar; some pilots flew their French machines to southern England, including both Stanisław Wielgus and Witold Retinger, who landed on the south coast in their French Potez bomber. Other Polish airmen crossed the Channel in boats. Indeed, no means of escape was overlooked by the Poles in their determination to continue the fight. Lieutenant Stanisław Wandzilak, for example, led a party of forty mechanics to the French coast, seizing transport by force and eventually reaching England by sea – upon reformation of the PAF in Britain, Wandzilak was praised for his 'coolness and initiative'. Throughout the summer of 1940, in fact, until as late as

October 1940, Polish airmen continued to arrive in England – here they were most welcome reinforcements indeed.

Blackpool became the central clearing depot for the free Poles, who now found themselves in another foreign country having to learn another unfamiliar language. Given the chaos of the time, and language barrier, things understandably took time to get organised. Eventually, though, two Polish fighter squadrons were formed: 302 'Poznań' Squadron on 10 July 1940, the same day as 310 (Czech) Squadron, and on 2 August 1940, 303 'Tadeusz Kościuszko Warsaw' Squadron followed all three foreign squadrons, due to the ongoing language difficulties, operated a 'double-banking' system, whereby RAF officers occupied the senior positions of command, shadowed by their Polish and Czechoslovak counterparts. All three of these first foreign squadrons were equipped with Hurricanes, 302 and 310 Squadrons being based at Duxford and participating in 12 Group 'Big Wing' operations, whilst 303 Squadron went to Northolt in 11 Group. In addition to the language difficulties, the Poles, however, had no experience of flying the RAF's new, modern, monoplane fighters, so time for this conversion also had to be factored in before they could be made operational. Because of these issues, Air Chief Marshal Dowding was initially cautious about committing these squadrons to battle, but all three fought valiantly in the Battle of Britain, 303 Squadron, declared operational on 30 August 1940, ultimately emerging as the conflict's highest claiming fighter squadron. Other Polish pilots, with a good grasp of English, were posted to RAF fighter squadrons from August 1940, serving alongside men from Britain and its Commonwealth, and other free foreign nationals, including French, Belgian and Dutch airmen. Indeed, as Dowding later acknowledged, without the Poles in particular, who formed the largest number of free foreign airmen, the Battle's outcome could have been very different.

On 12 September 1940, 308 'City of Krakow' Squadron was formed at Speke, under the command of Flight Lieutenant Stefan Laskiewicz, whose first pilots were Flight Lieutenant Mieczlaw Wiorkiewicz and Pilot Officers Stanisław Wielgus, Feliz Szsyka, Ryszard Koczor, Wladyslaw Chciuk and Wladyslaw Bozek, with Sergeant-Pilots Wladyslaw Majchzk, Mieczlaw Parafinski, Ernest Watolski and Pawel Kowala.

308 'CITY OF KRAKOW' (POLISH) SQUADRON

The Poles of 308 Squadron around the 'Baginton Oak', a well-known local landmark near their airfield and inn of the same name. Amongst them are Pilot Officers Felix Szyszka (in forage cap behind Flight Lieutenant Jasionowski (holding the dog); Pilot Officer Stanisław Wandzilak (extreme right, front row), and Flying Officer Stanisław Wielgus (extreme left, back row), and Sergeant Tadeuz Hegenbarth (in forage cap, behind and between the two officers wearing service caps).

17 September 1940, saw 308 Squadron receive its first aircraft, Fairey Battle JP6687, in which the pilots practised 'circuits and bumps'. As personnel continued arriving, on 27 September 1940, the Squadron moved to Baginton, near Coventry, setting up HQ in the large Oak public house, adjacent to the huge Baginton oak tree landmark. Then, 308's new Hurricanes began arriving. Based in the West Midlands, by day the Poles were able to continue their training largely unmolested by the *Luftwaffe*, the intention being that 308 Squadron would provide protection to both the nearby industrial city and the Armstrong Whitworth factory on Baginton airfield, producing the Whitley bomber. The RAF CO was Squadron Leader J.A. Davies, supported by Flight Lieutenants J.G. Younghusband and Young, although on 29 September 1940, command was formally passed

The Poles have gone but Baginton's timeless oak remains.

The 'Oak' Inn at Baginton, where 308 Squadron set up its unofficial HQ.

to the Polish Flight Lieutenant Mieczlaw Wiorkiewicz. The British pilots remained with the Squadron, however, although sadly Davies was killed, striking a balloon cable, on 16 October 1940. Interestingly, the following day 'Pilot Officer Thomas was posted as Adjutant' [ORB]: this was, in fact, Forest Frederick Edward Yeo-Thomas, later to find fame as a daring Special Operations Executive agent in enemy occupied France – codenamed 'The White Rabbit' (whose story was serialised for television in 1967 with Kenneth More playing Yeo-Thomas).

After the defeat of the German daylight bomber offensive by 30 September 1940, the enemy switched to night attacks, less accurate but the trade-off being able to largely operate with impunity as Britain's night defences were so inadequate. That autumn the terrible night Blitz on British cities began – and on the night of 14 November 1940, 515 German bombers battered Coventry during Operation *Moonlight Sonata*, an attack lasting from 2000 hrs to 0600 hrs. Intended to devastate the city's manufacturing area, the target was marked by the radio-beam-guided *Pfadfinders* of *Kampfgruppe* 100, as the bombers flew shuttle runs to and from their bases in France. Great damage was caused, not least to the city centre, which suffered destruction of two-thirds of its buildings, including Coventry Cathedral, and 4,300 civilian properties. A third of the city's factories were destroyed, and many damaged, over 500 people were killed. That terrible night, 308 Squadron's personnel took to the shelters, but the Duty Officer, Pilot Officer Zbysznski and other airmen extinguished incendiaries and helped out where possible. Three Poles approached what they thought was an airman descending by parachute, only to be killed when what was actually a parachute mine exploded – all three, AC1 Franciszek Krzeminski, and AC2s Josef Jurkowski and Edward Cebula, were killed. In the morning, some of 308 Squadron's ground staff marched to the aerodrome, 'through streets laden with debris and houses on fire all around' [ORB]. So terrible was the raid, in fact, that a new word entered the English language: 'Coventration'.

Inevitably, after such a raid, German reconnaissance bombers were active during daylight, obtaining photographic evidence of the devastation. On 20 November 1940, the three Polish airmen killed that terrible night were buried at Baginton's St John the Baptist churchyard – and as personnel left,

A formal 308 Squadron function at Leamington Spa's Clarendon Hotel, 1941.

one of these bombers passed overhead, escaping because the alarm was raised too late. The following three days, repeat performances followed – all of which changed on 24 November 1940. That day, *Leutnant* Herbert Hollstein (navigator and aircraft captain), *Feldwebel* Helmut Schwingshakl (pilot), *Unteroffizier* Gustav Koch (flight engineer) and *Gefreiter* Hans Gran (air gunner), of 3/(F)/123 based at Paris-Buc were briefed at 0800 hrs to photograph Coventry. The Ju 88 flew from Buc to Brest, where the aircraft was re-fuelled before pressing on towards England at 24,000 feet. Across the Channel, that morning a Wing Commander Oliver, a 12 Group staff officer, visited Baginton to check on the Poles' training. In the afternoon, Oliver joined Pilot Officer Grudzinski and Sergeant Mieczlaw Parafinski on a battle climb practice flight – which would prove fateful for the 3/F/123 Ju 88 crew.

At 1530 hrs, Wing Commander Oliver noticed a condensation trail over Coventry, and climbed the Hurricanes to investigate. At 20,000 feet over the city, the 'bogey' was seen to be wither a friendly Blenheim or a Ju 88, which were very similar in appearance. Reaching 26,000 feet, the Hurricane pilots pursued the aircraft north for five minutes, after which it turned south in a shallow dive. Using maximum boost, the Hurricanes followed, Parafinski overtaking his leader and identifying the machine as a Ju 88. The Pole delivered a quarter attack whilst Oliver fired from long-range before blacking out whilst turning sharply in an attempt to get on the enemy's tail. When the Wing Commander recovered, he saw the Ju 88 some distance to the south, still under attack by Parafinski. Eventually, the bomber's starboard engine was set alight, enabling Oliver to close within 50 yards and watch the fuselage erupt into flame as the bomber went in at high speed. The pursuit had taken the fighters south-east across Warwickshire and into Gloucestershire, the Ju 88 crashing at Coates Manor, near Cirencester, killing its crew: Parafinski had recorded 308 Squadron's first kill, adding this to the He 111 he destroyed over Warsaw on 1 September 1939. That night a party ensued at the Baginton Oak, and in recognition of his achievement, Sergeant Parafinski received the Squadron's first Cross of Valour. Sadly, during another battle climb exercise, on 26 February 1941, Parafinski was killed when his Hurricane crashed at Cottesbrook, Northamptonshire; oxygen system failure was believed to be responsible. On 1 December 1940, a week after Parafinski's Coates Manor success, 308 Squadron was declared operational.

By the spring of 1941, more Polish fighter squadrons had been formed, and with administration now better

The grave of Sergeant Mieczylaw Parafinski in Baginton churchyard, who claimed 308 Squadron's first victory but later killed in a flying accident.

organised it was arranged for Polish pilots who had served to date in RAF squadrons, to be posted to Polish fighter squadrons. On 13 March 1941, Pilot Officer Franciszek Surma arrived, followed by Pilot Officer Jerzy Poplawski four days later. On 29 March 1941, Flight Lieutenant Marian Pisarek arrived from 315 Squadron, becoming a flight commander on 308 – decorated with the Virtuti Militari and Cross of Valour, Pisarek had claimed two victories over Poland, and four more enemy aircraft destroyed over England, and others damaged, whilst flying with 303 Squadron from Northolt. All three new pilots were veterans of the Battle of Britain – and of whom much more later.

As previously related, 308 Squadron was ordered to re-equip with Spitfires on 2 April 1941, the aircraft chosen being the old Mk IAs currently being flown by 65 Squadron at Kirton. As of the following day, the Poles began collecting the Spitfires, R6644 arriving on 10 April 1941. Five days later, Pilot Officer Stanisław Wielgus and Sergeant Muchowski scrambled, thus making 308 Squadron's first operational Spitfire flights. Over the next few days, 308 Squadron operated a mixture of Hurricanes and Spitfires, until 18 April 1941 when conversion to the Spitfire was complete. In the Baginton hangar, R6644 was prepared for flight, receiving its new fuselage code of ZF-H, and, very likely, both the red and white chequered square of the PAF and 308 Squadron's winged arrow crest. The Spitfire would not make its first known flight with the Poles, however, until 6 May 1941.

Pilot Officer Stanisław Wielgus

During the spring of 1941, 308 Squadron's pilots flew in sections of two, often patrolling the Leamington Spa area of Warwickshire and, further afield, the Kidderminster area of Worcestershire. At 1525 hrs on 6 May 1941, Pilot Officer Wielgus scrambled in R6644 on a patrol taking him 40 miles from Baginton. With him was Pilot Officer Franciszek Surma, in X4477; the section returned to Baginton at 1555 hrs after an uneventful sortie. It would be the only flight Wielgus would make in ZF-H.

Born the eldest son of a carpenter-farmer in Miedzierza, Konecki, Poland, on 17 November 1912, Wielgus was older than most of his contemporaries. Educated at Kawęczyn and Konskich, he developed at interest in aviation modelling and history, was a keen athlete and became a scout. Obliged to undertake military training, Wielgus first joined an infantry regiment before requesting a transfer to the PAF. In 1937, he successfully completed pilot training at Dęblin and was commissioned, joining the Krakow Squadron as a second lieutenant. Between 23 September 1938–10 October 1938 he flew special operations with the Silesia Group, receiving praise from General Wladyslaw Bortnowski. That year,

Flying Officer Stanisław Wielgus.

Wielgus became a gliding instructor, and the following year qualified as a physical education instructor. The outbreak of war found him serving with the Krakow Squadron's 122 Flight, serving as a liaison officer. He also flew the RWD-8 aircraft operationally, reconnoitring airfields and delivering fuel to various flying units. On 11 September 1939, he arranged the delivery of three petrol tankers to Chelm by the railway service, and the following night flew to neutralise an agent signalling to German aircraft – for which feat he later received the Virtuti Militari, Poland's highest award for gallantry.

On 17 September 1939, 122 Flight left Poland for Chernivtsi, Wielgus eventually reaching France via Beirut and Marseilles, signing in at the collecting point in Lyon. Between 26 May 1940 and 17 June 1940, he served with the French at Chateauroux aerodrome, then flying with Witold Retinger to Tangmere, via Bordeaux and Nantes. On 12 September 1940, having been commissioned into the RAFVR, Pilot Officer Wielgus joined the newly formed 308 Squadron at Speke. He then went with the Squadron to Baginton, making numerous Hurricane and Spitfire flights, before going south with the Squadron in June 1941.

We will learn more of Wielgus' exploits in Part Two.

A SPITFIRE'S STORY: THE INVISIBLE THREAD

Pilot Officer Jerzy Poplawski

On the evening of 7 May 1941, Pilot Officer Jerzy Poplawski practised dusk landings in R6644 for twenty-five minutes – although unrecorded by the 308 Squadron Form 541, this sortie is documented in his log book, which also confirmed the Spitfire's individual code letter as 'H'; it was his only flight in ZF-H. Poplawski also flew R6644 on 10 May 1941, to patrol base, returning safely at 1245 hrs after an uneventful twenty-five minutes.

Born in Hodel, Poland, on 1 October 1919, and known informally as 'Jurek', Poplawski achieved his early ambition to become a pilot and, according to his flying log book, became a cadet at the 'Officers' Flying School, Dęblin 1937', passing out with a commission in 1939. Initially, he was posted to a light-bomber squadron, flying PZL 23 'Karas', but before he could fly operational sorties after the German invasion on 1 September 1939, Poplawski was evacuated to Romania. From there, he and comrades travelled to France, arriving in Marseilles on 29 October 1939, then made their way to England, landing on 27 January 1940:

> I was first stationed at RAF Eastchurch when I arrived in England from France, and the first town in knew was Sheerness. In the future, every time I flew over Sheerness and Eastchurch I couldn't help thinking of those first days in England and the happiness I found after escaping from Poland following the German invasion.

At Eastchurch, Poplawski was commissioned as a pilot officer in the RAFVR, spending June and July 1940 at the Elementary Flying Training School, Carlisle. On 12 August 1940, Pilot Officer Poplawski was sent to the Army School of Cooperation at Old Sarum for evaluation, where he was selected for fighters. Consequently, on the same day, Poplawski reported to 5 OTU, Aston Down, for conversion to Hurricanes. On that day, he was checked out by Flying Officer Martindale in the Tiger Moth, in which type he spent the rest of that week flying various solo training flights.

308 'CITY OF KRAKOW' (POLISH) SQUADRON

Pilot Officer Jerzy Poplawski (left) with an unknown fellow 308 Squadron pilot at Baginton in March 1941. The Hurricane's nose art appears to be an African warrior's shield and weapons with the legend 'Rhodesia'.

A SPITFIRE'S STORY: THE INVISIBLE THREAD

On 20 August 1940, Pilot Officer Maloney flew dual with Pilot Officer Poplawski in a Harvard, and after a number of 'Circuits and landings' in both that type and a Miles Master, Pilot Officer Poplawski first flew a Hurricane on 25 August 1940. On 5 September 1940, his operational training was considered complete, during which he had flown 18.15 hours on Hurricanes. His Flight Commander, Flight Lieutenant Prosser Hanks DFC (see Chapter Two) assessed the young Pole's performance as 'average'. Next stop was 111 Squadron at Drem, in Scotland. Having already been heavily engaged in the Battle of Britain, flying from Croydon and Debden, 111 had been sent north to re-build and re-fit, there to receive replacement pilots and provide them further training. On 13 September 1940, Jurek made his first flight with 'Treble One', a formation practice sortie, after which days were spent on such training exercises as dogfighting, aerobatics and air firing. On 21 September 1940, Pilot Officer Poplawski qualified for the Battle of Britain Clasp to the 1939–1945 Star when he scrambled with 111 Squadron to intercept an unidentified radar plot. The sortie was uneventful – but having flown an operational sortie between 10 July 1940 and 31 October 1940, the Pole was now one of the Few. On 26 September 1940, having accumulated more experience on Hurricanes, Pilot Officer Poplawski was posted to 229, at Northolt, on the outskirts of north-west London, in 11 Group's frontline:

> I spent most of my Battle of Britain time with 229 Squadron, commanded by Squadron Leader Freddy Rosier, who later retired as a most distinguished and senior air marshal. I knew him and his wife very well. Although I did not shoot anything down during the Battle of Britain, I did fire at several enemy aircraft. I think that I was so excited that I trembled too much and as a result my aim was not good!

Pilot Officer Poplawski's first operational flight with 229 Squadron's 'B' Flight was a patrol from Northolt on 2 October 1940. Thereafter, he was a regular member of 229 Squadron's operational line-up, flying patrols daily. On 6 November 1940, 229 Squadron took off at 1430 hrs to patrol the Croydon Line at 15,000 feet. The Hurricanes were vectored to Kenley and Horsham where they encountered 10/10ths cloud reaching from 2,000–24,000 feet. Blue Section became separated from the rest of the squadron in the bad visibility, Sergeant Frank Twitchett landing at Hatfield, where an undercarriage leg buckled upon touch-down; Pilot Officer Poplawski, however, was missing. No news was received of his status for some time – then, with relief, it was learned that he had forced-landed at Streatley, west of Hitchin, having run out of fuel. And so, with the worsening winter weather, the patrols went on, every day, until on 15 November 1940, 229 Squadron flew to Wittering in 12 Group, there to rest for a week. On 22 November 1940, the Hurricanes flew to another new base, Speke, there to provide some protection to Liverpool and Manchester, and from where endless convoy patrols were flown over the Irish Sea. Poplawski would make his last patrol with 229 Squadron on 7 March 1941, after which he travelled to Baginton, there to join 308 Squadron:

> When I was posted to 308 (Polish) Squadron, I found some friends of my own age or thereabouts, but most of them were already experienced pilots in Poland, and that had to be respected. As I remember, at first, I used to fly on the wing of my Flight Commander, but I don't recall his name now. This was really the start of my active war, in action against the enemy, because the Battle of Britain itself had been quiet for me.

Amongst those new friends, was Pilot Officer Franciszek 'Franek' Surma, as Jurek explained in that first letter:

> Franek Surma was a good friend of mine, a bit shy when you talked to him. Perhaps we were all a bit quiet, trying not to think of tomorrow. It would be wrong to say that we had no fear. After all, we were human beings and as such we all knew what fear was. But we also had a code of how we conducted our lives, a sense of duty, that made us control our fear. And that fact was perhaps the most important in our lives. We both talked about it a lot.

General Sikorski with pilots of 315 (Polish) Squadron at Ballyhalbert, County Down, on 14 August 1943 – Squadron Leader Poplawski was commanding (standing, centre). After the war, he emigrated to Argentina, settling in Buenos Aires, where he died, aged 84, on 21 June 2004.

> We had a mascot, a black 'Scotty' dog which was particularly attached to Franek Surma, and vice-versa. Another friend of 'Scotty's' was a pigeon, who used to follow wherever the dog went. When 'Scotty' stopped and rested, the pigeon either stood next to her or just simply stood on her back. This little story is perhaps important background minutia because Franek liked 'Scotty' very much and the dog responded to him more than anyone else.

Pilot Officer Poplawski would also go south with 308 Squadron in June 1941 – as will be related in Part Two.

Sergeant Tadeuz Hegenbarth

Sergeant Hegenbarth first flew R6644 on 8 May 1941, scrambling at 1410 hrs with Pilot Officer Bozek (R6980) to patrol Kidderminster, landing at 1505 hrs after an uneventful sortie.

Tadeuz Ryszard Hegenbarth – informally known as 'Tadek' – was born on 29 December 1917 at Recklinghausen, Germany. Known to have been a pilot and 'Kapral' (sergeant) in the pre-war PAF, it is known that he was in Salon, France, on 20 May 1940, and Clermont on 7 June 1940. After arriving in England, he was at the Blackpool depot, where he was made a sergeant in the RAFVR and posted to 308 Squadron at Speke.

Again, Sergeant Hegenbarth would go south with 308 Squadron in June 1941, and we will hear more of his exploits in Part Two.

Sergeant Tadeusz Hegenbarth.

Pilot Officer Franciszek Surma

At 1520 hrs on Sunday, 11 May 1940, Pilot Officer Surma scrambled from Baginton in R6644, with Sergeant Stanisław Widlarz (R6894), to patrol Kidderminster at 27,000 feet. It would be the last flight R6644 would ever make…

Pilot Officer Franciszek Surma pictured at Baginton, spring 1941.

Chapter Six

The Crash

Over Worcestershire's world-famous Malvern Hills, the inspiration for Sir Edward Elgar's rousing *Land of Hope and Glory*, the R6644's engine suddenly burst into flame. Oil then covered the windscreen, whilst smoke billowed into the tiny cockpit. Although standing orders dictated that a wheels-up forced-landing should be made, unable to see, owing to the oil and voluminous smoke, Pilot Officer Surma turned the aircraft away from the built-up area below and baled out above open fields.

Unsurprisingly, the high drama over the sleepy Worcestershire beauty spot that Sunday lunchtime attracted great interest.

Schoolboy Harry Cleaton:

> I was walking along the main Worcester Road in Malvern, between Great Malvern and Link Top on the Malvern Hills. I had just reached the leathercraft factory and sat down on a low stone wall to admire the view. I could see a Spitfire over Malvern Link, flying towards Worcester, but it was trailing a thin plume of black smoke and losing height rapidly. This was an astonishing sight, and then the pilot baled out! I ran all the way to North Malvern Police Station, in Newtown Road, but when I arrived, breathless, the local bobby, PC Jack Calder, was just leaving on his push bike to find the crash site.

Mr Davies, Malvern's Chief Air Raid Warden, was walking his dog along Pickersleigh Road when R6644 passed over him, trailing smoke. He ran to the nearest house, No. 9, and called Malvern Police Station, giving the

THE CRASH

Station Officer a running commentary of events until the aircraft disappeared from his view.

Schoolboy Jimmy Thomas:

> We had been playing an early season game of cricket on Malvern Link Common and were walking home when we saw the Spitfire. When the pilot baled out we just couldn't believe it! The Spitfire pitched down vertically, and we reckoned that both plane and pilot would make landfall in the Madresfield area. We immediately jumped on our push bikes and pedaled [*sic*] off furiously in that direction!

Bill Pritchard, a 21-year-old milkman working for Bennett's Dairy of Worcester:

> I was driving my milk truck down Jennet Tree Lane, which leads from Malvern Link to Callow End and knew nothing of the crashing Spitfire until there was an explosion in the field to my right, near the junction of Jennet Tree and Hawthorn Lanes. Naturally I was absolutely startled and stopped immediately. Good job I did, as a length of aluminium 3 feet long hit the road directly in front of me; had I still been driving it would have gone straight through my windscreen! I realised then that it was an aircraft and not a bomb that had caused the explosion, so I climbed over a newly laid hedge and hurried to the crash site, although I realised that if the pilot was still in the plane he would be beyond any help. As I made across the field I was puzzled by someone shouting at me, but looking around there was no-one else on the scene but me. Then I looked up and saw the pilot coming down on his parachute, shouting at me to keep away from the burning wreckage because of dangerous exploding ammunition. The parachutist drifted over me, towards the cottage at the junction of the two lanes, so I returned to my truck, picked up the piece of aircraft in the road and took it home as a souvenir.

A SPITFIRE'S STORY: THE INVISIBLE THREAD

R6644 had impacted in a field behind a row of council houses on Jennet Tree Lane; Charlie Knight was only four at the time, but vividly recalled that it was the first time he had seen both a parachute and fire engine.

Inside the nearby cottage on the junction of Jennet Tree and Hawthorn Lanes, Mrs Probert was having lunch with her daughter, Vi, who was enjoying

Above: The cottage at the junction of Hawthorn and Jennet Tree Lanes, Madresfield, in which Land Girl Vi Farrant was having a tea break when Pilot Officer Surma landed by parachute in the adjacent field.

Left: Land Army: Vi Farrant.

THE CRASH

a rare weekend off from her work in the Land Army, and two evacuees; Vi remembered that:

> We were startled by the explosion and all four of us dashed outside to investigate. We could see a pall of smoke rising and assumed a stray bomb to be the cause. As we turned around to go back inside we were amazed to suddenly see a parachute disappearing over the back of our cottage! We ran into the adjacent field and watched an airman land before gathering up his parachute. Our instinct was to go to him and help, but then we had second thoughts as he could have been a German! I can't remember what was said between us but I do recall that he had a foreign accent which sounded a bit German.

Having collected up and removed his parachute, Pilot Officer Surma walked across the lane and looked at the wreckage of his Spitfire, which was burning fiercely in a small crater whilst other debris was scattered on the surface over a wide area. By now literally hundreds of people were arriving, by various modes of transport, from the directions of both Malvern and Callow End. Local lad Neville Grizzell had just enough time to give the pilot a Woodbine before the Pole was ushered away by a doctor and PC Calder. Hurrying to the scene along Hawthorn Lane were a group of airmen from a nearby

Men of the Hawthorn Lane searchlight site.

A SPITFIRE'S STORY: THE INVISIBLE THREAD

The crash site of Spitfire R6644, near the tree, in a field on the south side of Jennet Tree Lane, owned by the Madresfield Estate.

Looking towards the crash site, which is beyond the hedge and in the next field, from behind the Surma Memorial, close to where the pilot landed by parachute.

THE CRASH

searchlight site, who took charge of the situation and confirmed Surma's identity.

The area was farmed by the Page family, who took the pilot to their Bosworth Farm where he was made most welcome until transport arrived to return him to Baginton. At the crash site, the searchlight airmen and local police then had to fend off souvenir hunters. Young air cadet Ken Davies, son of the Chief Air Raid Warden, was rapidly on the scene managing to purloin a much-coveted piece of Spitfire wreckage. Young Harry Cleaton was not so fortunate, though, as en route his push bike suffered a puncture, meaning that he could not get to the crash site until the following day. By then the site was so well guarded, the recovery team being on site, that the schoolboy was unable to acquire a souvenir. These events, however, would remain indelibly etched upon the memories of all who had witnessed the drama take place.

So ended the 'life' of Spitfire Mk IA R6644, just one of some 22,000 Spitfires produced, with a total of 266.10 flying hours. 118 flights

A SPITFIRE'S STORY: THE INVISIBLE THREAD

Above left and above right: In 1941, the area was farmed by the Page family of Bosworth Farm – where these photographs were taken whilst Pilot Officer Surma awaited transport back to Baginton. The originals were given to the author by Jake Page on the day the crash-site was located in 1987.

have been identified, for a total of 94.35 hours – the substantial number of outstanding and untraceable hours having largely been flown at 5 OTU and by 616 Squadron. Twenty-seven pilots have been identified as having flown R6644, ten of which did not survive the war, and five of whom became prisoners of war – statistics indicating the uncertainty of life for a fighter pilot.

PART TWO

Chapter Seven

Flying Officer Franciszek Surma VM KW

Franciszek Surma – known as 'Franek' – was born on 1 July 1916, at Rybnik, in the Galkowicz district of Poland. His parents, Franciszek and Tekla Surma were peasant farmers and also had three daughters, all of whom were older than Franek and doted on the baby boy in their family. A clever child, Franek won a scholarship to attend the grammar school at Galkowicz, of which the family was justly proud; a model son, even after long days of study, Franek would always help out on the farm. In 1928, he continued his education in Żory, and at that time decided to become a pilot. Eight years later he enlisted

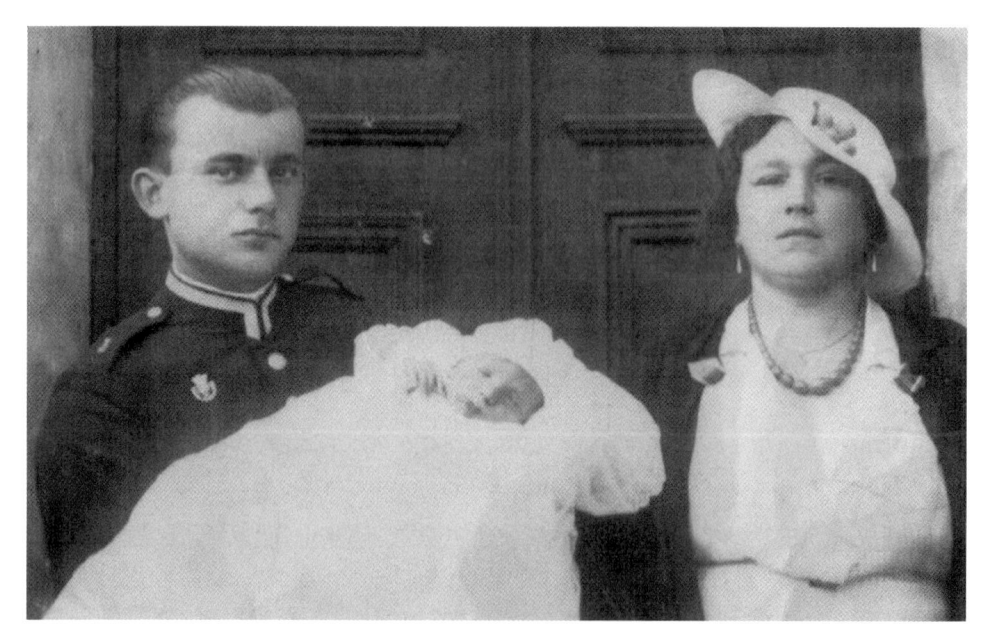

Officer Cadet Surma at a family christening in Poland before the war.

in the PAF and volunteered for aircrew training. According to his personal file, Franek Surma was passed as category 'A' fit for duty, and considered 'very physically fit and an excellent mathematician'.

Every Polish service pilot also had to complete basic infantry training, so although Cadet Surma was on the strength of the Air Force Officer Cadet Training School in Dęblin, he completed his infantry experience with 4 Company of the Polish Cadet School. That over, Franek started *ab initio* flying training in April 1939, when a Cadet Staff Sergeant. In July 1939, Officer Cadet Surma received his 'wings', a silver eagle clutching a laurel wreath, and his file recording that he was 'well above the average both physically and intellectually. He shows initiative and enthusiasm, and is an example to his comrades to whom he displays maximum loyalty'. Posted to the Krakow Squadron, Surma flew the little P.IIc fighter: a dream had come true.

After the German invasion and collapse of Poland in September 1939, Franek Surma's route to England was via Romania, Syria and France. Initially billeted at 51 Pool, Eastchurch, his combat experience over Poland, and early grasp of English, marked him for immediate posting to 6 OTU at Sutton Bridge. There Pilot Officer Surma, as he now was, learned to fly the Hawker Hurricane. Having successfully concerted to that type, on 20 August 1940, with the Battle of Britain in full swing, Surma reported to North Weald, in 11 Group, to fly Hurricanes with 151 Squadron. The young Pole's first operational flight was five days later, when his flight was deployed to operate from the forward base at Rochford. Five days later he opened his account against the *Luftwaffe*, claiming a He 111 'probable' over the Thames Estuary. On 1 September 1940, 151 Squadron was rested, having suffered eleven pilots killed during the Battle of Britain to date, and flew north, to Digby. After a period of leave it was decided that the Squadron's two Poles, Pilot Officers Franek Surma and Jan Orzechowski, being fresh to the fray, should return south and report to 607 'County of Durham' Squadron, based at Tangmere.

No. 607 Squadron was an auxiliary unit and, having also fought in France, had suffered heavy casualties since returning to the combat zone a few days previously. Having joined 607 on 10 September 1940, Surma made his first operational flight from Tangmere four days later. The Squadron was making up to six operational sorties a day at this busy time, and on 17 September

A SPITFIRE'S STORY: THE INVISIBLE THREAD

Pilot Officer Surma at readiness, 607 Squadron, Tangmere, September 1940.

1940, Surma chased an Me 109 off Sergeant Lansdell's tail. Although the Pole managed several quick bursts, the enemy fighter made off into cloud. During that action Pilot Officer Harry Welford was shot down, possibly by *Hauptmann* Neumann of I/JG 27, but, although slightly wounded, he safely forced landed at Bethersden. Harry remembered 607 Squadron's Polish pilots:

> Jan Orzechowski was a short, stocky and rather serious man. He smoked cigarettes incessantly and used a cigarette holder. The Polish officers tried to strike a certain pose, I suppose, to keep up with us rather casual Britishers. They were extremely good pilots, but quite mad and totally fearless Surma, who was with me in 'B' Flight, was a bit more relaxed and met us halfway, probably because he spoke more English than the others.

On Thursday, 26 September 1940, the Germans heavily bombed Supermarine's Spitfire factory at Woolston, Southampton, the works having been targeted several times over recent days. On this occasion, KG 55's He 111s reached their target virtually unchallenged – and devastated it.

Combat ensued over the Isle of Wight, Portsmouth and at sea, 6–12 miles south of the Needles, between 1550 and 1630 hrs, 607 Squadron arriving on the scene just as the raiders started bombing. After an initial head-on charge, as usual the Squadron was split up and pilots thereafter fought independently. Some 20 miles out to sea, south of St Catherine's Point, Surma found a gaggle of Ju 88s at 15,000 feet:

> I saw a bomber break away from the enemy formation and tried to overtake him. At the same moment I saw an Me 109 gliding down above and behind the Ju 88s. I followed the enemy aircraft for a considerable distance and, when several miles south of St Catherine's Point I made two or three long bursts from 100–150 yards on the tail of the enemy aircraft, which immediately went into a dive and crashed into the sea.

The gutted Supermarine factory after the devastating raid of 26 September 1940 – on which day Pilot Officer Surma destroyed an escorting Me 109 off St Catherine's Point.

A SPITFIRE'S STORY: THE INVISIBLE THREAD

Harry Welford:

I do recall an amusing anecdote concerning Franek Surma and the events of 26 September 1940. We had a very intrepid and garrulous fighter pilot in Jim Bazin's 'B' Flight called 'Chatty' Bowen, who seemed to enjoy continued success in combat. Franek envied Chatty's success and wished that he could borrow some of his luck. Chatty was known to carry a stuffed toy elephant as a mascot, and Franek pleaded with and cajoled Chatty into lending it to him for a sortie. After much argument and persuasion from other members of the Flight. Chatty agreed to lend Franek the mascot to fly with, but only on a sortie he was not flying himself. Franek was instructed to return the mascot to Bowen's Hurricane the moment he landed. Later, Surma returned jubilant as he had destroyed a 109, and as promised he returned the mascot to his rigger, who replaced it in the cockpit of Bowen's Hurricane. Chatty, however, just couldn't find the mascot on his next trip and cursed Surma for not returning it. On that sortie Chatty was shot down and it was assumed that his change of luck was due to Surma not having returned the toy elephant. The twist to the tale is that when the salvage team recovered the wreck of Bowen's Hurricane from the Isle of Wight, they discovered the elephant in the cockpit; it was believed that the mascot had fallen from the gunsight and jammed the rudder pedals!

The time that Franek and I were together in 'B' Flight was extremely short, only six days, but the loss of life occurred so rapidly that the experiences of a lifetime could be crammed into less than even that short time. Franek was the sort of chap who was immediately popular and when we had a beer in the evening he would teach us how to say '*Nostravia!*', which means 'Good health' in Polish. He impressed me. The story about the mascot I probably got second hand off a Squadron chum whilst I was in Ashford hospital, as the incident occurred after I was shot down,

FLYING OFFICER FRANCISZEK SURMA VM KW

but the story is certainly true to the characters of both Chatty and Franek. Before I was wounded Franek was trying to borrow the mascot, and used to infuriate Chatty – who was, after all, a senior pilot whilst Surma was very junior – beyond all reason by calling him his 'Lovelee boy'!

On 11 October 1940, 607 Squadron was rested, having also lost eleven pilots killed that summer. A week later, Pilot Officer Surma was posted to another 11 Group RAF fighter squadron, 46, at Stapleford. He arrived on 18 October 1940, along with several other replacement pilots, but three days later was posted to 257 Squadron at North Weald. During the early stages of the Battle of Britain, that squadron had flown from Northolt but suffered heavy casualties. This led to a change in command, the charismatic Squadron Leader Robert Stanford-Tuck regenerating the Squadron.

On 28 October 1940, Surma engaged a He 111 in an inconclusive combat over Romney and Folkestone. The enemy bomber was credited as

Pilot Officer Surma being taught the game of 'pax' by his flight commander on 607 Squadron at Tangmere, Flight Lieutenant Charles 'Chatty' Bowen – who is wearing a highly prized German *schwimmveste*.

a 'probable', but the following day Pilot Officer Surma was not so lucky: that afternoon the Me 109 fighter bombers of II/LG 2 attacked North Weald at low level, supported by JG 26 Me 109 fighters. Flight Lieutenant Peter Brothers was at tea in the officers' mess when the raiders struck: 'We all dived under the table! My car, an open 3-litre Bentley, was parked outside and I was livid to find that a near miss bomb had filled it with soil, which took forever to clean out!'

As the raid came in, twelve Hurricanes were actually taking off. Sergeant Girdwood's aircraft left the ground but slapped back down by a bomb blast; the pilot was burned to death. Flight Lieutenant Blatchford got up safely and engaged, but was hit by a 109 and forced to crash land. The 257 Squadron Intelligence Officer, Flying Officer Geoffrey Myers, described what happened to Pilot Officer Surma:

> Red 2, Pilot Officer Surma, saw the bombs falling as he was taxying over the aerodrome. A bomb exploded on his left-hand side as his aircraft was running up. The explosion jerked him, but he took off satisfactorily. He noticed four enemy aircraft flying over our hangar between 4–5,000 feet, and also saw many planes on his right, which he took to be Hurricanes.
>
> When he climbed to about 3,000 feet he heard an explosion in his cockpit, which filled with white smoke. His plane went into a spiral dive, he no longer had control so opened the Perspex. After a moment the Hurricane came out of its dive and leveled out, but soon began diving to starboard. After trying to bring it out of this second dive without success, he attempted to bale out. By this time he had lost height to 1,500 feet. After struggling to get out of the cockpit he baled out at about 1,000 feet and made a safe parachute descent, landing in a tree top near an inn at Matching. After quickly convincing the Home Guard that he was Polish and not German, he was given two whiskies and driven back to the aerodrome. He had lost both of his flying boots when jumping out of the plane, received a black eye but was otherwise unharmed.

FLYING OFFICER FRANCISZEK SURMA VM KW

No evidence can be found confirming Larry Forester's claim in his Stanford-Tuck biography *Fly For Your Life* that a group of French soldiers nearly lynched Surma after his parachute landing, on account of the confusion caused by his accent and because the Pole was allegedly wearing a German leather flying jacket supposedly seized from an enemy bomber he had destroyed in Poland (this was, in fact, put to Wing Commander Stanford-Tuck in 1987, who avoided answering the question…).

What is certain is that Pilot Officer Surma had been shot down by *Hauptmann* Gerhard Schöpfel, *Kommandeur* of III/JG 26 – and fortunately lived to tell the tale.

Three days later, Surma was flying again, November 1940 continuing with more convoy patrols from Martlesham Heath. December 1940 saw little activity, the weather unsuitable for much flying. On 6 December 1940, Sergeant Bennet's Hurricane was tipped on its nose by high winds whilst taxiing, and Surma, in V7052, stalled on approach to Clacton, landing in a

Hauptmann Gerhard Schöpfel, *Kommandeur* of III/JG 26, who shot down Pilot Officer Surma on 29 October 1940 – coincidentally also responsible for shooting down another pilot of R6644, namely Flying Officer Casson, on 9 August 1941.

field short of the runway. The verdict was that the Pole had misjudged the wind strength, which was over 40 mph.

On 16 December 1940, Pilot Officer Surma was posted to 242 Squadron, flying Hurricanes again, at Martlesham. Commanded by the legless Squadron Leader Douglas Bader, 242 Squadron had been central to the Duxford Wing's operations during the Battle of Britain, and its swashbuckling CO similarly central to the controversy arising. During the winter of 1940/41, 242 was providing aerial cover for coastal convoys off the east coast, Surma flying seventeen such patrols. Of the young Polish fighter pilot, Squadron Leader Bader reported that he was 'A very competent fighter pilot who understands English well on the R/T'.

On 14 March 1941, Pilot Officer Surma took his leave of 242 Squadron to join 308 'City of Krakow' Squadron, equipped with rather old Hurricanes at Baginton, near Coventry. Joining him would be others of the Polish Few, including Flight Lieutenant Marian Pisarek and Pilot Officer Jerzy 'Jurek' Poplawski. Many years later, Squadron Leader Poplawski wrote to me from his home in Argentina:

> Franek Surma and I were close friends. We were both veterans of the Battle of Britain, although he was a much more distinguished pilot than me, and we were of a similar age. He was a rather deep person, perhaps even a little reserved. Perhaps we were all like that, trying not to think of tomorrow. It would be wrong to say that we were not afraid, after all we were just ordinary human beings, and as such we all knew what fear was. But we also had an unwritten code of conduct in our lives, a sense of duty that helped us control our fear. That code was possibly the most important influence on our lives. Franek and I discussed it a lot.

Because the night Blitz was reaching its zenith, enemy reconnaissance aircraft were regularly active over the Midlands during daylight hours. At 1125 hrs on Wednesday, 26 March 1941, Pilot Officer Surma led Pilot Officer Bozek and Sergeant Kremski off from Baginton to intercept one such intruder. The Ju 88 was sighted over Leamington and attacked, the German pilot immediately jettisoning his bombs. Much to the delight of 308 Squadron, the combat progressed until it was over the airfield at 3,000 feet, but the raider somehow escaped, albeit trailing smoke. The Poles were credited with a third of a probable each.

As we have seen, 308 Squadron converted to Spitfires in April 1941, and on 11 May 1941, Pilot Officer Surma baled out of R6644 near Malvern due to an engine fire – which brings the reader up to date with his personal story, enabling our return to the Poles at Baginton.

The Polish Virtuti Militari and Cross of Valour gallantry awards, both of which were awarded to Flying Officer Surma.

Chapter Eight

308 'City of Krakow' Squadron and the Non-Stop Offensive

On 1 June 1941, 308 Squadron moved south, to RAF Chilbolton, a 10 Group airfield in Hampshire and the Middle Wallop satellite. There the Poles exchanged their Spitfire Mk Is and IIs for Mk Vs, and undertook gun firing practice at Chesil Beach with 118 Squadron. On 24 June 1941, 308 Squadron moved again, this time to RAF Northolt, the home of No. 1 Polish Fighter Wing. Flying from Northolt the squadron provided cover to convoys off

A Spitfire of 308 Squadron returns safely to RAF Northolt in 1941.

Portland Bill, Swanage and Bournemouth, but, more importantly, Northolt was within striking distance of enemy occupied France; it was in that direction that the Polish Wing would be engaged.

From November 1940 onwards, the Germans had continued daylight fighter and fighter-bomber sweeps, which had been employed during the Battle of Britain's final phase. These incursions ceased in mid-December 1940, resuming on a reduced scale in February 1941. In the meantime, lone Ju 88s continued their *Störflug* operations, harassing attacks on the British aircraft industry, using cloud cover to safely reach and withdraw from their targets. Although the main aerial battle was being fought after dark, clearly Fighter Command remained under pressure to defend Britain in daylight – and the dreadful night attacks were perceived by Fighter Command's new chief, Air Marshal Sholto Douglas, to be 'a softening up… for an invasion of Britain in the spring of 1941'. Although the crisis of summer 1940 had passed, the spectre of a seaborne invasion, therefore, remained a constant shadow.

Before Douglas left the Air Ministry to take up his new appointment at Fighter Command, he met with Air Chief Marshal Charles 'Peter' Portal, the Chief of the Air Staff, to discuss the future of day fighting. Portal had recently been visited by the service's first CAS, the so-called 'Father of the RAF', Lord 'Boom' Trenchard, who, before the Second World War, had been a confirmed 'Bomber Baron', thinking so little of fighters that he considered them 'necessary only to keep up the morale of one's own people'. Now, though, the former CAS insisted that the fighters' time had come, and, the Battle of Britain won, it was time for Fighter Command to go over to the offensive and 'lean towards France', advocating sweeps across the Channel similar to tactics used over the Western Front during the First World War. At first, Douglas was unconvinced, pointing out that those operations were costly, and that cross-Channel operations were likely to be 'too severe for the results that we would be likely to achieve'. Nonetheless, Portal instructed to Douglas to produce a report on the matter, which he did, writing 'a very full appreciation with the object of proving that a policy of offensive patrols over northern France was not a good one'. Afterwards, however, Douglas had a re-think, concluding that his 'arguments were pretty feeble', and that they actually supported the prospect that 'an offensive policy for fighters against the German air force in northern France was the right one'. Consequently, Douglas had to inform Portal that he had changed his tune, and was, after all, 'in favour of Trenchard's idea'. Nonetheless, Douglas knew that caution would have to be exercised, and that his fighters must not 'just go belting over there looking for trouble'. On 21 October 1940, the Air Staff then formally directed Fighter Command to prepare for these offensive fighter operations. So it was that soon, Douglas's young pilots would start 'carrying the war to the enemy'.

On 20 December 1940, Flight Lieutenant Christie and Pilot Officer Bodie of 66 Squadron crossed the Channel at low-level and strafed the enemy airfield at either Berck or Le Touquet. This 'Mosquito' raid set the scene, in fact, for the New Year ahead.

On Christmas Day 1940, Air Marshal Douglas held a conference of squadron commanders at Fighter Command HQ, Bentley Priory, at which the new 'Non-Stop Offensive' was outlined:

> Broadly speaking the plan, which we now adopted, visualized two kinds of offensive operations. In cloudy weather, small numbers of fighters would cross the Channel under cover of the clouds, dart out of them to attack any German aircraft they could find, and return similarly protected. In good weather fighter forces amounting to several squadrons at a time, and sometimes accompanied by bombers, would sweep over Northern France. The codenames chosen for these operations were respectively 'Mosquito' (later changed to 'Rhubarb' to avoid confusion with the aircraft of that name) and 'Circus'; but in practice it was necessary to restrict the name 'Circus' to operations with bombers, and fulfilling certain other conditions…
>
> Rhubarb patrols began on 20 December 1940, and provided valuable experience alike for pilots, operational commanders, and the staffs of the formations concerned. I encouraged the delegation of responsibility for the planning of these patrols to lower formations, and many patrols were planned by the pilots themselves with the help of their Squadron Intelligence Officers.

It was obvious from the start that in many cases pilots engaged on these patrols would not meet any German aircraft, and that being so they were authorised to attack ground targets. Douglas, though, nonetheless emphasised that the primary objective was the destruction of enemy aircraft.

On 27 December 1940, Air Vice-Marshal Keith Park was replaced as AOC-in-C 11 Group, covering London and the south-east, by 'Big Wing' protagonist, Air Vice-Marshal Sir Trafford Leigh-Mallory, formerly AOC 12 Group. Leigh-Mallory summed up the new offensive outlook: 'We have stopped licking our wounds. We are now going over to the offensive. Last year the fighting was desperate. Now we're entitled to be cocky'.

Operations of a large scale began on 9 January 1941, when five RAF squadrons – sixty fighters – swept uneventfully over France. At the time, Wing Commander David Cox was an RAFVR sergeant-pilot in 19 Squadron, and remembered that: 'When only fighters appeared the Germans were content to stay on the ground and let Fighter Command waste fuel. To provoke the enemy, Blenheim bombers (of 2 Group, Bomber Command) joined the Offensive, and later even four-engined Stirlings. This resulted in quite a sharp reaction from the German fighters.'

These operations' component fighter squadrons deployed thus:

> Close Escort: Surrounding and remaining with the bombers at all times.
>
> Escort Cover: Protecting the Close Escort fighters.
>
> High Cover: Preventing enemy fighters getting between the Close and Escort wings.
>
> Target Support: Independently routed fighters flying directly to and covering the target area.
>
> Withdrawal Cover: Fighters supporting the return flight, by which time escorting fighters would be running short of fuel and ammunition.
>
> Fighter Diversion: A wing, or even wings, eventually, creating a diversionary sweep to keep hostile aircraft from the target area

during 'Ramrod' operations, this being similar to a Circus but involving the destruction of a specific target.

During the Battle of Britain, Group Captain A.B. 'Woody' Woodhall had been Station Commander and Duxford's 'Boss Controller', who wholeheartedly supported the 'Big Wing' concept and was a personal friend of both Air Vice-Marshal Leigh-Mallory and Squadron Leader Douglas Bader. In his memoir, *Soldier, Sailor, Airman Too*, he wrote that these mass fighter formations of 1941 were: 'a formidable force, and some wag christened it the "Beehive", because the sedate bomber formation, flying in perfect formation and surrounded by a weaving mass of faster Spitfires, looked just like a swarm of bees circling their parent hive – and so "Beehive" became its code name'.

On 10 January 1941, Circus No. 1 was despatched against ammunition supplies hidden in the Forêt de Guines. Blenheims of 114 Squadron were closely escorted by the Hurricanes of 56 Squadron, forward support being provided by the North Weald Hurricane squadrons: 242 and 249. 302 Squadron's Hurricanes and 610 Squadron's Spitfires flew target support; the Spitfires of 41, 64 and 611 Squadrons were high cover, and finally 74 and 92 Squadrons' Spitfires brought up the rear. This represented some 120 fighters and six bombers, and was a complete reversal of the defensive role previously undertaken by Fighter Command – and one for which Hurricanes and Spitfires, intended as short-range interceptors, were not designed or intended. It was Fighter Command's pilots who now faced a two-way Channel crossing on a single engine with limited fuel, and combat either over the sea or enemy-occupied territory. On this initial operation, I and II/JG 53 responded and engaged the RAF fighters: one Hurricane and a Spitfire were destroyed for no German loss – rather setting the scene for the 'season' ahead.

Circus No. 2 went ahead on 2 February 1941, with Blenheims of 139 Squadron targeting Boulogne docks. And so it went on – relentlessly, during the 'season' of 1941.

On 27 June 1941, 308 Squadron flew its first sweep over France, during which Pilot Officers Surma and Szyszka shared the destruction of an Me 109

No. 1 Polish Fighter Wing forming up over Northolt for yet another offensive operation over France in 1941.

whilst strafing the *Luftwaffe* airfield at St Omer. Unfortunately, on that day, one of mass Rhubarbs, the Poles lost their recently appointed Wing Leader, Wing Commander Piotr Laguna, shot down by ground fire whilst strafing an airfield near Calais. It was a busy time, the Poles in action daily, either sweeping over north-west France or escorting bombers in these complex Circus operations.

On 28 June 1941, 308 Squadron provided medium escort cover to bombers attacking Lille – during which sortie, at 0845 hrs over Hazebrouck, Pilot Officer Wielgus claimed one Me 109 destroyed:

> On the return journey from the target on Circus 26, my Section was flying at 5,000 feet when we saw four Me 109Fs flying about 500 feet below us and preparing to attack a Hurricane. I dived on one enemy aircraft from astern and gave it one short burst from machine-guns, as a result of which flames poured out of the engine. This stopped, so I gave it another burst when it dived down steeply, broke out in flames and dived down towards the ground.

A SPITFIRE'S STORY: THE INVISIBLE THREAD

Sergeant W. Majchryzyk also claimed a 109 destroyed at the same time and location, these being 308 Squadron's first combat claims since joining No. 1 Polish Fighter Wing.

On 2 July 1941, Pilot Officer Surma flew Spitfire P8387, on a bomber escort sortie between 1140 hrs and 1335 hrs:

> Bad atmospheric conditions. Consequently, no reinforcements met at rendezvous over France. Squadron left alone with 303 in big fight. Flight Lieutenant Kawsik and Sergeant Kowala are missing. Pilot Officer Kudrewicz wounded, machine riddled. Squadron Leader Pisarek, after being chased over the Channel by Jerries, lands at Manston with machine riddled. [ORB]

Above left: Pilot Officer Bruno Kudrewicz – who survived the war and emigrated to New Zealand.

Above right: Pilot Officer Wladyslaw Bozek, one of 308 Squadron's original pilots when formed at Speke.

308 'CITY OF KRAKOW' SQUADRON AND THE NON-STOP OFFENSIVE

109s destroyed were claimed by Pisarek, now commanding 308 Squadron, Pilot Officer Kudrewicz, Pilot Officer Bozek and Sergeants Widlarz and Zielinski, the latter and Kudrewicz also claiming a probable each. Flight Lieutenant Kawsik, however, was killed, and Sergeant Kowala was captured.

Such offensive sorties continued on a daily basis, weather permitting. On 12 July 1941, 308 Squadron provided high cover to bombers attacking Hazebrouck marshalling yards, Pilot Officer Syszka and Sergeant Zielinski claiming Me 109s – but Flying Officer Wielgus, as he now was, was missing. The following day, amidst torrential rain and thunder, his body was picked up off Dover; one of the original members of 308 Squadron and a pilot of R6644, Stanisław Wielgus was buried at Northwood on 17 July 1941.

The evening of 17 July 1941, saw 308 Squadron on another sweep – but alone, 306 Squadron having been sent on a different course. North of St Omer, 308 Squadron was attacked by sixty Me 109s, Squadron Leader Pisarek immediately ordering his pilots into a defensive circle, with weavers, and zig-zagged back to the coast. Owing to repeated enemy attacks by III/JG 26, defensive circles had to be reformed several times, but somehow the Poles kept together and fended the Germans off. Three 109s were claimed destroyed and two probables, but three 308 Squadron Spitfires, having taken off late and straggling behind the main formation, were missing: Pilot Officers Stefan Maciejowski, who captured, and Jan Syszka, who was killed; Sergeant Tadeusz Hegenbarth, another pilot of R6644, was never seen again.

Flying Officer Wielgus's grave at Northwood – note the unique shape of the Polish headstones.

A SPITFIRE'S STORY: THE INVISIBLE THREAD

Squadron Leader Marian Pisarek, 308 Squadron's highly respected commander – he would not survive the war.

The 308 Squadron diarist was critical in his summing up of the operation: 'Not understandable why the Squadron is sent over by itself just after a wing has been over and brought the Jerries out. Lucky that the whole Squadron was not wiped out.' [ORB]

22 July 1941 saw 308 Squadron sweeping Dunkirk, St Omer and Gravelines. Enemy aircraft were shot-up on the ground at St Omer and Guines airfields, and on the return flight Pilot Officer Surma destroyed a 109E, which he caught attacking a Spitfire between Guines and the French coast. The combat took place at just 200 feet, the Spitfire pilot clearly watching the 109 crash into the ground at 1350 hrs, near St Omer. The following day, 308 Squadron flew a lunchtime escort, on a similar sortie on 24 July 1941, Squadron Leader Pisarek and Pilot Officer Jakubowski collided over the target; although both pilots returned to Northolt safely, despite significant damage to their Spitfires.

Bad weather at the beginning of August 1941 saw a slight reduction in operations, although both Pilot Officer Stampel and Sergeant Bruzda were missing from a sweep over St Omer on 7 August 1941, 308 Squadron having been bounced by twenty Me 109s. Two days later, Northolt's Wing Leader, Wing Commander Rolski flew with 308 Squadron, sweeping from Dunkirk to Gravelines, claiming a Me 109 destroyed, as did Pilot Officer Retinger. On 14 August 1941, the whole Northolt Wing swept over the Pas-de-Calais, 308 Squadron flying at 22,000 feet. This time, it was III/JG 26 which came off worse, which 308 Squadron spotted climbing – and having the advantage of height and surprise, attacked the Germans with 315 Squadron, whilst 306 covered them from above. The Northolt Wing claimed fifteen Me 109s destroyed, four by 308 Squadron in addition to two probables. Only *Unteroffizier* Heinrich Holzenkämpfer was killed, and *Obergefreiter* Heinrich Wälter baled out wounded, in reality, the high overclaiming ratio indicating just how chaotic this combat was. As the combat travelled towards the coast, elements of I/JG 26 and JG 2 arrived on the scene, followed by 6/JG 26 in their new Fw 190s. The Germans claimed five Spitfires destroyed for no further loss – 306 Squadron suffered three pilots killed, whilst 308 lost Pilot Officer J.B. Kremski.

On 29 August 1941, Squadron Leader Pisarek led 308 Squadron as top cover on Circus 88 to Hazebrouck; over the coast, the Poles were attacked by 'Masses of Jerries', a running battle ensuing all the way to mid-Channel. Once more, Pisarek's skilful leadership kept his Spitfires together, although Pilot Officer J.R. Bechtner was shot down and killed.

During September 1941, the autumnal weather was poor, again curtailing operations. This month, 308 Squadron upgraded its Spitfire Mk IIs for the newer Mk VB, which boasted a more powerful Merlin engine and two 20mm Hispano cannon in addition to four .303 Browning machine guns – weapons that could either be fired together, or individually.

On the afternoon of 4 September 1941, 308 Squadron swept over France yet again, as Circus 93 targeted the Mazingarbe ammonia plant. At 1625 hrs, Pilot Officer Jurek Poplawski recorded his first combat success:

> The Squadron was approaching Fruges at 28,000 feet when eight or more Me 109Fs were sighted, flying below. Twelve more were seen above at about 32,000 feet. These attacked us and as one of them, after diving, began to climb, I turned to my left and made a head-on attack. I got within 50 yards and fired two bursts from both my cannon and machine-guns. I saw my bullets striking the cockpit area when the enemy aircraft turned onto its starboard wing and went into a vertical dive, which became a spin. I followed it down to 10,000 feet and saw it crash into a wood. Having become separated from the Squadron I returned to Northolt alone.

From that operation, Sergeant Kowalski failed to return; hit by flak, the Pole baled out over France and was captured.

A SPITFIRE'S STORY: THE INVISIBLE THREAD

On 16 September 1941, Flying Officer Surma, having been promoted, made his first flight in a Spitfire Mk VB, AB930, ZF-J. That day, 308 Squadron's 'A' Flight engaged thirty Me 109Fs over Gravelines, Surma, leading Red Section, claiming destroyed a 109 destroyed, confirmed by his wingman, which his wingman, Sergeant Warchal. Pilot Officer Poplawski claimed a victory in unusual circumstances:

> I saw one Me 109 passing on my starboard side and decided to chase him. As I did so I observed tracer bullets converging about 30 yards in front of me and, turning sharply to the right, saw one Me above, and I was attacked by another from the rear at the same time.
>
> I saw my Squadron in front of me but was unable to catch up with them. I lost height in a series of turns, keeping careful watch on my attackers. I flew low across the Channel, pursued by Me 109s, which kept me under fire. I continued taking evasive action and, when about 5 miles out to sea, the Me on my starboard side was about to attack. I saw tracer bullets emerging from the Me on my port side and turned towards the Me on my starboard side.
>
> I then throttled back and as soon as the Me had overshot, I pulled up and got above and dived towards him. Realising that as soon as he straightened out he would be in immediate range of my guns, he continued to dive and failed to pull out in time. The aircraft skidded into the sea and I saw half the fuselage and tail submerge. Meanwhile, the other Me had climbed and was circling over the first, but made no further attempt to attack me.
>
> No rounds fired!

On 20 September 1941, the Polish Wing flew as Escort Cover Wing on Circus 100, to Rouen. Over the target Flying Officer Surma and his wingman, Sergeant Jan Okroj, became separated. The latter was flying Surma's now usual Spitfire, AB930, and was attacked by three Me 109s. From long range, their cannon shells damaged his tail unit but somehow Okroj outran his

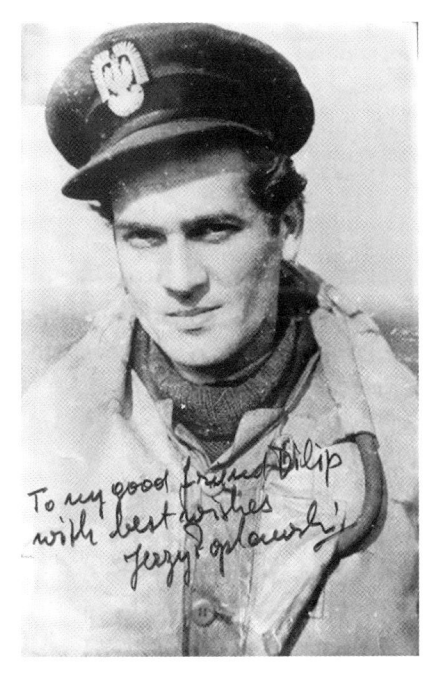

Above left: Pilot Officer Jurek Poplawski at Northolt in 1941.

Above right: Sergeant Jan Okroj.

assailants and forced-landed at Thorney Island. The Spitfire was so badly damaged, however, that it was sent to Heston Aircraft Ltd for repair.

During that sortie Flying Officer Surma destroyed two more 109s, almost certainly from JG 2, both of which crashed in flames:

> I was White 1, leading a section of four. As the bombers turned over the target our formation turned to starboard. I saw an Me 109F below and slightly ahead. I dived on him and got on his tail. The pilot saw me and climbed slightly. I closed to 20–30 yards and gave a long burst, after which pieces fell off the enemy aircraft in all directions, which then burst into flame. It turned over to starboard and plunged down in flames and smoke. I then saw tracer bullets on the port side of my cockpit. I turned to starboard and dived away, losing sight of my No. 2, Sergeant Okroj. I followed the formation, trying to re-join the

A SPITFIRE'S STORY: THE INVISIBLE THREAD

Above and below: Canon shell damage to the tail of Spitfire ZF-J, AB930, when being flown by Sergeant Okroj. Franek Surma would ultimately be reported missing in this machine.

nearest squadron. As I made progress in catching one of them up, I saw a yellow-nosed Me 109F climbing and trying to get into position to attack the bombers. I climbed, at the same time turning over and getting above and to his rear. As I attacked this Me, I saw another and went into a dive. I had a good turn of speed so I followed him quite easily, giving him a long burst at 6–7,000 feet, from 80 yards. The Me caught fire, I got closer and fired another burst from about 40 yards. More flames and clouds of smoke came out and the enemy aircraft spiraled down. Pilot Officer Zbiechowski also saw it going down.

Surma then engaged a third aircraft:

As I was too low to re-join the Squadron I flew low to the Channel. About 10 miles out to sea I caught sight of the bombers – they were on my starboard side. As it was quiet I managed to join a squadron on the port side, by which time I could see the English coast, and saw an Me 109F making off after attacking a Spitfire. Behind the Me were three Spitfires in line astern. I maneuvered to cut off the Me's escape but the Spitfires abandoned their quarry for some unknown reason. The enemy aircraft climbed and I tried to get on his starboard side and into the sun. At that moment the German turned to port and looked back, and-as I was at the same height he saw me. This Me had its undersurfaces painted in the same blue as our Spitfires, and the upper surfaces were camouflaged in green and brown, as our aircraft used to be, no doubt to confuse us.

The German pulled over on his back, I followed and got him below me. We started a dogfight but he kept on circling and made several attempts to reverse our positions. The Me was superior in engine power and climbed away very easily. My only possible tactics were to turn either to port or starboard to cut in on him. All this time the enemy aircraft was gaining height and attempting to shoot me down, but his ammunition was wasted as

A SPITFIRE'S STORY: THE INVISIBLE THREAD

I took care to keep out of his axis of fire. I was unable to fire at him as I was unable to get into a sufficiently favourable position to do so. As the position became a stalemate we both broke off at the same time.

German fighters, however, were not painted to resemble Allied aircraft. More likely, it was actually another Spitfire. Also, could that explain why the three Spitfires broke off their pursuit? Did the pilot Surma attacked realise that his assailant was another Spitfire, I wonder, or did he too assume this to be a 109? 'Friendly fire' was an understandable mistake in the heat of battle, especially at this time when the Me 109F was still a comparative newcomer to the action and was so dissimilar to its predecessor, the angular Me 109E, but more like the curvaceous Spitfire. Such a scenario of mistaken identity was not uncommon, even for experienced and successful fighter pilots.

Pilot Officer Kazek Budzik with his Polish wife, Helen, serving in the WAAF at 12 Group HQ. The couple stayed in England after the war, setting up home in Nottingham.

On this day, 308 Squadron received a new replacement pilot: Pilot Officer Kazimierz 'Kazek' Budzik, the son of an army officer murdered by the Russians when the Polish officer corps was slaughtered at Katyn:

> I have no doubt that during the early part of the war the Polish formations were superior to those used by the British squadrons who flew in tight vics of three, in which each pilot has to be constantly aware of his neighbour's position to avoid collision. In that kind of formation you just cannot concentrate on searching for the enemy. They also flew in line astern, watching each other's tails instead of searching the sky. I have seen Me 109s latch onto the end of one of these formations and shoot a couple of aircraft down before disappearing, the rest of the formation oblivious to what has happened. Our formation was loose, stepped up, and in line abreast, just like the Germans. You were far enough away from your neighbour not to have to worry about collisions and so could search for the enemy. Each Spitfire was stepped up according to the sun's position, each aircraft therefore covering the other. Again, just like the Germans, in combat our four aircraft broke into pairs. It was eventually adopted by the RAF who called it the 'Finger Four', the Germans of course called it the '*Schwärm*'. It was certainly the safest formation to be in.
>
> When I first commenced flying operationally I could fly a Spitfire – but flying and fighting in one is a very different matter. On my first trip with 308 Squadron I was detailed to fly as No. 2 to the CO, Squadron Leader Marian Pisarek. Someone said to me, 'Pisarek is the best there is. Go where he goes, do what he does, watch him like a hawk and you will be alright, you will come home.' I took that advice and on my first few trips I stuck to Pisarek's tail like glue, all the way to the target and back again. I was so intent on following him, though, that I saw virtually nothing of what was going on around me. The more experienced pilots could fly, fight and search the sky all at the same time, which is why they were so successful. The most successful pilots

were those who would hold their fire until they were so close to the enemy that they could not miss. My problem was always that I opened fire too early, I was just unable to keep calm enough for all this sneaking up behind people – I just wanted to let them have it immediately I saw them!

The Polish squadrons were sometimes criticised by the British for using Polish over the R/T in a dogfight. I think that this was a little unfair as we could not speak English all that well anyway. When you have a split second to warn a comrade of danger, instincts take over and you just do not have time to convert your thoughts from Polish to English.

It was strange going off to war for an hour or so, then coming back to clean and comfortable living conditions with good food in the Mess. It was strange being shot at one minute but being back in London the next, possibly having a drink in a pub just a short while after escorting bombers to a target in France. People have got the impression that we fighter pilots had it easy, but what they fail to consider is that we flew long tours of operational duty. That type of flying in those circumstances caused great stress but I do not think people generally appreciate that.

When I first went to Northolt in September 1941, I went to put my kit in a room. I was met by a pilot who told me not to use a particular bed, as all who had done so had been killed. I have thought about this a lot and am sure that this was Franek Surma.

On 27 September 1941, Flying Officer Surma probably destroyed a yellow-nosed Me 109F during a Circus to Amiens, and Poplawski destroyed another, which the latter reported as 'burning nicely as it crashed into a row of houses west of Amiens.' The 109, however, had previously riddled the Pole's Spitfire with bullets, damaging it so badly that Poplawski had to crash-land at Biggin Hill.

On Circus 107, which took place on 12 October 1941, the Northolt and Kenley Wings escorted bombers attacking St Omer, 308 Squadron flying as

308 'CITY OF KRAKOW' SQUADRON AND THE NON-STOP OFFENSIVE

A pilot of 308 Squadron prepares for a sortie – note the unusual location of the Polish Air Force chequered square, usually seen below the exhaust ports.

forward support at 24,000 feet. Flying Officer Surma, wingman to Squadron Leader Pisarek, reported that:

> I was leading the right hand four aircraft. Having been warned over the R/T that our aircraft had been engaged by 109s, we wheeled round, re-crossing the French coast south of Le Touquet. Over the Channel I saw two Me 109s flying far apart in line astern, as though following a combat. I took evasive action by flying into the sun and the Me's passed below, unaware of my presence. I dived on the tail of the second Me and fired three short bursts into its tail from above at 100–150 yards range. The leading Me took evasive action and dived out of sight. My victim turned over onto its back and I fired another burst from about 80 yards. Whilst it was in that position white smoke poured from the Me 109, which then went into a steep dive. Bright flames then came from the Me, which went into a steep dive. Bright flames then came from the 109 which was burning fiercely as it crashed into the sea.

The following day saw Pilot Officer Poplawski notch up 308 Squadron's fiftieth aerial victory when he destroyed a 109 between Mardyck and St Omer. Another important occasion occurred on 28 October 1941, when Flying Officer Surma was awarded Poland's coveted gallantry decoration, the Virtuti Militari, 5th Class. He was now an 'ace' fighter pilot, having destroyed five enemy aircraft, probably destroyed two more, and damaged another, plus a third share in a damaged Ju 88. In an impressive ceremony at RAF Northolt, the 25-year-old Pole received his medal from General Sikorski, the Polish Prime Minister in exile.

During the first week of November 1941, 308 Squadron flew on several Ramrod operations, supporting 'Hurribombers', and participated in a Polish Wing sweep to St Omer on 7 November 1941. With deteriorating winter weather, however, the air-fighting 'season' of 1941 was drawing to a close; the last Circus of the year was flown on 8 November 1941. Sadly, it would be a disaster for Fighter Command.

Chapter Nine

Circus 110: One of Our Spitfires is Missing...

Circus operations were complex, sometimes involving hundreds of aircraft. Having flown his first operational sortie with 308 Squadron on 12 October 1941, Flight Lieutenant Kazek Budzik, as he became, remembered that:

> When we were to fly an operation, the Squadron would be on stand-by: one hour, half an hour, and so on, until we would have a briefing with all of the pilots who would be taking part in the operation. This would include pilots from the whole wing, not just 308 Squadron. We would first of all be told what kind of

A Spitfire Mk VB under fire.

sortie we were to fly, whether it was a fighter sweep or a Circus, or whatever. At this time in the war, 1941, these operations were usually to escort a small number of bombers attacking a target in France, intended to provoke a reaction from German fighters and codenamed 'Circus'.

On the wall of the briefing room was a big map. This would show the formation's route to and from the target, and indicate rendezvous times. The Wing Commander (Operations) would then give us a briefing on the tactics to be used, identify the air leaders, and your individual position in the wing formation. Later on at Northolt the Wing Leader was Alexander Gabzewicz, a big, awe-inspiring, man who had destroyed a German bomber on the first day of the war in Poland; I never thought he was afraid of anything, but after the war I once told him how terrified I always was at briefings. He surprised me by saying that he was probably more scared than me but just couldn't show it!

After the briefing we would go to our Spitfires and start the cockpit checks, sign the Form 700, that sort of thing. When complete we would pause for a few moments and then start our engines, taxying forward into position for take-off. All the pilots would be watching the leader. When he moved forward we all followed him and took-off, not always together, sometimes in twos and threes, but always straight after each other and roughly in the formation in which we had been ordered to fly. Once airborne, we would do one circuit of the airfield, to make sure we had everyone together, and slot into our allotted positions. Then, we would head for the rendezvous with the bombers.

Sometimes, the German fighters, usually Me 109s, would harass the formation, known as the 'Beehive', because that's what it looked like, with swarms of fighters escorting just a few bombers, even before we crossed the English coast. At that stage there would only be a couple of them and they would be very high up, diving down as if to attack but pulling up at the last minute, just being a nuisance and trying to distract our pilots.

CIRCUS 110: ONE OF OUR SPITFIRES IS MISSING…

It would be later, over France, that we would encounter large formations of Me 109s. I also remember that we used to think the ones with yellow noses were particularly aggressive, as if from an elite unit.

Our targets were often Le Havre, Brest, Boulogne, Calais, Amiens and Lille. All of these targets were heavily defended by flak. As the formation approached the target you could see black puff-balls of smoke from exploding flak shells, getting bigger and bigger, and closer and closer, all the time. It also got thicker as more guns opened fire. From that distance the flak bursts looked like harmless smoke, but when you got near to it you could see a fire burst inside the smoke ball. The flak didn't really bother Spitfires at that time as we could fly fast and, as we were so manoeuvrable, we could fly above or around concentrations of flak. It certainly didn't bother me personally at that time, flying at relatively high altitude, but later on, attacking ground targets at low-level after D-Day, I was shot down by flak twice in a month.

The reason I describe the flak is because the bomber crews could not fly above and around it. The main concentration of flak was over the target when the bombers commenced their run. Therefore they had to fly straight and level through a murderous hail of fire. I cannot emphasise enough my respect for the bomber crews; they were extremely brave men, all of them: they could not deviate from their bombing run to save themselves, I want to make that point very clear.

Over the target, after the bombers had dropped their bombs, there was a little confusion as the formation tried to stay together and get out as quickly as possible. The flak would still be banging away as the bombers turned after their bombing runs. The close escort Spitfires squadron now had to remain with the bombers and protect them on the return journey across the Channel. Now the Me 109s would start repeatedly attacking the formation, all the way back to England. The top and medium cover squadrons would mix it with the Me 109s and soon a huge dogfight would develop as the formation withdrew. As a result, these squadrons would soon be scattered, the pilots often coming home in ones or twos. Only the close cover squadron would stay with the bombers, come what may.

Close cover escort would only leave the bombers when safely over the English coast and close to their base. We would then return to Northolt and be de-briefed by the intelligence officer. That is when we would file any combat claims or report any observations of interest.

Circus 110 took place on Saturday, 8 November 1941.

On that day, twelve Blenheims were despatched to attack the railway repair sheds at Lille, the bombers escorted by no less than eleven Spitfire squadrons. The Northolt Wing's Polish squadrons were detailed to fly top (308 Squadron) cover at 16,000 feet, medium (315) cover at 15,000 feet, and close (303) escort at 14,000 feet. Covering this Escort Wing was to be the Exeter Polish Wing, its squadrons flying at 17,000 feet, 18,000 feet and 20,000 feet. The Kenley Wing provided high cover, at 21,000 feet, 23,000 feet and 26,000 feet, whilst the 12 Group Wing provided rear support at 20,000 feet, 21,000 feet and 23,000 feet, along with the Biggin Hill Wing, flying at 24,000 feet, 25,000 feet and 28,000 feet. The escort force, therefore, comprised fifteen squadrons, a total of 180 Spitfires.

What could possibly go wrong?

Everything.

At 1105 hrs, the Polish Wing Leader, Wing Commander Tadeusz Rolski, led his wing off from Northolt, completing an orbit of the airfield before setting off to rendezvous with the bombers over Manston. No. 308 Squadron was first to arrive, and orbited. On cue, the two other Northolt squadrons, 303 and 315, arrived simultaneously with the bombers (although only six Blenheims were met, instead of the intended twelve) and all set course for France.

Unfortunately, whilst completing their turn, 308 Squadron had been blinded by the bright sun and lost sight of the 'beehive'. Wing Commander

Rolski could see that 308 was turning the wrong way, but was unable to communicate via R/T due to the essential requirement for silence at this early stage of the operation. Instead, the Wing Leader violently rocked his wings to attract attention, but to no avail. Eventually, Squadron Leader Pisarek, commanding 308 Squadron, had no option but to break radio silence and inform Ground Control that his Squadron had missed the rendezvous. 'Ops' then vectored Pisarek towards the bombers, and 308 Squadron forlornly set off in pursuit – but would never catch up. Northolt's 303 and 315 Squadrons, and the Exeter Polish Wing, were well ahead with the Blenheims, crossing the enemy coast east of Gravelines.

The build-up of RAF aircraft had not gone unnoticed by the Germans, however, and all but one Jafü 2's defending fighter unit were scrambled in good time. This large number of Me 109s and the new, deadly, Fw 190, was able to climb and position themselves down-sun, ready to pounce. The main RAF formation soon passed over Bethune before hitting the target and turning for home over Arras. Covering the bombers' withdrawal were five Spitfire squadrons; although these units were in their correct position whilst the bombers were outward bound, they were ahead of their prescribed co-ordinate on the return journey, throwing the bombers and escorting squadrons into confusion.

The Blenheim's passage over France had already attracted accurate flak, and after leaving the target eight Me 109s were spotted beneath the Allied formation. Although the Germans repeatedly attacked from below and behind, all of the Blenheims were brought home safely. RAF fighter pilots subsequently claimed four Me 109s and one Fw 190 destroyed, three 109s damaged and a 190 damaged.

No. 308 Squadron, however, unable to locate the main formation after missing the rendezvous, was instead vectored to patrol from Dunkirk to Calais, between 16,000 feet and 25,000 feet. Towards the end of their patrol time, when fuel was running low, the Squadron was jumped by a large force of I/JG 26 Me 109Fs. The Poles were immediately split up and, owing to the lack of fuel, obliged to disengage and head home. After losing their attackers, 308 Squadron's pilots, in ones and twos, found and joined the main formation, also homeward bound.

A SPITFIRE'S STORY: THE INVISIBLE THREAD

Back at Northolt, Pilot Officer Poplawski reported that at 1145 hrs, 'over the French coast':

> I went to the assistance of a Spitfire that was being attacked by an Me 109F. I got on the Me's tail and from 200 yards above I gave a short burst from my cannons. I saw an explosion in the starboard wing and the Me turned onto its side with the starboard wing down. I fired another burst from both my machine-guns and cannons. Volumes of black smoke appeared from the Me which started to dive down sideways. As four Me 109s were approaching to engage me, and were higher, I decided to join a formation of our aircraft in the distance.

Pilot Officer Poplawski damaged a Me 109F, which he believed was attacking Flying Officer Surma.

CIRCUS 110: ONE OF OUR SPITFIRES IS MISSING...

Pilot Officer Tadeusz Stabrowski reported that at the same time, 'Five miles north of French coast':

> I saw a Spitfire being attacked by an Me 109F and went to its assistance, engaging the enemy aircraft from above and astern. I gave it a burst of fire from both cannon and machine-gun at 300 yards. The Me wobbled badly and I knew that I had hit it. I followed up my attack and fired three more bursts. The Me quivered and wavered more and more, thick black smoke pouring from the underside of the fuselage. It dived towards the sea near the French coast. Being short of ammunition and petrol, and a long way from base. I could not chase the Me and so returned to England.

Pilot Officer Tadeuz Stabrowski damaged the same Me 109. Reported missing off Dieppe in 1943, more recently Stabrowski's remains were identified through DNA testing, having been buried as unknown in a French coastal cemetery.

The only German fighters lost against Circus 110 were two Fw 190s, the pilot of one of which was killed. Three more enemy aircraft were damaged in crash-landings, which could have been combat related and one of which may even have been the 109 clearly damaged by Poplawski and Stabrowski, who appear to have attacked the same enemy aircraft simultaneously but independently.

Fighter Command lost fourteen pilots on Circus 110, including three squadron commanders and a wing commander. Two Spitfires failed to return to Northolt: W3944, PK-A, flown by Squadron Leader W. Szczesznewski, commander of 315 Squadron, believed to have been hit in the fuel tank by flak, who was later reported as a prisoner, and, AB930, ZF-J, flown by Flying Officer Surma, who was posted 'Missing'. As happened so often, nobody knew what had happened to him, and the Squadron's diarist concluded that the day was 'very depressing'.

Circus 110 was to be the RAF's last full-scale operation of 1941, and was not a success. The Fighter Command Intelligence Report lamenting that 'errors on navigation and timing, accentuated by a high wind, led to the failure of an elaborately planned complex of operations. Fourteen pilots of Fighter Command lost in a single day'.

On 12 December 1941, the survivors of 308 Squadron were rested at last, after six months of continuous operations, and flew north to rest and re-fit at Woodvale.

But what fate had befallen Flying Officer Franek Surma?

In 1987, from his home in Buenos Aires, Squadron Leader Jurek Poplawski remembered that:

> The whole flight lasted an hour and fifty-five minutes. I believe that it was Franek's Spitfire being attacked by at least one 109. The German attack was both sudden and shocking in its ferocity. We tried to assist the Spitfire but I soon had a warning of 'Break left!' from Squadron Leader Pisarek, which I did. Apparently, there were even more 109s coming down to attack and so, as I was also short of fuel, I couldn't hang around. Therefore I did not see what ultimately happened to either Franek or the 109 that I had attacked.

CIRCUS 110: ONE OF OUR SPITFIRES IS MISSING...

> I also recall that there was another 109 between me and that which was shooting at the Spitfire, but that is really all I can remember of that action, which was fairly early on in my operational career. I flew throughout the war, and so much happened later, in Normandy and Germany, for example, that it is difficult to recall that fleeting moment in 1941 with any more clarity.

Sadly, Squadron Leader Pisarek was killed later in the war whilst leading the Polish Wing, but his wingman on Circus 110, Pilot Officer Kazek Budzik, remembered:

> Pisarek told me to stay close to him, which I did. As Pisarek shouted 'Break!' to Poplawski, then I must have been with him in the area that Surma was killed, but I must admit that as I was so inexperienced and concentrating so hard on staying with Pisarek that I didn't see much of what was going on around me. I do remember a 109 flashing across my windscreen and Pisarek yelling at me to fire. Of course Surma was an experienced pilot, an ace. I hardly knew him but I remember thinking at the time that he had been very unlucky to be killed like that.

Squadron Leader 'Gandy' Drobinski flew on Circus 110 with 303 Squadron: 'I knew Franek Surma from PAF days before the war and also remember him in the Mess at Northolt. He was a very good pilot. Circus 110 was a long sortie of nearly two hours, escorting bombers over France to Lille. For much of the flight we were over France and vulnerable to attacks from German fighters. Not everyone liked that particular target.'

On 16 November 1945, after the Second World War had ended, the Air Ministry received a letter from the British Red Cross Committee, which was in receipt of an enquiry from a Miss Jane Jones of Osterley, Middlesex, asking for information regarding Flying Officer Surma's fate, and details of his grave; unfortunately, nobody knew what had happened to the Polish ace, and as his remains and last resting place had not been found, there was nothing to tell Miss Jones. Like countless other lost souls, after the necessary lapse of time without news, Surma's death was presumed for official purposes and he remains missing.

Who, then, shot down Flying Officer Franek Surma? German combat records suggest that the enemy pilot responsible was *Hauptmann* Johannes Seifert, the 25-year-old *Kommandeur* of I/JG 26, who claimed a Spitfire NW of Dunkirk at 1305 hrs (continental time), but whether just over land or out to sea is unrecorded.

Could it be, perhaps, that Flying Officer Surma's remains were recovered but buried in France as 'Known unto God'?

None of the unknown airmen buried in cemeteries from Ostend to Dieppe are recorded as being Polish, however, and only one grave presents as a possibility: an unknown airman buried in Dunkirk Town Cemetery (Plot 2, Row 2, Grave 44), date of death 8 November 1941. Enticingly, Commonwealth War Graves Commission records state 'Body recovered from a Spitfire'. Exasperatingly, though, there was no other information available regarding the location of that crash, or details of the aircraft concerned, and nor has anything else been discovered in surviving French records. We know that 308 Squadron was attacked over the French coast at

Hautpmann Johannes Seifert, *Kommandeur* of I/JG 26, who may have shot down Flying Officer Surma on 8 November 1941.

CIRCUS 110: ONE OF OUR SPITFIRES IS MISSING...

Dunkirk on 8 November 1941, the natural assumption being that Flying Officer Surma crashed into the sea – but that is not certain. It would have been equally possible that his Spitfire crashed on land, close to the French coast. So, there is certainly a possibility that this unidentified burial could be Surma.

An examination of Fighter Command losses for the day in question indicates a total of five other Spitfire pilots missing, in addition to Surma. Two of them, pilots of 72 Squadron, can be discounted from this investigation, having been lost south of Le Touquet, so some distance south of Dunkirk. The remaining three squadrons are all from the 12 Group Digby Wing: that morning, the Canadian 412 Squadron had flown to West Malling, to operate with its fellow Canadian 411 Squadron, and 616 Squadron. Pilot Officer

Above left: The unknown airman's grave in Dunkirk Cemetery.

Above right: Wing Commander Douglas Scott AFC, Digby's Wing Leader, who was also shot down and killed in action on 8 November 1941, and whose grave can be found next to the unknown casualty of that day's fighting.

Jeff West, a New Zealander, serving in 616 Squadron, recalled that the day had not started well as breakfast was 'only half ready', and that the Wing Leader, Wing Commander Douglas Scott AFC, was 'annoyed, and justifiably so'. Things failed to improve, however, and in his diary, West described Circus 110 as a 'Shambles'. A late breakfast, though, was the least of Wing Commander Scott's worries that day.

According to the 412 Squadron ORB: 'The Wing was instructed to proceed to a patrol line east of Dunkirk but reached the French coast earlier than ordered and so proceeded to patrol the coastline NE of Dunkirk, where a heavy and accurate AA barrage was encountered, which split the Wing formation. E/A joined battle and individual fights followed. Wing did not reach the patrol line east of Dunkirk.'

The 616 Squadron ORB states that the Wing '… proceeded into France over Dunkirk. Twelve Me 109s were seen 3,000 feet above and about to dive down to attack our Squadron, so the latter broke sharp left to manoeuvre for position'.

No. 411 Squadron ORB: '… The Squadron went on a sweep over France, circled Dunkirk and encountered terrific flak'.

Wing Commander Scott's formation had actually been attacked not by Me 109s but by Fw 190s of Hauptmann Müncheberg's II/JG 26, north of Dunkirk. The Wing Leader himself was shot down and killed, his final message being 'I guess I'm too old for this, boys', which at thirty-three may well have been the case. Scott is buried in Dunkirk Cemetery – next to the unknown airman of interest.

The main weight of the Fw 190's attack fell on 412 Squadron – which lost three pilots:

> Squadron Leader Christopher Bushell (Spitfire Mk VB, W3959).
> Pilot Officer Kenneth Raymond Ernest Denkman (Spitfire Mk VB, W3952).
> Sergeant Owen Fraser Pickell (Spitfire Mk VB, AD270).

All three pilots also remain missing, their casualty files confirming that they were shot down over Dunkirk.

CIRCUS 110: ONE OF OUR SPITFIRES IS MISSING...

The following are the corresponding German claims (continental time):

Hauptmann Müncheberg	Spitfire	Loon Plage (Dunkirk)	1307 hrs
Hauptmann Müncheberg	Spitfire	NNE Dunkirk	1315 hrs
Oberleutnant Ebersberger	Spitfire	N Dunkirk	1304 hrs
Feldwebel Glunz	Spitfire	15 km N Calais	1308 hrs

It is believed that Müncheberg shot down Wing Commander Scott, who crashed on land and was the Spitfire hit over Loon Plage. The other three claims were all over the sea, and doubtless concern 412 Squadron's three missing pilots.

All three were Canadian, and their uniforms would have included the 'Canada' shoulder flash. The headstone of the unknown airman in question at Dunkirk is that of a British or Commonwealth serviceman, but gives no indication as to nationality – unlike the case of Flight Lieutenant Stabrowski, which specifically identified him as Polish. Other Polish pilots, however, have been buried under Commonwealth, not Polish, headstones, the case of Flying Officer Franciszek Gruszka at Northwood refers, for example. We also know that this was not an airman's body washed up on 8 November 1941, but actually recovered from a Spitfire shot down that day.

According to Flying Officer Surma's casualty file, he was 'shot down over France'.

It would seem, then, that that there is a realistic chance that this unknown airman in Dunkirk Cemetery could be Flying Officer Surma, given that the three missing Canadians appear to have been shot down over the Channel. Even taking those losses into account, there remains a one in four chance. Unfortunately, unlike the case of Flight Lieutenant Stabrowski, because this grave is in a British War Cemetery, and given current policy, there would be no possibility of a DNA comparison with Flying Officer Surma's family members – and only that would resolve what is a vexing question.

On 2 November 1948, the PAF Memorial was unveiled beside Western Avenue, near the north-eastern edge of Northolt airfield. The rear of the Memorial records the names of 1,241 Polish airmen out of the total of 2,408 who were killed in action during the Second World War – including the names of Flying Officers Surma and Wielgus, and Sergeant Hegenbarth. On the base of the Memorial's plinth, topped by an eagle about to take flight, are these simple but moving words:

> I Have Fought A Good Fight, I Have Finished My Course.
> I Have Kept The Faith.

Indeed, this is surely true of all those pilots who flew Spitfire R6644, regardless of nationality.

The Polish Air Force memorial at Northolt.

Postscript

The Legend Lives On...

In 1985, I was a young police officer at Malvern, and learned from a friend, Andy Long, that Spitfire R6644 had crashed nearby, its Polish Battle of Britain pilot having safely baled out, only to be reported missing six months later. We both became so fascinated by the story that we soon traced eyewitnesses via

Dilip Sarkar (standing centre), Andy Long (standing left), and Sean Kelly (kneeling, third left) of the Malvern Spitfire Team at R6644's crash site in March 1987 with eyewitnesses, from left, Ken Davies, Neville Grizzell, Jim Thomas, Charlie Knight and Bill Pritchard, and aero modeller Mick Brown.

A SPITFIRE'S STORY: THE INVISIBLE THREAD

Malvern Spitfire Team members Geoff Cole and Andy Long passing the magnetometer over R6644's impact spot, March 1987.

the local media and pieced together a detailed story. Moreover, the Spitfire's Form 78, detailing the units with which it served, provided us with the basic data required to undertake further research at the Public Records Office (now The National Archives). A list of pilots who had once flown R6644, which had an impressive total of 266 flying hours, was subsequently obtained and research began to trace any survivors or the relatives of casualties.

The story of Franek Surma himself particularly interested me personally, for two reasons: firstly because at the time, Poland remained behind the Iron Curtain, and although it was known that Poles had fought during the Battle of Britain, there was a distinct lack of detail available, especially in English, and especially concerning the stories of individual units and airmen; secondly, I was so moved by the fact that he had no known grave. The desire to record and share more widely at least part of the Polish contribution, and if possible discover Surma's fate, became primary factors driving the project.

THE LEGEND LIVES ON...

Then, of course, there was the Spitfire story, in itself romantic and inspirational enough all on its own.

Over the next year our project grew enormously, and we received permission from the MOD, the landowner, Madresfield Estate, and the tenant farmer, Mr Nugent at Lower Woodsfield, to excavate the crash site of R6644.

Crop rotation, however, dictated that the site could not be excavated until September 1987, so in October 1986 Andy and I co-founded the Malvern Spitfire Team to undertake the project. We also decided to make the excavation a public one, to raise money for the RAF Association's 'Wings Appeal', and involved the local branch. The Team brought together a small group of people with diverse backgrounds and ages, all wanting to provide an individual marker to Flying Officer Surma. We decided to build a cairn of granite, hewn from the nearby Malvern Hills, and erect this at the roadside in Jennet Tree Lane, near to where Pilot Officer Surma had landed by parachute. Support was also forthcoming from the local ATC Squadron, 1017, and the MOD Participation Committee approved a fly-past by both the Battle of Britain Memorial Flight and a Tornado GR1 of 65 Squadron (with which unit R6644 had flown). The icing on the cake was when the Polish Air Force Association in Great Britain accepted our invitation to unveil our modest memorial. It was a privilege indeed to learn that two Polish Battle of Britain Spitfire pilots, both of whom remembered Franek Surma, would perform the honours: Squadron Leaders Bolesław 'Gandy' Drobinski DFC and Ludwik Martel VM KW.

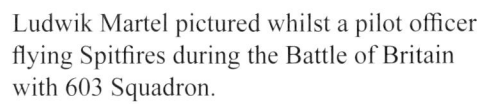

Ludwik Martel pictured whilst a pilot officer flying Spitfires during the Battle of Britain with 603 Squadron.

A SPITFIRE'S STORY: THE INVISIBLE THREAD

Squadron Leaders Martel and Drobinski on the day R6644's crash site was excavated and they jointly unveiled the Surma Memorial, 12 September 1987.

'Operation Spitfire', the recovery of Spitfire R6644 and the unveiling of the Surma Memorial took place on Saturday, 12 September 1987 and remains one of the most moving experiences of my life. It seemed that the whole of Worcestershire had turned out to support us, so engaged with the story had local people become, after months of press coverage and a significant amount of cash and publicity was raised for the 'Wings Appeal'. The excavation indicated that the Spitfire had hit a layer of very hard clay and granite just a few feet below the surface, shattering all major components. Nevertheless, disappointing though was initially, many small artefacts were found, the biggest being a piston and liner, the most impressive being the tiny de Havilland badge from the extreme front of the aircraft's propeller spinner cap. All of the finds were laid out for display on a long table whilst team-member Bob Morris, an engine fitter with 66 (Spitfire) Squadron during the

THE LEGEND LIVES ON...

Battle of Britain, identified the artefacts for our special guests, innumerable members of the public and the press.

Malvern Hills District Council hosted a civic reception for our Polish and other VIP guests, whose number included many former Spitfire personnel, in a marquee at the crash site. It was a poignant occasion, made more so when the council chairman, Mrs Lyn Norfolk, explained that her own father remained missing in action from the Second World War. Squadron Leader Martel spoke on behalf of the Polish delegation and, moved close to tears, described how honoured he was to have been invited to such a unique event, and how indescribably moved both he and his colleagues were that so many people had turned out to remember a young Polish flier whom they had never met. 'Perhaps', he said, 'the motto of the Malvern Spitfire Team is true: "The Legend Lives On"'.

Although bad weather grounded the Battle of Britain Memorial Flight at St Athan, Jennet Tree Lane was absolutely packed when the time came for Surma's memorial to be unveiled. The two Polish pilots walked with the team and the guard of honour, provided by the local ATC squadron, the few yards to the memorial. It was incredible to see the huge crowd of people part ahead of us, and I will never forget the words that Squadron Leader Drobinski said to me that day: 'In 1945 we Poles were not invited to participate in the great victory parade, such was the

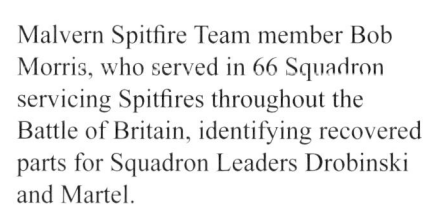

Malvern Spitfire Team member Bob Morris, who served in 66 Squadron servicing Spitfires throughout the Battle of Britain, identifying recovered parts for Squadron Leaders Drobinski and Martel.

A SPITFIRE'S STORY: THE INVISIBLE THREAD

The recovery of what little remained of R6644 well underway by the Malvern Spitfire Team.

The crash site reinstated the following day, looking towards the world-famous Malvern Hills.

situation with Stalin, and we could not even go home. Britain gave us a home and, all these years later, you have now given us our victory parade. It was worth the wait'.

Around the cairn were clustered journalists and television cameras, and during the dedication service Reverend Eric Knowles said that 'Flying Officer Surma's sacrifice is an example to us all of how to serve our country, our friends and our God'. Squadron Leaders Drobinski and Martel solemnly stepped forward and removed the Polish Air Force ensign from the memorial – the first such commemoration for an individual Polish airman in the UK. The atmosphere was incredibly charged, the crowd silent as wreaths were laid by the Polish Air Force Association, RAF Association and the Malvern Spitfire Team. As the last wreath was set down a strong gust of wind suddenly shook the tree beneath which the memorial was built; in the prevailing atmosphere it was easy to imagine that this was Franek Surma's spirit coming to rest. I certainly hope it was.

In June 1988, the artefacts recovered from R6644's crash site became the centre-piece of a major exhibition featuring the Malvern Spitfire Team's research at Tudor House Museum in Worcester. The opening event was

The crowd in Jennet Tree Lane during the memorial service. Holding the PAF wreath is Mr Tadek Krysztik, Secretary of the former PAF Association in GB.

A SPITFIRE'S STORY: THE INVISIBLE THREAD

Above left: The Rev. Alan Knowles, chaplain of the local 187 (ATC) Squadron, who took the memorial service.

Above right: The modest memorial cairn commemorating Flying Officer Surma, built by the Malvern Spitfire Team, using granite hewn from the nearby hills, which was the first such tribute to an individual Polish fighter pilot in the UK.

attended by numerous Battle of Britain pilots and other VIPs, but the ribbon could only be cut by one man, so far as we were all concerned: Flight Lieutenant Kazek Budzik VM KW, Squadron Leader Pisarek's wingman on Circus 110. The exhibition was a huge success, attracting 10,000 visitors in just a few months. Consequently the time allocated to our exhibition was extended, and it then became a travelling show, seen at numerous aviation museums, cultural centres and schools across the UK.

In October 1987, members of our Team were invited to lunch at the HQ of the Polish Air Force Association in Great Britain, in London, hosted by Air Vice-Marshal Maisner, and our friends Squadron Leaders Drobinski and Martel. It was both a great surprise and honour to be made an 'Honorary Pole' and made an honorary member of the Association, both of which things I proudly accepted on behalf of the Team. Certainly back then, the Polish wartime air effort really was largely hidden history – unlike today,

THE LEGEND LIVES ON...

The largest R6644 artefact recovered – a piston and liner from the Spitfire's Merlin engine – still bearing traces of the fire.

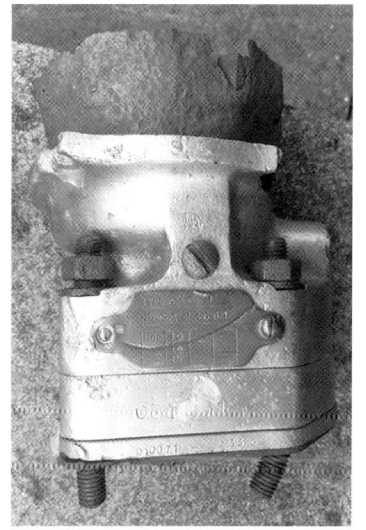

Above left: The screw-in disc of R6644's propeller hub, which had punched out an amount of spinner cap upon impact – including the tiny de Havilland badge. Although the majority of remaining paint is the original black, traces of sky still exist.

Above right: R6644's Constant Speed Unit, hurriedly fitted to existing Spitfires in the field during the Battle of Britain by de Havilland engineers.

A SPITFIRE'S STORY: THE INVISIBLE THREAD

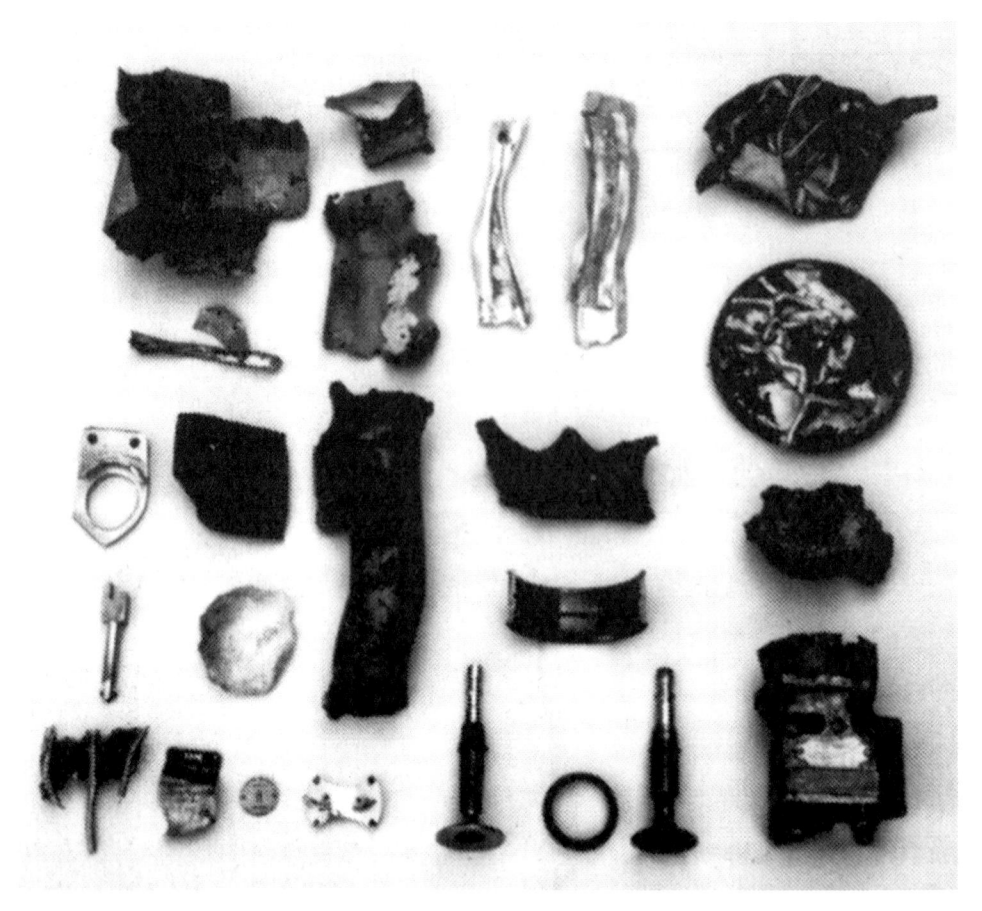

A selection of recovered R6644 artefacts, including the cockpit door latch, valves and other engine items, instrument and radio parts, airframe skinning and armoured glass. It is clear that R6644 impacted at high speed and into hard ground, shattering into fragments. These artefacts are now curated and exhibited by the Laguna Spitfire Legacy Project, on the author's behalf.

nearly 40 years later, when so much more information is available that no longer are the Poles 'The Once Forgotten Few'; I am proud to have played a pioneering role in that long overdue process.

In those days, the Polish community in England was comparatively small, this being before the open migration of more recent times. Moreover, because Poland was still part of the Soviet Bloc and behind the 'Iron Curtain', Polish war veterans here tended to maintain a low-profile, and certainly had no wish to draw attention to themselves to the possible detriment of their families living in Poland under Soviet rule. Because of all this, communication with Poland

THE LEGEND LIVES ON...

Above: The conserved R6644 artefacts displayed in Tudor House Museum, Worcester, at the Malvern Spitfire Team's *Spitfire!* exhibition in 1988. The artefacts are now on loan to and curated by the Laguna Spitfire Legacy Project and frequently on show to the public at various events. Details of the Laguna project can be found in the Bibliography.

Right: Flight Lieutenant Kazek Budzik VM KW, who opened the exhibition in October 1988.

A SPITFIRE'S STORY: THE INVISIBLE THREAD

Left: In 1992, the author presented an R6644 souvenir to Squadron Leader Ron Stillwell DFC DFM AE, who flew R6644 with 65 Squadron.

Below: An R6644 souvenir was also presented to Air Vice-Marshal David Scott-Malden CB DSO DFC, who flew the Spitfire whilst training in 1940.

was at best erratic, at worst completely unreliable, relying upon the post; this was, of course, long before the digital age, social media and the instantaneous personal communication platforms we enjoy today. Consequently, efforts to trace the Surma family initially failed, but early in 1989, Polish Spitfire enthusiast Kryzstof Choloniewski, placed an appeal on my behalf in the

THE LEGEND LIVES ON...

Krakow newspaper. Out of the blue, in February 1989, a letter arrived in my post, which remains the most moving piece of correspondence I have ever received; it was from Franek Surma's two surviving sisters, Elzbiete Morcinek, aged 80, and Otylia Paszek, aged 76:

> We were delighted and extremely moved to learn of your project, the knowledge of which affected us considerably. At last we will learn the whole truth regarding the fate of our dear brother. We are the only surviving family of Franciszek Surma and came from a long line of peasant farmers, 'Franek' being the youngest child. We all adored him, as did everyone who knew him. He was a very good child, very obedient and hard working. At school in Zory he passed his exams and decided to become a pilot. On this issue he opposed his parents' wishes for the one and only time. None of us agreed with us his plans, for we considered joining the air force to be a very dangerous affair and so were afraid for our little brother. Our concern made no difference as he was decided and would not consider any alternative. We do not regret now that we did not succeed in changing his mind as we now know that he was a hero. Two of our family, in fact, were killed by German pilots: the Germans bombed a school in Wieszniowice in Czechoslovakia and hit a house on the opposite side of the street, where our sister lived and who was killed instantly.
>
> After Franek completed his education at Zory he moved to Krakow and joined the air force. At this time he wrote about attending a course at the Reserve Officers Cadet School for infantry at Rozane. He also attended cadet schools in Rawicz and Deblin.
>
> We were always delighted to see Franek when he was on leave and our parents would organise parties. He looked wonderful in his uniform. He was an extremely cultured, intelligent and gallant young man. We were all very interested to learn of his flying exploits and listened to his stories with bated breath. On one of his few visits he even brought home a parachute to show us how safe it was to jump.

Two days before war broke out he made several aerobatic and low passes over every house occupied by a member of our family. We remember running out of the house in a state of great excitement! We all knew that this was Franek but we were scared to death by his aerobatic antics! In Galkowicz there stood a large oak tree and this shook violently as Franek passed overhead, so low was he. We understood that this was a sign to say that our little brother was going away.

During the war we received a letter from Franek via Holland. He let us know about the dispatch of two other letters and some money. Only one of those letters reached us. Via Portugal we received parcels from him, known as 'Signs of Life', containing tins of sardines. Our joy was not for the food but the knowledge that the sender was still alive. Can you imagine our great joy? Those were the only happy moments in those cruel days. After the war ended we received another parcel, which made us happy because we assumed that Franek was still alive. But we waited in vain for him to come home. Finally we asked the Red Cross to try and discover whether he was still alive. Eventually we received confirmation that our dear brother had failed to return from an operation in 1941 and was probably killed in the cold waters of the English Channel. We also received his medals and photographs. The news of this tragedy drove us all to the utmost depths of despair.

Since that time, more than forty years have now passed and we are happy that Franek's memory is alive, not only with us. At our 'Memory Room' in Gadawa his photograph is displayed in a place of honour. Also you, in far-away England, have not forgotten him. We are so proud of our brother. We are also astonished at your achievements as such a young man, and want to shake your hand for all you have done. Kindly express our gratitude to everybody who has contributed to the commemoration of Franek Surma. We are most grateful to his friends, the chaplain and the people of England. It is hard to express our thanks in words; there are no words that could adequately express the feelings of two old people who have kept alive in their hearts the memory of their dear brother.

Through your project you have awakened our memories and shown how wonderful people can be. Many special thanks go to you and we will be praying for your success in life, prayers for someone now very dear to us. May God take care of you and your organisation. We are so happy that there is still someone to light a candle for Franek on All Souls Day. We are happy because the memorial erected to him serves as his grave, a symbol he can see from heaven. We have always worried about Franek having no known grave, but now we are at peace, thanks to you.

Further words would be superfluous.

Incredible scene from the launch of the author's original version of the R6644 story, The Invisible Thread, at the Abbey Hotel, Great Malvern, in September 1992. On the same day, a new charity, The Surma Memorial Trust, founded by the author, was launched, supported by local businesses, proceeds from the sale of a print by the artist Mark Postlethwaite GAvA, depicting R6644 over Malvern, signed by numerous of The Few present, were donated to the Trust. These monies were distributed to projects working to improve the quality of life for youth.

A SPITFIRE'S STORY: THE INVISIBLE THREAD

Above: The irrepressible Kazek Budzik back in a Spitfire at the 1992 launch.

Opposite above: Revered guests at the 1992 launch; from left: (* indicates one of 'The Few') Dr Gordon Mitchell, Wing Commander Bernard Jennings*, Fred Roberts (an armourer during the Battle of Britain); Flight Lieutenants Hugh Chalmers, Peter Hairs*, Tadek Turek (Polish) and Michael Graham; Mr Bob Morris (Malvern Spitfire Team member and fitter IIE on 66 Squadron during the Battle of Britain); Mr Bob Morton and Squadron Leader 'Buck' Casson* (both of whom flew R6644); Flight Lieutenants William Walker*, Kazek Budzik (Polish), Richard Jones* and Ken Wilkinson*. The author went on to host numerous, even bigger gatherings, at book signings throughout the rest of the decade and well into the next.

Opposite below: Heroes all. Another 1992 launch photograph, the following adding to the line-up in the previous photograph: Group Captain Gerry Edge* (extreme left); *Luftwaffe* wartime pilot Hans 'Peter' Wulff (fourth left); Flight Lieutenant Harry Welford* (fifth left); Flying Officer John Lumsden (Malvern Spitfire Team Chairman and post-war Mosquito pilot, extreme left, back row); Flight Lieutenants Peter Taylor (third from right, back row), and Tadek Dzidsic (Polish, extreme right). These events were absolutely fantastic, providing the public a unique opportunity to meet heroes from the pages of history – we will not see their like again.

THE LEGEND LIVES ON...

Bibliography

Pilots' Flying Log Books (ranks as at the time of flying R6644)

Squadron Leader H.F. Burton
Squadron Leader G.A.L. Manton
Flight Lieutenant P.P. Hanks
Flight Lieutenant J.I. Kilmartin
Flight Lieutenant C.H. MacFie
Flying Officer B.E.F. Finucane
Pilot Officer L.H. Casson
Pilot Officer H.S.L. Dundas
Pilot Officer W. Read
Pilot Officer F.D.S. Scott-Malden
Pilot Officer A.F. Vokes
Sergeant H. Baxter
Sergeant A. Johnson
Sergeant D. Kingaby
Sergeant R.A. Morton
Sergeant R.L. Stillwell
Sergeant J. Stokoe

Pilots' Diaries

Pilot Officer L.H. Casson
Pilot Officer F.D.S. Scott-Malden

BIBLIOGRAPHY

Pilot Officer J. West
Sergeant V. Lowson

The National Archives

Operations Record Books:
5 OTU: AIR29/682
1 PRU: AIR29/414
1 Sqn: AIR27/1
19 Sqn: AIR27/252
46 Sqn: AIR27/460
56 Sqn: AIR27/528
65 Sqn: AIR27/593
66 Sqn: AIR27/600
92 Sqn: AIR27/46
229 Sqn: AIR27/1418
242 Sqn: AIR27/1471
256 Sqn: AIR27/1523
257 Sqn: AIR27/1526
131 Sqn: AIR27/940
111 Sqn: AIR27/866
308 Sqn: AIR27: 1678
411 Sqn: AIR 27/1803
412 Sqn: AIR27/1805
485 Sqn: AIR27/1983
601 Sqn: AIR27/2068
602 Sqn: AIR27/2074
607 Sqn: AIR27/2093
611 Sqn: AIR27/2109
616 Sqn: AIR27/2126

Combat Reports:

19 Sqn: AIR50/85
56 Sqn: AIR50/104

65 Sqn: AIR50/25
257 Sqn: AIR50/100
308 Sqn: AIR50/120
602 Sqn: AIR50/166
603 Sqn: AIR50/167
616 Sqn: AIR50/176

Casualty Files:

Wing Commander B.E.F. Finucane: AIR 81/13337
Squadron Leader C. Bushell: AIR81/10212
Flying Officer F. Surma: AIR81/10179
Pilot Officer K.R.E. Denkman: AIR81/10213.
Pilot Officer V. Lawson: AIR81/16044
Sergeant A.H. Johnson: AIR81/9762
Sergeant O.F. Pickell: AIR81/10195
Sergeant P.G. Rose: AIR81/6213
Sergeant D. Foulger: AIR81/5865

Unpublished Sources

Dilip Sarkar Archive, correspondence.

Films

Things to Come, directed by William Cameron Menzies (London Films, 1936).
The Gap, directed by Donald Carter (Gaumont-British Instructional, 1937).
The Warning, edited by R.Q. McNaughton (British National Films, 1939).
The Lion Has Wings, directed by Michael Powell, Adrian Brunel and Brian Desmond Hurst (London Films, 1939).
Battle of Britain, directed by Guy Hamilton (Spitfire Productions, 1969).

BIBLIOGRAPHY

YouTube

Pathe News broadcast by Don Kingaby, 'The 109 Specialist', January 1941: https://www.youtube.com/watch?v=FoWFLPeVgww

Dilip Sarkar's YouTube Channel: https://www.youtube.com/channel/UC-gHoncnHqdgIZ6xNfe4Chg

Books

Aders, G. and Held, W., *Chronik: Jagdgeschwader 51 'Mölders'*, Motorbuch Verlag, Stuttgart, 2009

Anon., *We Speak From the Air: Broadcasts by the RAF*, HMSO, London, 1942

Calder, A., *The People's War: Britain 1939–45*, Jonathan Cape Ltd, London, 1969

Boot, H. and Sturtivant, R., *Gifts of War: Spitfires and Other Presentation Aircraft in Two World Wars*, Air-Britain (Historians) Ltd, Tonbridge, 2005.

Caldwell, D., *The JG26 War Diary: Volume One, 1939-1942*, Grub Street, London, 1996

Cornwell, P.D., *The Battle of France Then & Now: Six Nations Locked in Aerial Combat, September 1939 – June 1940*, Battle of Britain International Ltd, Harlow, 2007

Douglas, MRAF Lord, *Years of Command: A Personal Story of the Second World War in the Air*, Collins, London, 1966

Dundas, Sir H.S.L., *Flying Start: A Fighter Pilot's War Years*, Stanley Paul, London, 1988

Foreman, J., *Battle of Britain: The Forgotten Months*, Air Research Publications, New Maldon, 1988

Foreman, J., *RAF Fighter Command Victory Claims of World War Two, Part One 1939-1940*, Red Kite, Walton-on-Thames, 2003

Foreman, J., *RAF Fighter Command Victory Claims of World War Two, Part Two 1 January 1941–30 June 1943*, Red Kite, Walton-on-Thames, 2005

Foreman, J., *1941, Part 2: The Blitz to the Turning Point*, Air Research Publications, Walton-on-Thames, 2008

Forrester, L., *Fly For Your Life: The Story of R.R. Stanford Tuck DSO DFC and Two Bars*, Companion Book Club, London, 1956

Franks, N.L.R., *Air Battle for Dunkirk: 26 May–3 June 1940*, Grub Street, London, 2006

Franks, N.L.R., *RAF Fighter Command Losses of the Second World War, Volume 1, Operational Losses: Aircraft and Crews, 1939–41*, Midland, Hersham, 2008

Galland, General A., *The First and the Last*, Cerberus Publishing, Bristol, 2001

Hillary, R., *The Last Enemy*, MacMillan & Co. Ltd, London, 1942

Quill, J.K., *Spitfire: A Test Pilot's Story*, John Murray Ltd, London, 1983

Lisiewicz, Squadron Leader M. (ed.), *Destiny Can Wait: The Polish Air Force in the Second World War*, William Heinemann Ltd, London, 1949

Lucas, P.B., *Malta, The Thorn in Rommel's Side: Six Months that Turned the War*, Stanley Paul, London, 1992

Mitchell, G., et al, *R.J. Mitchell, World-Famous Aircraft Designer: Schooldays to Spitfire*, Nelson and Saunders Publishers, Olney, 1986

Morgan, E. and Shacklady, E., *Spitfire: The History*, Key Publishing, Stamford, 1987

Price, A., *The Spitfire Story: Revised Second Edition*, Arms & Armour, London, 1995

Prien, J., *Jagdgeschwader 53: A History of the 'Pik As' Geschwader, March 1937-May 1942*, Schiffer Military History, Atglen, PA, 1997

Ramsay, W. (ed.), *The Battle of Britain: Then & Now, Mk V*, Battle of Britain Prints International Ltd, London, 1989

Ramsey, W. (ed.), *The Blitz Then & Now: Volume 1*, Battle of Britain Prints International Ltd, London, 1987

Ramsey, W. (ed.), *The Blitz Then & Now: Volume 2*, Battle of Britain Prints International Ltd, London, 1988

Russell, C.R., *Spitfire Odyssey: My Life at Supermarines 1936–1957*, Kingfisher Railway Productions, Southampton, 1985

BIBLIOGRAPHY

Shores, C. and Williams, C., *Aces High: A Tribute to the Most Notable Fighter Pilots of the British & Commonwealth Forces in WWII*, Grub Street, London, 1994

Shores, C., Cull, B. and Malizia, N., *Malta: The Spitfire Year, 1942*, Grub Street, London, 1991

Wynn, K., *Men of the Battle of Britain: A Biographical Directory of the Few*, Frontline Books, Barnsley, 2015

Zamoski, A., *The Forgotten Few: The Polish Air Force in World War II*, Pen & Sword, Barnsley, 2022

Websites

The National Archives	www.nationalarchives.gov.uk
Commonwealth War Graves Commission	www.cwgc.org
Battle of Britain Memorial Trust CIO	www.battleofbritain memorial.org
Kenley Revival Project	www.kenleyrevival.org
Battle of Britain London Monument	www.bbm.org
Polish Airmen's Association UK	www.polishairmensassociation.org.uk
Dilip Sarkar	www.dilipsarkarmbe.com
Laguna Spitfire Legacy	www.lagunasspitfirelegacy.org

Other Books by Dilip Sarkar

Spitfire Squadron: No. 19 Squadron at War, 1939–41
The Invisible Thread: A Spitfire's Tale
Through Peril to the Stars: RAF Fighter Pilots Who Failed to Return, 1939–45
Angriff Westland: Three Battle of Britain Air Raids Through the Looking Glass
A Few of the Many: Air War 1939–45, A Kaleidoscope of Memories
Bader's Tangmere Spitfires: The Untold Story, 1941
Bader's Duxford Fighters: The Big Wing Controversy
Missing in Action: Resting in Peace?
Guards VC: Blitzkrieg 1940
Battle of Britain: The Photographic Kaleidoscope, Volumes I–IV
Fighter Pilot: The Photographic Kaleidoscope
Group Captain Sir Douglas Bader: An Inspiration in Photographs
Johnnie Johnson: Spitfire Top Gun, Part I
Johnnie Johnson: Spitfire Top Gun, Part II
Battle of Britain: Last Look Back
Spitfire! Courage & Sacrifice
Spitfire Voices: Heroes Remember
The Battle of Powick Bridge: Ambush a Fore-Thought
Duxford 1940: A Battle of Britain Base at War
The Few: The Battle of Britain in the Words of the Pilots
Spitfire Manual 1940
The Sinking of HMS Royal Oak *in the Words of the Survivors* (re-print of Hearts of Oak)

OTHER BOOKS BY DILIP SARKAR

The Last of the Few: Eighteen Battle of Britain Pilots Tell Their Extraordinary Stories
Hearts of Oak: The Human Tragedy of HMS Royal Oak
Spitfire Voices: Life as a Spitfire Pilot in the Words of the Veterans
How the Spitfire Won the Battle of Britain
Spitfire Ace of Aces: The True Wartime Story of Johnnie Johnson
Douglas Bader
Fighter Ace: The Extraordinary Life of Douglas Bader, Battle of Britain Hero (re-print of above)
Spitfire: The Photographic Biography
Hurricane Manual 1940
River Pike
The Final Few: The Last Surviving Pilots of the Battle of Britain Tell Their Stories
Arnhem 1944: The Human Tragedy of the Bridge Too Far
Spitfire! The Full Story of a Unique Battle of Britain Fighter Squadron
Battle of Britain 1940: The Finest Hour's Human Cost
Letters from The Few: Unique Memories of the Battle of Britain
Johnnie Johnson's 1942 Diary: The War Diary of the Spitfire Ace of Aces
Johnnie Johnson's Great Adventure: The Spitfire Ace of Ace's Last Look Back
Sailor Malan – Freedom Fighter: The Inspirational Story of a Spitfire Ace
Spitfire Ace of Aces – The Album: The Photographs of Johnnie Johnson
The Real Spitfire Pilot, being the previously unpublished original manuscript of Spitfire Pilot, by Flight Lieutenant David Crook, with introduction, commentary and photographs by Dilip Sarkar
Bader's Big Wing Controversy: Duxford 1940
Bader's Spitfire Wing: Tangmere 1941
Spitfire Down: Fighter Boys Who Failed to Return
Forgotten Heroes of The Battle of Britain
Faces of The Few
Spitfire Faces
Arise to Conquer: The Real Hurricane Pilot by Wing Commander Ian Gleed, introduction, commentary and photographs by Dilip Sarkar

Free French Spitfire Hero: The Diaries of and Search for René Mouchotte (with Jan Leeming)

I Had A Row with a German by Group Captain Tom Gleave, introduction by Dilip Sarkar

Battle of Britain: The Finest Hour in Cinema

Battle of Britain: The Movie (contributor to and publisher of the now late Robert Rudhall's original edition (2000), and editor and substantial contributor to 2022 revised edition)

Faces of HMS Royal Oak: *The 'Mighty Oak' Disaster at Scapa Flow*

Battle of Britain Volume 1: The Gathering Storm – Prelude to the Spitfire Summer of 1940

Battle of Britain Volume 2: The Breaking Storm – 10 July 1940–12 August 1940

Battle of Britain Volume 3: Attack of the Eagles – 13 August 1940–18 August 1940

Battle of Britain Volume 4: Airfields Under Attack – 19 August 1940–6 September 1940

Battle of Britain Volume 5: Target London – 7 September 1940–17 September 1940

Battle of Britain Volume 6: Daylight Defeat – 18 September 1940–30 September 1940

Battle of Britain Volume 7: The Final Curtain – 1 October 1940–31 October 1940

Battle of Britain Volume 8: The Battle of Britain Remembered

Index

5 OTU 25–6, 29–31, 37–8, 45, 56, 63, 68, 82–4, 96, 165, 180, 216, 228
6 OTU 25, 131, 231
7 OTU 151, 163, 171, 181, 187, 195, 200
51 OTU 82
53 OTU 78
57 OTU 181
58 OTU 61, 85
60 OTU 85

10 Group 25, 104, 120, 240
11 Group 23–5, 47, 52, 57, 69, 85, 90, 102, 104, 138, 159, 166, 174, 195, 208, 218, 231, 235, 243
12 Group 24–5, 49, 56, 65, 68, 71, 92, 94, 100, 102, 104, 126, 133, 166, 174, 179, 182, 184, 195, 201–202, 208, 212, 219, 243, 262, 269
212 Group 109, 112

1 Squadron 26–7, 33–4, 37, 109
3 Squadron 130
11 Squadron 72
17 Squadron 19
19 Squadron 9, 17, 19, 30, 56, 68–73, 75–6, 104, 166, 182, 243
21 Squadron 72–3
29 Squadron 82
32 Squadron 127, 133
33 Squadron 109
41 Squadron 142, 179, 244
46 Squadron 99–100
54 Squadron 47, 52, 54, 66, 87, 129, 171, 181–2
56 Squadron 40, 45–8, 123, 244
64 Squadron 61
65 'East India' Squadron 19, 71, 88, 95, 105, 140, 159–60, 162–3, 165–9, 172, 174, 176, 178–9, 181–2, 184, 187, 195, 200–202, 214, 275
66 Squadron 86, 89, 100–104, 242
72 Squadron 269
73 Squadron 34
74 'Tiger' Squadron 11, 105, 151, 244
79 Squadron 132 3, 135
85 Squadron 93
92 'East India' Squadron 56–61, 127, 244
110 Squadron 73, 87
111 Squadron 8, 42, 61, 218
114 Squadron 244
117 Squadron 112–13

118 Squadron 240
122 Squadron 169–70
129 Squadron 179
131 'County of Kent' Squadron 86
134 Squadron 79
135 Squadron 87
139 Squadron 244
145 Squadron 105–107, 121, 142
151 Squadron 231
152 Squadron 72–3
213 Squadron 109
222 Squadron 59, 85–6, 100
226 Squadron 142
229 Squadron 218–19
234 Squadron 71
238 Squadron 109
242 Squadron 238, 244
253 Squadron 30
255 Squadron 94
256 Squadron 84–5
257 Squadron 30, 39–40, 66, 235–6
260 Squadron 110
263 Squadron 51, 78
264 Squadron 92, 100–102, 105
266 'Rhodesia' Squadron 56, 71, 140, 166, 181–2, 201
302 'Poznan' Squadron 208, 244
303 Squadron 48, 208, 214, 263, 267
306 Squadron 247, 249
308 'City of Krakow' Squadron 129, 202–16, 219–21, 239–40, 244–50, 255–9, 262–3, 266, 268
310 (Czech) Squadron 208
315 Squadron 214, 248, 263, 266
402 Squadron 201
411 Squadron 269–70
412 Squadron 269–71
452 Squadron 164, 195, 197
485 Squadron 163–4
501 Squadron 61
601 'County of London' Squadron 48, 56
602 Squadron 197–8
603 'City of Edinburgh' Squadron 30, 51–2, 66, 78
605 'County of Warwick' Squadron 43–4
607 'County of Durham' Squadron 231–3, 235
609 'West Riding' Squadron 118, 120
610 Squadron 121, 123, 129, 142, 144, 244
611 'County of Lancashire' Squadron 63, 65, 105, 119, 125–8, 244
616 'South Yorkshire' Squadron 89–96, 105, 108, 112, 117–121, 123–4, 128–9, 131–2, 136–7, 140, 142, 145, 149, 151, 153, 156, 159, 228, 269–70

Abbeville 86, 133–4
Aeberhardt, Pilot Officer Robert 30, 69
Agazarian, Pilot Officer Noel le Chevalier 31, 63–4
Aikman, Pilot Officer 199–200
Air Ministry 6–9, 12, 23, 45
Airthief, Operation 19
Ark Royal, HMS 41
Aston Down, RAF 23–5, 31, 37, 39, 45–7, 57, 59, 67, 71, 83, 88, 99, 177, 196, 206, 241, 267

INDEX

Bader, Wing Commander Douglas 33, 65, 95, 105, 107–108, 111, 119–23, 128–9, 140–5, 148, 153, 155, 157–8, 196, 238, 244
Baginton 202, 209, 212–15, 219, 221, 227, 238–9
Bajan, Flight Lieutenant 203, 205
Balfanz, *Oberleutnant* Winfried 54
Barclay, George 64–5
Bartley, Squadron Leader Tony 60, 174
Battle of Britain Memorial Flight 275, 277
Barwell, Squadron Leader 100
Baxter, Sergeant Humphrey 182–5, 200
Beachy Head 142, 144, 181
Beaverbrook, Lord 12, 20, 27
Bellamy, Sub-Lieutenant Viv 83
Benedict, Operation 78
Bentley Priory 42, 242
Biggin Hill 47, 56–9, 69, 132–6, 256
Bircham Newton, RAF 77, 84
Bird, Pilot Officer Alec 38–9
Blatchford, Flight Lieutenant 236
Bodie, Pilot Officer 242
Boothman, Flight Lieutenant J.N. 5
Bortnowski, General Wladyslaw 215
Bradwell Bay 47, 82
Brize Norton 118, 131
Broadhurst, Air Vice-Marshal Harry 112, 114, 116, 123, 133
Brown, Pilot Officer Peter 'Sneezy' 119
Bruce, Sergeant Alfred Eric Andrew 125–6
Budzik, Pilot Officer Kazimierz 'Kazek' 255, 259, 268, 280

Bulman, P.W.S. 'George' 7
Burgess, Flight Lieutenant George 41
Burma, RAF 49, 87
Burt, Sergeant Alfred 65
Burton, Squadron Leader Howard 'Billy' 90, 92, 95–116, 120, 138, 142–3, 145–6, 151, 158
Bushell, Squadron Leader Roger 56–7, 270

Cambridge University 62
Camm, Sydney 7–8
Casson, Pilot Officer Lionel 'Buck' 93, 108, 118, 130–1, 133, 138, 142, 144–5, 148–9
Catterick 52, 84, 142, 171
Chalmers, Sergeant Hugh 183
Chamberlain, Neville 12
Chilbolton, RAF 240
Christie, Flight Lieutenant 242
Churchill, Winston 3, 12, 20, 37, 78, 90
Circus 110, 259–72
Clisby, Flying Officer 34, 37
Coltishall, RAF 40, 49, 77, 90, 103–104, 128, 138, 151
Cox, Wing Commander David 243
Cranwell 31, 33, 62, 84, 99, 104, 111, 121, 151
Crowley-Milling, Flight Lieutenant Denis 123, 145
Cunningham, Pilot Officer Wallace 71, 75, 77

Davies, Sergeant Clifford 76
Davies, Squadron Leader J.A. 209, 211

Debden 61, 85, 174–5, 218
Derby, Operation 129
Dewy, Pilot Officer Robert 30
Dickson, Flight Lieutenant 33
Dixon, Pilot Officer Lancelot Steele 82
Douglas, Air Marshal Sholto 40, 241
Dover 2, 46, 56, 66, 103, 107, 118, 121, 137, 141, 164, 195, 201, 247
Dowding, Air Vice-Marshal Hugh 6–7, 23–5, 28, 36, 40, 89, 91, 100, 126, 208
Driscoll, Flying Officer 170
Drobinski, Sqaudron Leader Bolesław 'Gandy' 195, 207, 267, 275–7, 279–80
Dundas, Group Captain Sir Hugh 'Cocky' 43, 93–4, 116–24, 128, 138, 142–4, 151
Dunkirk 15, 37, 56, 88–9, 102–103, 111, 118, 127, 129, 133, 141, 149, 159, 184, 188, 198, 207, 248, 263, 268–71
Dunlop, Operation 41
Dutton, Squadron Leader Roy 71, 195
Duxford, RAF 9, 19, 40, 56, 65, 68, 70–1, 92, 96, 100, 102, 104–105, 119, 121, 125, 139–40, 166, 208, 238, 244
Dynamo, Operation 37, 102, 107, 127–8

Eagle, HMS 41
Edmunds, Pilot Officer 73, 76
Edwards, Pilot Officer Dennis Victor 113
Egan, Sergeant Eddy 51
Elkington, Flying Officer John 'Tim' 78, 82

Fenton, Group Captain Jimmy 109, 112
Finucane, Flying Officer Brendan E.F. 'Paddy' 173, 193–201
Flax, Operation 111
Foulger, Sergeant 200–202
Fowlmere, RAF 30, 56, 65, 71, 92, 104–105, 119, 139

Galland, Major Adolf 201
Gaunce, Squadron Leader Elmer 142
Gillam, Flight Lieutenant Denys 119
Glaser, Pilot Officer David 181
Grangemouth 78, 85
Gruska, Flying Officer Franciesk 159

Haines, Flying Officer 69–70
Halahan, Wing Commander Patrick 'Bull' 26–7, 34
Halton, RAF 197
Hal Far, RAF 42
Hamilton, Flying Officer Harry 125–6
Hanbury, Squadron Leader Osgood 'Pedro' 112, 114
Hancock, Wing Commander Pat 31
Hanks, Group Captain 26, 31–42, 218
Harwell, RAF 84
Hawarden 151, 163, 171, 181, 187, 195
Haysom, Wing Commander G.D.L. 109
Hegenbarth, Sergeant Tadeuz 221, 247, 272
Hendon 24, 87, 125
Hendon Air Pageant 33
Hillary, Pilot Officer Richard 28, 31, 63–4

INDEX

Hogg, Sergeant 92
Holland, Flight Lieutenant Bob 60, 72–3, 191, 286
Hornchurch, RAF 19, 42, 47, 51–2, 54, 56, 61, 65–6, 86, 88, 106, 142, 159, 165, 173, 187, 195, 198–9, 201
Howes, Pilot Officer Peter 63
Hunt, Sergeant Doug 103
Hunter, Squadron Leader 100

Jakubowski, Pilot Officer 248
Johnson, Sergeant Arthur 178–9, 182
Johnson, James Edgar 'Johnnie' 44, 94, 104–105, 112, 122–3, 139, 142
Jones, Flight Lieutenant Jerry 92, 105

Kendall, Pilot Officer John 86
Kenley, RAF 47, 69, 90, 99, 104–105, 112, 118–19, 128, 136–7, 142, 158, 164, 195, 197–8, 218, 256, 262
Kilmartin, Flying Officer John 'Iggy' 27, 29, 31
Kingaby, Sergeant Donald Ernest 51, 55–61
Kirton 89–90, 93–6, 105, 119, 139, 142, 151–2, 159, 162, 166, 174, 178, 182, 185, 187, 195, 200, 202, 214
Knowles, Squadron Leader E.V. 45, 279
Kowalski, Sergeant 249

Laguna, Wing Commander Piotr 245
Lane, Squadron Leader Brian 69, 71
Lawson, Squadron Leader Walter 'Farmer' 70–1, 73–6
Leconfield 85, 89, 118, 131, 136

Leigh-Mallory, Air Vice-Marshal Sir Trafford 40, 100–102, 126, 243–4
Llandow, RAF 20, 22–3, 78
Lock, Flight Lieutenant Eric 200
Long, Andy 273–4
Lowson, Sergeant Victor 171–7, 201
Lund, Pilot Officer J.W. 'Tommy' 63

MacFie, Flight Lieutenant Colin 93–4, 105, 120, 124–30, 138, 142, 151, 157
Machacek, Flying Officer 106
MacLean, Wing Commander Angus 191–2
Maffett, Pilot Officer 30
Malan, Squadron Leader 'Sailor' 105–106, 151
Manby 92
Manlove, Pilot Officer Richard 38–9
Manton, Squadron Leader Graham Ashley Leonard 'Minnie' 42–9
Marble Arch 109
Marsh, Pilot Officer 72–3
Martel, Squadron Leader Ludwik 275–7, 279–80
Martlesham Heath 45, 85, 102, 104, 127, 167, 237–8
McComb, Squadron Leader James 127
McDevette, Sergeant Thomas 128–9
McEvoy, Group Captain Theodore 48
McMullen, Squadron Leader 174–6
McSherry, Flying Officer James 113
Merston, RAF 142
Messerschmitt, Willy 7, 61, 108, 120
Middle East, RAF 108, 181
Middle Wallop 78, 120, 240

Milton, Flying Lieutenant 124–6, 170
Mitchell, Reginald Joseph 4–8, 11, 20
Mölders, Major Werner 48, 122
Moonlight Sonata, Operation 211
Mould, Pilot Officer 34–5, 37
Myers, Flying Officer Geoffrey 236

Northolt, RAF 8, 48–9, 86, 129, 164, 202, 208, 214, 218, 235, 240–1, 245, 248–9, 256, 258, 260, 262–4, 266–7, 271
Norwood, Pilot Officer Robin 180–2
North Weald 39–40, 45–8, 66, 85, 142, 231, 235–6, 244

O'Neill, Squadron Leader John 48–9
Okroj, Sergeant Jan 250–2
Olbrecht, *Leutnant* Heinz 114
Oliver, Wing Commander 212–13
Orzechowski, Pilot Officer Jan 202, 231–2

Parafinski, Sergeant 208, 212–13
Park, Air Commodore Keith 28, 102, 243
Pease, Pilot Officer Peter 31, 63
Pembrey, RAF 19, 57, 85
Pinkham, Squadron Leader 69
Pisarek, Flight Lieutenant Marian 205, 214, 238, 246–9, 255, 257, 263, 266–7, 280
Poplawski, Pilot Officer Jerzy 214, 216–20, 238, 249–51, 256, 258, 264, 266–7
Portal, Air Chief Marshal Charles 'Peter' 241–2
Portreath, RAF 112, 114

Quill, Jeffrey 14–17

Read, Pilot Officer William Albert Alexander 77–8, 82
Redhill 163, 166, 174, 197
Robertson, Air Commodore E.D.M. 104
Robinson, Squadron Leader Marcus 90, 136
Rochford 45–6, 89, 118, 159, 231
Rolski, Wing Commander Tadeusz 248, 262
Rose, Sergeant Peter Garratt 185–93
Ross, Sergeant William 85

Sanders, Squadron Leader P.J. 'Judy' 57
Saunders, Flight Lieutenant G.A.W. 'Sammy' 87, 195
Scott, Wing Commander Douglas 270–1
Scott-Malden, Pilot Officer David 62–7
Selsey Bill 59–60, 140, 167
Smith, Pilot Officer Don 105
St Athan 20, 22–5, 277
St Omer 106, 141, 158, 174, 179, 184, 195, 245, 247–8, 256, 258
Stabrowski, Pilot Officer Tadeusz 265
Stainforth, Flight Lieutenant G.H., 5
Stampel, Pilot Officer 248
Stenton, Corporal 83–7
Stillwell, Sergeant Ron 165–70, 175–6, 181
Stokoe, Sergeant Jack 49–52, 54–5
Strang, Pilot Officer Robert 162–4

INDEX

Strike, Operation 111
Surma, Pilot Officer Franciszek 'Franek' 214, 219–22, 225, 227, 230–9, 244, 246, 248, 250–1, 253–4, 256–8, 266–9, 271–2, 274–7, 279, 284–6
Sutton Bridge 45, 69–70, 131, 136, 231
Sykes, Sub-Lieutenant John 83
Szczeszniewski, Squadron Leader W. 266

Tangmere, RAF 33–4, 56, 95–6, 105–108, 120, 122, 128–9, 140–4, 148, 153, 158–9, 162–3, 166–7, 174, 181, 187, 195, 215, 231
Tarrant, Flight Lieutenant Hugh 176
Tern Hill, RAF 88
Trenchard, Major General 'Boom' 2–3, 28, 31–2, 43, 49, 84, 241–2
Tuttle, Wing Commander G.W. 188
Twitchett, Sergeant Frank 219

Victorious, HMS 41, 78–9
Villa, Squadron Leader John 'Pancho' 179, 181
Vokes, Pilot Officer Arthur Frank 67–72, 76–7
Vulcan, Operation 111

Walker, Flight Lieutenant Peter 'Johnnie' 26, 34
Warchal, Sergeant 250
Wareing, Sergeant Phillip 119, 138
Weaver, Flight Lieutenant Steve 'Squeak' 46, 48
Welford, Pilot Officer Harry 232
Westhampnett 96, 122, 141–2, 167
West, Sergeant Jeff 121, 142, 269–70
West Malling 47, 82, 166, 174, 184, 269
West Ruislip, RAF 87
White Waltham 20, 165
Wielgus, Pilot Officer Stanislaw 207–208, 214–15, 245, 247, 272
Williams, Sergeant R.H.A. 184
Wittering, RAF 56, 70, 84, 94, 140, 181, 185, 201, 219
Woodhall, Group Captain A.B. 143, 244
Woodhouse, Squadron Leader 121–2

Yaxley, Group Captain Robert Gordon 113–14, 116
Younghusband, Flight Lieutenant J.G. 202, 209